£2.49

ANNE

◆

THE PRINCESS
ROYAL

ANNE

♦

THE PRINCESS
ROYAL

Her Life and Work

Brian Hoey

GRAFTON BOOKS

A Division of the Collins Publishing Group

LONDON GLASGOW
TORONTO SYDNEY AUCKLAND

Grafton Books
A Division of the Collins Publishing Group
8 Grafton Street, London W1X 3LA

Published by Grafton Books 1989

British Library Cataloguing in Publication Data
Hoey, Brian
Anne: the Princess Royal
1. Great Britain. Anne, Princess, daughter of
Elizabeth II, Queen of Great Britain
I. Title
941. 085'092'4

ISBN 0-246-13557-3

Photoset by Rowland Phototypesetting Ltd
Bury St Edmunds, Suffolk.

Printed in Great Britain by
Hartnolls Ltd, Bodmin, Cornwall

CONTENTS

PROLOGUE

The bare announcement from Buckingham Palace at 12 noon on Thursday 31 August 1989 that the Queen's only daughter and her husband are to live apart conceals a great deal of heart-searching and behind-the-scenes activity that has been occupying the attention of a small number of people for several months.

It has been a closely guarded secret known only to a handful of the Princess's companions, but this is no sudden decision by the Princess Royal and Captain Phillips. They have been considering the move for some time and the major consideration has been the welfare of their children, Peter and Zara. What would be the best for them and when could the announcement be made so that it would do them the least harm?

After nearly sixteen years of marriage, what has suddenly gone wrong? Actually, nothing has gone suddenly wrong – it's been a gradual process that has taken several years to come to a head. And it has nothing to do with recent stories in the press about private letters belonging to the Princess Royal being stolen or about Mark's alleged involvement with an Indian call-girl, though neither of these incidents did the marriage any good, of course. The simple truth is that Anne and Mark have just grown apart. There is no third party involved; if there was there would be no question of Mark remaining at Gatcombe, even if he is now to live in another part of the estate. If either he or his wife were seriously involved with someone else, he would have had to move away.

The state of the marriage has been a source of gossip and rumour for many years. The couple's long absences from each other and their separate lifestyles have attracted stories in the press all over the world almost since the day they were married in 1973. Mark has been seen in the company of attractive women – nearly all business acquaintances, as it happens – thousands of miles from home, while the Princess has been portrayed as a wife who has thrown herself into a frantic round of official engagements, simply to keep her mind off less pleasant thoughts.

Mark has rarely accompanied his wife on official duties, and this was agreed by both of them many years ago. He has always been less than comfortable in public and after a couple of none too successful appearances alongside the Princess it was decided that he would pursue his own career, and she would carry on alone.

In the early days of their marriage they enjoyed a common bond mainly through their mutual love of horses. They were both competitors at international level and their interests were completely bound up in their own and each other's equestrian careers. The problems started when Princess Anne stopped competing at top level and began widening her public role. Mark remained completely immersed in the world of horses, while she took on a wide variety of different jobs. Her presidency of the Save the Children Fund alone has brought her a tremendously high profile in the field of international famine relief. She meets Presidents and Prime Ministers on equal terms and speaks with authority on a variety of important and at times controversial issues.

Mark has endeavoured to carve an independent career for himself, with a great deal of success. He is said to earn over £400,000 a year, but it is still all concentrated on horses. What has happened to their relationship is that he has simply been left behind. They no longer share the same interests and after sixteen years of marriage they have grown bored with each other. They may have fallen out of love, but they still like one another and share a deep affection for their two children, whose welfare is still their number one priority.

This is as amicable an arrangement as it is possible to get in the circumstances; Mark will continue to organize his many business interests from his new home, while his wife will remain as mistress

of Gatcombe Park, which is what she has always been. When the
Queen bought Gatcombe from the family of the late Lord Butler in
1976, as a present for the couple, the title of the house was put in
the Princess's name alone, and it has remained so. Mark has
never owned any part of Gatcombe, but he has made a significant
contribution to the maintenance and upkeep of the estate. So the
question of dividing any communal property does not arise, and in
any case no mention of a divorce has yet been made.

The Queen is naturally deeply saddened by the separation, and
Prince Philip will be a source of encouragement and strength to his
daughter during this very difficult time. The relationship between
the Princess and her father has always been close – never more so
than it is right now.

I have known the Princess Royal and Mark Phillips for nearly
twenty years. In that time I have come to like them both and
admire them for their independent attitudes. Perhaps it is these very
attributes that have now brought about this latest break in a royal
marriage. It is always sad when a marriage breaks up; it is even
more difficult when it happens in the full glare of publicity. In the
coming months they are going to have to try to carry on with their
lives as usual – but apart. The Princess has no intention of reducing
her public engagements, and they will both continue to conduct
themselves with the dignity they have always shown. Perhaps the
world will respond by showing them the sympathy and compassion
they need. They are both survivors; I wish them equal happiness
in whatever direction their lives now move.

Brian Hoey
September 1989

ACKNOWLEDGEMENTS

I am indebted to a great many people for their help and encouragement in writing this book. Many of them gave their assistance on
the understanding that I would respect their anonymity and I am
glad to do so – so my thanks to them has to be in general terms.
Nevertheless, I hope they will accept my appreciation even though
they cannot be named individually.

My greatest thanks must of course go to the Princess Royal
herself. When I first mentioned the idea of writing a second book
with her as the subject, she was less than enthusiastic, saying, 'What
else is there to say?' But when I eventually persuaded her that there
was indeed a great deal more to say, she agreed to cooperate –
albeit reluctantly at first. Her Royal Highness cleared the way for
me to accompany her on official visits (as part of the team) and
allowed me to talk to friends and Household without any pre-
conditions. She also gave me interviews about her life and work
and at no time did she ask for editorial control of the manuscript.
Ma'am, I am glad to be able to record my grateful thanks to you.

Similarly, Captain Mark Phillips spoke freely when I asked him
to comment on various aspects of the Princess's life.

I cannot rate too highly the contribution made by Lieutenant
Colonel Peter Gibbs, Private Secretary to the Princess Royal. All
the interviews were arranged by him personally and nothing was
too much trouble when it came to getting the facts right. Without
him this book simply would not have been written.

All the other members of the Household were equally helpful and I am grateful for this opportunity of publicly thanking them all: the Hon. Maddy Loudoudis, Assistant Private Secretary, Jo Hockley, Sue White and Jane Hambling in the office, who have all been patient in the extreme with my never-ending queries. The ladies-in-waiting put up with my presence on several royal visits, when I'm quite sure they could have done without any extra burdens. They were all helpful and I'm sure they will understand if I name only the three in particular with whom I came into the most frequent contact: the Hon. Mrs Legge-Bourke, the Countess of Lichfield and Mrs Timothy Holderness-Roddam.

Philip Robinson spoke frankly and honestly about the job of being a royal policeman and also smoothed the path for me on a number of occasions. I am grateful to him and also to his colleagues, Peter Schmidt, Barry Wilkinson and Jeff Fuller.

Others to whom I owe a debt of gratitude include Nicholas Hinton, Peter Valpy, Canon Bill Down, Tom Scott, Marjorie Langford, John Haslam, David and Dinah Nicholson, Malcolm Wallace and Dick Palmer.

For Grafton Books my publisher Richard Johnson has been a constant support and Katherine Everett an enthusiastic and knowledgeable picture researcher. Janice Robertson was responsible for the editing of the manuscript and Mike Shaw my agent nursed the project from conception to birth.

Finally, I would like to emphasize that at no time has there been any pressure from Buckingham Palace or Gatcombe Park to omit any facts and all views expressed, unless otherwise stated, are mine and mine alone.

Brian Hoey
May 1989

INTRODUCTION

'I don't come here looking for trouble. I come here to see if I can help.' The Princess Royal is speaking at the end of her most recent African tour on behalf of the Save the Children Fund, when she was asked if she became involved in any of the political troubles of the countries she visited. That is the basis of her philosophy: never mind the politics, let's get on with the job of helping those in need, whether they are refugees in Marxist-controlled countries such as the Sudan, orphans in any of the one-party states of the African continent or young mothers in India and Bangladesh whose urgent need is education in basic hygiene. The Princess Royal, who is still known as Princess Anne in most of the countries throughout the world, has been involved in public life since she was eighteen, when she stood in for her father, the Duke of Edinburgh, and presented leeks to the Welsh Guards at a St David's Day parade.

Her involvement with Save the Children, the charity with which she is most closely identified these days, goes back to New Year's Day 1970, the day on which she became its President. She is its sixth President in its seventy-year history and only the second woman to have held the position. Her great-aunt, the late Countess Mountbatten of Burma, did the job from 1949 to 1960.

But even though Save the Children gets most of the publicity and is the main reason for her 'high profile', let us not forget that Her Royal Highness is actively involved with nearly a hundred other organizations, all of whom take a proprietorial interest in their royal patron, and she, in turn, gives them as much time as she can.

Riding for the Disabled claims a great deal of her attention and her diary always includes visits to RDA outposts in remote parts of the British Isles and overseas. Similarly, London University, of which she is Chancellor, also demands much of her time. She attends nearly every degree ceremony – and this can mean up to 1800 graduates passing before her at the Royal Albert Hall in a single sitting.

Her Royal Highness is now in her fortieth year and for more than half her life she has been a full-time member of the 'Royal Firm' as her late grandfather King George VI called it. In between she has found time to become one of the outstanding riders of her time, winning the European Three-Day Event Championship in 1971 when she was just twenty-one, and representing Britain at the 1976 Olympic Games in Montreal. She has also married, brought up two children and helped to manage a large country estate and farm in Gloucestershire.

The Princess Royal and Mark Phillips have tried to solve an almost impossible problem – how to blend two busy careers, lived in the unremitting glare of publicity, with a secure private life. The difficulty comes when two people, who appeared at first glance to have so much in common, discover that they have simply grown apart. Nine times out of ten there isn't even a third party involved; it is just a case of one partner being left behind as the other develops wider interests.

The Princess travels the world on behalf of her many organizations, meeting prime ministers and presidents and people from all walks of life. Mark is a businessman who also has overseas commitments, but the only lengthy absence is during the autumn when he has to go to Australia and New Zealand to fulfil contracts arranged for him by International Management Group, the company owned by the world's leading sports agent Mark McCormack. Much of his time is now spent at the new three-million-pound equestrian centre at Gleneagles in Scotland which bears his name. As one of the world's top riders, it is important for Mark to be seen at his various business venues. He knows, and his sponsors realize only too well, the value of having someone with his name and reputation present as often as possible when the paying customers are around. Nobody wants to go to a Mark Phillips' riding course if Mark Phillips isn't there in person.

All this has placed considerable pressure on their marriage during the past sixteen years when they have always maintained a dignified silence in the face of the many rumours that have broken out – at times with monotonous regularity. The Princess has persisted with her huge round of public engagements, though continually dogged by the paparazzi, at home and abroad, during periods when she must have longed for the sort of privacy royalty could command in the past.

The Princess Royal regards Gatcombe Park as home. Buckingham Palace, where she retains a small suite of bedroom, sitting room and dining room, is 'the office'. It is from here that she operates for all London engagements, but she does not often spend the night. As a family the Phillipses have this in common: both parents are obsessive about preserving their children's privacy.

Peter, the Queen's first grandchild, was born in 1977, and his sister Zara in 1981. They are the only members of the Royal Family not to have titles (not even an Hon. before their names), and the Princess believes there is no reason why they should have. She says, 'They are not royal. The Queen just happens to be their grandmother.' This is one of the few subjects on which the Princess and her mother appear to disagree. It is said that the Queen would love to confer titles on both children, and of course if she wanted them to be known as Prince Peter and Princess Zara it is fully within her power to make it happen. But so far Her Majesty has bowed to the wishes of her daughter, and the older they get, the more difficult it becomes to change their styles and titles. Peter is at a prep school and will eventually go on to public school, but not, as was expected, his father's old school, Marlborough. Zara attends a local preparatory school in the village of Minchinhampton, less than a mile from home, to which she is taken every morning. Eventually she too will go to boarding school. They both mix with other children of their own age, go to birthday parties and invite their schoolfriends to theirs. There is no question of their being segregated or treated differently simply because of their mother's position. Not for them the high profile of the little Princes William and Henry, the children of the Prince and Princess of Wales, even though they are first cousins. Peter and Zara are not the constant target of photographers, although when they appear with the Queen or their own mother they do become the focus of attention. It's natural and understandable; but their fairly strict upbringing means that they are never in danger of becoming 'big-headed'. If one of them behaves badly, in private or in public, the Princess doesn't hesitate to administer a slap if necessary.

The whole question of titles – either for herself or others – is one which does not interest her a great deal. Her own title came through an accident of birth, and even though she is an absolute believer in the monarchy and the present system, she sees no reason why her husband should have been given an earldom simply because he was marrying her. The offer was made by the Queen – and politely but firmly declined. It's a decision they both agree was the right one at the time, and they have never thought it necessary to change their minds. The Princess's attitude to titles, which is well known in the royal family, may well have been partly the reason why it took so long for her to be created the Princess Royal. The Duke of Edinburgh was the first person to raise the subject (without his daughter's knowledge), some years ago, but it was not until 1986 that the Queen offered the title to her daughter – and it was accepted. Many people felt it was long overdue.

The social life of the Princess Royal revolves around a group of very close friends, most of whom share her interest in horses. But they don't all come from the 'horsey' set. Former world motor racing champion Jackie Stewart has been a close friend since he first met the Princess when they were voted Sports Personalities of 1971. The Princess Royal and Captain Phillips used to spend part of their holidays at the Swiss home of the Stewarts, and Jackie's wife Helen is a godmother to Zara. The Princess also enjoys the company of actors occasionally. She was delighted to join the film star Michael Caine and his wife at a private party to celebrate the fortieth birthday of the actor Anthony Andrews. Anthony and his wife Georgina have been close friends of Princess Anne and Mark for a number of years, and they share many interests including shooting and riding.

The Princess is a very loyal friend, standing by those close to her, especially when they are going through difficult times, as the Countess of Lichfield found out when she was divorced from her husband, Patrick, the Earl of Lichfield, one of the world's most famous and highly paid glamour photographers.

In recent years the Princess Royal's public image has undergone a 'renaissance'. She undertakes the toughest overseas tours to some of the poorest regions in the world and never flinches from dirt, disease or smells. Her foreign tours are in marked contrast to those undertaken by the other younger ladies in the royal family. She knows her role is not a glamorous one and consequently is not asked, nor wants to be, to glittering extravaganzas in Hollywood and Palm Springs. When she went to Los Angeles in 1984 it was to attend the Olympic Games in her capacity as President of the British Olympic Association, and her presence, briefly, in Hollywood was also in an official role, this time as President of BAFTA (The British Academy of Film and Television Awards). Nevertheless, she still enjoyed the bright lights of the film capital even if some of the Hollywood luminaries did confuse her with the Queen's sister, Princess Margaret.

The Princess of Wales and the Duchess of York may have become the most photographed women in the world in recent years, shown nearly always in glamorous situations, with rock stars, film and television actors and others from the world of the arts. But the Princess Royal makes the headlines when she describes Aids as 'a self-inflicted wound' at a serious conference on the disease. She has become one of the most respected members of her family, totally dedicated to public life and second only to the Queen in the number of engagements she undertakes throughout the year. She has matured into a gracious, elegant woman who, though she still does not suffer fools gladly – if indeed at all – has become a warm, compassionate and sincere person whose role in the royal family is unique.

The Princess is however fully aware of who she is and the position she holds within the hierarchy of her family, and no one is ever left in any doubt of that position. I was present at one of her public engagements when a photographer (of the chirpy Cockney variety) called out: 'Look this way, my love.' The reply was immediate, cutting and very regal: 'I am not your love' – almost immediately some else added sotto voce 'I am Your Royal Highness.'

She is able to continue her exhausting round of public engagements because she has the ability to keep her professional and private lives separate. Her children's welfare is the number one priority and she and Mark have always been in total agreement on this. Her Royal Highness was the first British princess in 900 years who was able to marry the man of her choice without any thought of political or monarchical expediency, and the man she chose to accept managed to retain his independence in spite of sharing his private life with the most public of figures for sixteen years.

In her own words, Princess Anne has said that she 'never was and never will be a fairytale princess'. This is undoubtedly true. She doesn't court the attentions of the tabloid press with outfits costing thousands of pounds every time she appears in public, and if she wears her hair in a new style nobody takes much notice. Instead she is known for the work she does rather than who is doing it. And that's the way she likes it. She doesn't care if some of the people in the underdeveloped Third World countries she visits for Save the Children don't know who she is. The fact that her presence might attract attention to the problems is enough to justify the visit in her eyes. If she is photographed looking tired and sweaty in some dust-covered, fly-blown desert where the temperature rarely dips below a hundred degrees Fahrenheit, she doesn't mind at all. The project in hand is the thing that matters, not her own image as a member of the most famous family in the world.

Princess Anne is totally supportive of the monarchy and any talk of change is quickly dismissed by her. 'The idea of opting out simply doesn't arise. I see no point in change simply for change's sake,' she says. Although she has been described as very much 'her father's girl' with many of the same characteristics – outspoken, abrasive and sarcastic – she has also inherited most of her mother's more likeable qualities. She is a caring mother, loyal to family and friends, devoted to her duty and compassionate without being sentimental. In fact she finds this last quality a positive asset in her dealings with the Save the Children Fund. In her view, 'It's no good my wringing my hands and saying "what's to be done?" when I visit a camp in which one in four babies die before they are five years old. It's much better if I can look at the problem dispassionately – or at least without showing too much compassion – and find out from the workers in the field what needs to be done and how I can help to get it done.'

In her everyday dealings with the other charities with which she is involved – and involved is the right word in her case – she continues to demonstrate a practical understanding of their problems, and her in-depth knowledge of the work they do has helped to make her so much more than just another royal figurehead. That is a role she has refused to play right from the start. Lavinia, Duchess of Norfolk, the person who persuaded her to join the Riding for the Disabled Association as its Patron back in 1970, soon realized her mistake. 'Patron is the title we give to someone who allows us to use his or her name on our letterheadings. They do not normally take any active part in our day-to-day activities. So I soon realized what a misnomer this was when applied to Princess Anne. She chaired our meetings from day one and demanded reports on everything that was going on. If we asked her to visit a remote branch in the north of Scotland or West Wales she would always fit it in somehow. So eventually we made the right decision and made the Princess our President instead of our Patron. And she really is a working President in every sense of the word.' The Princess puts it more succinctly, 'I simply swopped with the Duchess.'

The Princess Royal was born a royal princess with an impeccable family tree. She is a direct descendant of Queen Victoria through both her mother and father. Yet for much of her life she has been thought of as the 'odd one out' in the royal family – and not just by outsiders but by her relations too. It is a label she is fully aware of, but one about which she professes not to care. As the Queen's second child, Her Royal Highness has known from early childhood that her own position will always be inferior to that of her older brother the Prince of Wales, and indeed, these days, also to those of her two younger brothers the Duke of York and Prince Edward. If it is a situation that troubles her she does not show it, but it seemed in her younger days that she felt the need to prove herself over and over again. Prince Charles's destiny was predetermined from the moment of his birth. He was born to be king and his training began almost from the moment he could walk. His sister found it hard to accept that she was required to take second place, and as children she and Charles competed at almost everything; at least, she did. If they played a game in the nursery or garden Anne always strove that little bit harder to make sure she was the winner – and she usually was, partly because Charles has never felt the need to compete with anyone, and partly because he is by nature a more gentle person. Some years ago Princess Anne explained these early feelings, saying, 'I was always the "tail-end Charlie" and grew up being used to the fact.' And this very fact of being the permanent 'number two' perhaps made her feel she was also second best – at least for a time. So much so that she appeared to be something of a rebel from an early age. In fact it is only in the last ten years that she has ceased to become the 'odd one out' in the royal family. Her independence manifested itself in several ways: two of the most significant being the sport she chose to follow and the man she married.

Eventing is surely the toughest of all equestrian sports. One has to master three separate disciplines: dressage, cross-country and show jumping. It is also a sport in which individual effort and skill are all important; only rarely, in a team event such as the Olympics, does one have to consider other people. Her Royal Highness has experienced both the satisfactions and disappointments common to all competitors, and her talent, courage and hard work over many years have taken her to the top of her chosen sport.

Horses are no respecters of rank and, as Princess Anne herself told me, 'When I'm approaching a water-jump with fifty or sixty photographers clicking away like mad, television cameras zooming in to try and catch me going in head first and a couple of thousand spectators swarming all over the place, the only one who you can guarantee doesn't know I'm royal is the horse.'

Then when the time came for her to be married she chose to accept a man who was her peer only on the field of competition. Mark Phillips, himself an Olympic medallist, had few other qualifications to be a suitable husband for the Queen's only daughter. When they met he was a career army officer from a middle-class family in Wiltshire. He had no title and was not the heir to a great estate or fortune. What he did possess – and this is one of the qualities Princess Anne admires almost above all others – is the will to win. He is one of the most determined competitors in the world and his equestrian pedigree is immaculate. He was a world class horseman long before he even met the woman who was to become his wife, so in the early days of their friendship and subsequent courtship it was she who had to fight to keep up with him, not the other way around.

Since their marriage in 1973 they have each developed individual careers. Mark is an international businessman with interests in Australia, New Zealand and the USA as well as running a 1,000-acre farm at home (though in reality it is the farm manager who looks after the day-to-day organization while a farm office in Cambridge handles all the accounts). The Princess Royal has gone from strength to strength as a senior member of the royal family, carrying out public engagements in Britain and abroad in her own right or on behalf of the Queen. During her lifetime she has been the subject of a number of highly critical articles, accused at different times of being rude, quick to anger and impatient with others who are not quite as fast on the uptake as she is herself. But in all the thousands of words that have been written about her there has never been the slightest suggestion that she does not pull her weight. In the league table of royal duties, the number of engagements the Princess Royal carries out is exceeded only by the Queen. No one else comes anywhere near. It's a proud record but one which she herself is unaware of. She is at her best when doing something and is not a particularly avid spectator.

Another of her undoubted qualities is her courage. It was ably demonstrated in March 1974, when in the course of an attempt to kidnap her in The Mall, five people were shot; and in another context, her sporting courage was put to the test at the Olympic Games in Montreal in 1976. The Princess had fallen badly during the cross country section of the Three Day Event and was suffering from concussion and severe bruising. It would have been easy for her to retire from the competition. Nobody would have blamed her if she had. But she got back on her horse and finished the demanding course. I asked her some years later why she hadn't retired. Her reply was a classic example of royal understatement: 'I had told the team not to expect me to get back on if I was damaged – I was unconscious at the time!' Unconscious or not, her performance was still highly praised by her teammates.

I have known Princess Anne for nearly twenty years and watched her mature from a rebellious, forthright young lady who didn't hesitate to tell intrusive photographers to 'naff off', into a gracious, elegant woman of our time. If the photographers get in her way these days, she is still just as likely to invite them to leave in her own inimitable manner, but she has certainly lost the reputation she held for some years of being the least popular member of the royal family. Her work for Save the Children has been the biggest single factor in changing the image the public and the press had of her for such a long time. In fact the transformation can be traced accurately to 1982, when she undertook the toughest overseas tour ever experienced by a royal. She visited six African countries and covered more than 14,000 miles, seeing sights hitherto thought inconceivable for a member of her family: babies with distended stomachs and the faces of old men; young mothers trying to suckle infants when there was no milk in their breasts through famine, and dirt, disease and the smell of death everywhere. Reporters who had accompanied the Princess hoping for a good story about the state of her marriage (yet again) began to realize that here was a royal tour with a difference. In the first place they were not used to a daily programme that had always begun by 7.30 A.M. and rarely ended before midnight. They also thought that Princess Anne would follow the usual royal route and see only those sights the host country wanted her to see; with everything painted and polished before she arrived. But once the official part of the proceedings had been disposed of with as much speed as was diplomatically possible, it was into a Land-Rover wearing khaki drill trousers and with hair tied back and covered in a headscarf, and off into the bush. There was a polio immunization programme to see in Swaziland; a village health centre in Zimbabwe; an orphanage in Kenya – which she had first visited twelve years earlier – then on to Malawi to meet President Hastings Banda, one of her greatest supporters, and then to war-torn Somalia where thousands of refugees were literally starving to death. The Princess spoke to a number of field workers from SCF, and said, 'Tell me what you need and I'll make sure the right people hear about it.' Then it was on to North Yemen and finally into war-ravaged Beirut.

By now the press party had begun to realize how hard she worked and the stories which began to appear in the British newspapers were among the most favourable the Princess had ever known. Instead of the expected public relations exercise they found genuine news stories, and this was some time before Bob Geldof and his televised appeals which did so much to raise the public's awareness of the plight of Ethiopia's population. The reporters on that tour were so impressed with the work being done by Princess Anne that three of them became individual sponsors to orphaned children in Kenya and maintain them financially to this day.

Even the Princess noticed how her public image had changed. She said some time later, 'I did notice my miraculous transform- ation.' But even on that trip she would not pose specially for the photographers. They wanted to see her holding one of the pathetic babies, looking compassionate and maternal. She refused, saying, 'I don't do stunts.'

There has never been a time when she has not been of interest to the media, and has accepted this aspect of her life with resignation – except when competing at horse trials, for she regards this part of her life as 'private' as opposed to 'public'. In the same way that all the other members of the royal family like to preserve their privacy when not engaged on public duties, Her Royal Highness too believes she has a right to a private life. Perhaps she has, but it is a little naïve to expect the press to ignore her simply because she feels she is off duty. Editors are all too aware that some of the best stories and pictures occur when the subjects are relaxed, and the chance of catching Princess Anne in an unguarded moment or taking a spectacular tumble from her horse is too good to miss.

Recently however her relationship with the world's press seems to have settled down to a large extent. At least she is no longer voted, as she was in the USA in 1982, 'the person I would least like to interview'. And no longer does her photograph on the cover of a news magazine guarantee a drop in sales, as a German periodical claimed ten years ago. The Princess professes not to care about her image, saying, 'There's nothing I can do about it now anyway; it's too late.' However, she is honest enough to admit, 'It's nice when one reads something pleasant.'

Has she changed since the days when she carried on a series of running battles with the press? Is she more mellow and tolerant? She thinks not. 'The media is just showing me in a different light,' she says. 'I'm just the same as I've always been.' I am not too sure. To me she does seem slightly more tolerant and less likely to flare up the moment something goes wrong. Her close friend Jackie Stewart reckons I'm wrong. He says she is no different at all from when he first met her in 1971, but then his attitudes have probably changed also in the past eighteen years. One of Princess Anne's ladies-in-waiting put it perhaps best of all. 'She is no different now from the way she has always been,' she told me. 'The only surprise is that it's taken the rest of us such a long time to find out.'

One thing is certain. The Princess knows what she wants out of life and what her role is to be. She is totally confident of her ability to do her job and public awareness of her responsibilities has been heightened by both the changed attitude of the press and her response. The informal interviews with Michael Parkinson and Terry Wogan on television would not have been thought possible a few years ago. But today Her Royal Highness is confident of her own ability to handle such situations, and she is completely self-assured about the way she looks, dresses and behaves.

She may never inspire the sort of slavish devotion the Princess of Wales receives from the millions of readers of the tabloid press for whom she can do no wrong, but Princess Anne gets something else. She earns respect and admiration. In a recent poll in western Europe she was voted the person most people would like to see as the next British sovereign. It is a role she has never sought and one that she is most unlikely to take on as she is now seventh in line of succession to the throne. But the results of the survey give an indication of how people see the Princess Royal, not only in Britain but in other countries, most of which are republics to whose people the idea of an hereditary monarchy is repugnant. The feeling seems to be that, as royals go – the Princess Royal is OK.

CHAPTER
ONE

♦

A WORKING DAY

The time is 6.45 A.M. as the light comes on in the bedroom of the Princess Royal on the second-floor front of Buckingham Palace. It is still dark on this January morning and bitterly cold outside in the clear air with several hours still to go until dawn, as Her Royal Highness rises. There has been a late evening engagement in London the night before, which is why Her Royal Highness has been staying at the Palace. Normally she will drive back to Gatcombe as she spends as little time in London as possible. She bathes and dresses quickly and walks along the wide corridor lined with cabinets filled with china and porcelain and portraits of long dead ancestors. The tiny lift with its mirrored walls and plush bench along one side carries her silently to the ground floor where her police officer, Sergeant Jeff Fuller, is waiting. A brief good morning – she is not very talkative first thing – and they move through the Quadrangle Entrance to where her car is parked. It is a Reliant Scimitar, the same model she has been driving for nearly twenty years and bearing the number plate 1420 H which she has sported since it was given to her as a twenty-first birthday present by the men of the 14th/20th Hussars, the first regiment of which she became Colonel-in-Chief.

Jeff Fuller moves to the front passenger seat. He knows she will drive herself. None of the four police officers who take it in turns to act as her bodyguard has ever been allowed to drive the Princess.

They move swiftly through the North Centre Gate, acknowledging the salute of the uniformed constable on duty, and turn left into Constitution Hill. Even at this time of the morning the traffic is building up but most of it is coming into London and the roads leading to the M4 are reasonably clear. Once they have navigated the Chiswick flyover and settled onto the motorway the Princess is able to put her foot down and settle into the easy, relaxed style which allows her to drive without tiring for hours at a time. She is an expert at the wheel, flicking through the manual gearbox with the same sort of dexterity she uses when guiding one of her horses through a narrow gap in the field or over a fence. Her old friend, the former world champion Grand Prix driver Jackie Stewart, said that one of the first things he noticed about her was 'her strong workmanlike hands – equally good for driving or riding'. They are heading for Condicote in Gloucestershire, a remote hamlet on the outskirts of Stow-on-the-Wold, where David Nicholson, her trainer, is waiting. It is just after 8.30 when they turn into the yard at Cotswold House; Nicholson's other riders have just returned from first stables, which started at seven, and today, because of the trip from London, the Princess Royal is riding out second lot at nine o'clock.

She joins the rest of the string and takes her place on the horse that has been allocated to her by the trainer. It's not a special mount, reserved for her; she takes whatever is next in line to be worked. After an hour and a half of solid riding, they return to the stables and the Princess joins David Nicholson and his wife Dinah in the kitchen for a quick breakfast. This morning it is just coffee and kiwi fruit. Then, after telling them when she would next like to ride out (it all depends on her official programme), she drives off for the forty-minute journey to Gatcombe.

At home she parks on the gravelled drive in front of the house and goes upstairs to bathe and change for the first official duty of the day. Jeff Fuller moves around to the police officers' sitting room at the rear, to check with the office in Buckingham Palace whether there have been any last minute changes. There are none – there rarely is any alteration. Once the programme has been agreed and printed, they usually stick to it to the letter. By now another member of the team has arrived. She is one of the Princess's nine ladies-in-waiting, the Honourable Mrs Legge-Bourke, who has driven herself over the Severn Bridge from her home in South Wales. She is going to look after the Cardiff side of the day only; later on the Princess is leaving for a short foreign trip and for this she will be joined by another of the group.

Shân Legge-Bourke glances at her programme for the day. It has been photographically reduced to a size convenient for handbags and pockets and lists every movement planned for the two-hour visit. The names of all those the Princess will meet are also printed. Shân has checked earlier with Linda Joyce, then the Princess's dresser, to see what Her Royal Highness will be wearing. It's not so much to avoid clashing as to see if hats are the order of the day – they are not!

The lady-in-waiting and the policeman wait outside the front door and she curtseys as the Princess Royal emerges. A rather battered Land-Rover is waiting and the Princess moves automatically to the driver's seat. The others pile in for the short drive to the Top Field, where a helicopter of the Queen's Flight is ready for take-off. The crewman salutes but the pilot does not get out of the aircraft. The Princess does not stand on ceremony; she just wants to get on with the job. They take off immediately she is on board and strapped in, and head straight down the Bristol Channel for the South Wales coast. They don't talk because conversation is practically impossible inside the helicopter, just insert their ear plugs and enjoy the view. It's a beautifully clear day and they can see the traffic streaming across the Severn Bridge in both directions. The flight to Cardiff takes exactly half an hour. By road it would have been more than twice that and involved the police forces of four counties.

Meanwhile at Cardiff Heliport on the outskirts of the city's docks, all is ready for the royal arrival. It's been ready for hours. Six white police cars are drawn up alongside the landing area. The acting Chief Constable is on parade wearing his medals. Some thirty police officers are scattered around the heliport, both uniformed and plain clothes. There are six motor cycles to provide the escort and clear the route in advance. Two ambulances with fully equipped teams (including a couple of pints of blood of the Princess's group) are standing by, and a landing party from nearby RAF St Athan are in radio contact with the royal helicopter every second it is in the air. They report that the flight is two minutes late.

The official welcoming party is waiting inside the reception hall. It is led by Mrs Susan Williams, Lord Lieutenant of South Glamorgan, who, as the Queen's representative, has the responsibility of receiving the Princess on the county's soil. She will present Mr Dudley Fisher, High Sheriff, the Deputy Chairman of the County Council (who is here because the Chairman is away on holiday in Tenerife) and Mr Michael Boyce, the Chief Executive. Lastly, the man who owns the heliport is added to the list of those to be presented. As it happens he is the one with whom the Princess will have the longest conversation. She tells him that he should not have planted trees so near the landing area. He replies that he has been telling the County Council that ever since they planted them without his consent. Perhaps now they will take some notice.

As the gleaming red helicopter hovers into sight, the official party move out into the biting wind on the tarmac. The pilot lands without any problems and the first person out of the helicopter is the policeman who discreetly hands the royal pennant to the driver of the car in which the Princess will be travelling. It will be his last task to retrieve the pennant when they leave.

The Princess Royal steps down from the helicopter to be welcomed by the Lord Lieutenant. She is wearing a tailored coat in lovat tweed with a velvet collar, a silk scarf and leather boots. After the minimum of delays while she chats to the waiting officials she is ushered into the car and the convoy moves off. At every junction a police officer is stationed, holding up the traffic for just a few seconds until the royal car has passed. There is very little disruption and the whole operation swings into action like a well-oiled machine. It ought to, they have practised it often enough. The car immediately behind the Princess's swerves from side to side as the driver sees someone standing too close to the kerb – they are taking no chances. Everyone remembers the attempted kidnapping in March 1974.

Less than five minutes after landing, the Princess is being driven through the main gates of Cardiff Prison. There is another official greeting party, this time led by the Lord Mayor of the City, Councillor Bill Herbert. The Princess Royal is presented with a small bouquet of flowers by the granddaughter of the Governor and she moves towards the inner buildings of the prison. She is making the visit in her capacity as Patron of the Butler Trust, an organization which rewards high standards of prison work. She has already been to Birmingham, Holloway, Manchester, Norwich, Parkhurst, Wakefield and Barlinnie to look at the working conditions in Britain's prisons. It was while she was in Glasgow's notorious Barlinnie Gaol that she was, innocently, involved in a distressing incident. The Governor had arranged for her to see the maximum security wing and while there she was photographed talking to an inmate who was serving a life sentence for murder. When the mother of the victim saw the picture in the local press, she wrote a heart-rending letter to the Princess asking why she should be seen exchanging jokes with the man who had murdered her daughter. The Princess of course had been in no position to agree or refuse to be photographed; it was a normal press facility; but she understood all too easily how the photograph could have upset the lady and wrote a personal note back explaining the situation. There is no prospect of such an occurrence happening at today's visit. Cardiff is not a long-stay prison. Most of the 500 inmates are serving short sentences or are on remand.

A large press party is waiting inside the prison and the man in charge of them, Welsh Office press officer Elfed Bowen, who was awarded an MVO for his services to the Prince of Wales during an earlier tour, explains that he has had to restrict the number of cameramen and reporters. Many more had applied for accreditation than could be accommodated.

The first room the Princess sees is the visiting hall and, today being one of the official visiting days, it is packed with inmates and their families and friends. Prisoners sit on one side of a long table separated from their wives and families by a low glass screen. They are not supposed to touch across the screen but the warders turn a blind eye and a lot of kissing and cuddling is going on. A children's crèche in the room is run by the Women's Royal Voluntary Service and the Princess stops to talk to one of the ladies. She tells her she thinks it is a good idea and innovative to have such a crèche in a prison. It gives the husbands and wives a little time to themselves. There is also a small cafeteria where the visitors can buy tea, coffee and chocolate. The Princess is struck by the extreme youth of those present. The average age in this category B prison seems to be somewhere in the early twenties.

As the party moves to another part of the prison to see some of the inmates making jeans, the lady-in-waiting remarks on how fresh the atmosphere is inside. 'When we went to Barlinnie we were nearly knocked over by the smell as we went in,' she says. 'Obviously someone here has been busy with the fresh-air spray.' The Lord Lieutenant confirms this, saying that when she carried out her own personal 'recce' three weeks earlier, things had looked and smelt very different.

The Governor, Alan Rawson, is accompanying the Princess on her tour but he discreetly steps back and allows his staff and the inmates an opportunity to see the Princess and talk to her. He knows that she does not want to meet only the senior staff and officials, which is the usual case on a Royal visit, and takes a back seat for much of the two hours she spends inside his gaol. But he doesn't miss much and there is a lot of whispering between the officers accompanying the official party as he gives instructions about the next sector to be seen.

In one workshop the Princess stops to talk to an inmate who is cutting out a pattern for trousers. She asks him how long he has been in. 'Fourteen months,' is the reply. 'When are you getting out?' 'Friday, thank God.' (Today is Tuesday.) He revealed later that he was serving a sentence for deception. Was it worth it? 'Well, I'm going home to £40,000,' he answers with a grin. In a corner of the workshop the prison barber is giving an inmate a haircut. The Princess pauses for a moment, thinking that he is a member of staff. When he admits that he is also serving a sentence she seems slightly surprised that he should be doing this sort of job. Apparently it is common practice for the barber to travel around the prison and cut hair as and when he can. Cardiff Gaol has the most relaxed atmosphere of any of the prisons the Princess has seen so far. She meets one man though for whom the future looks bleak. He is just starting a life sentence and will be moved to another prison in a few days. After his talk with the Princess he says how different she looks from her pictures: 'Much younger and better looking. I could even fancy her.'

To the constant rattle of keys and chains the Princess moves around on her first visit to a Welsh prison. She meets an officer who has served for twenty-three years and remembers that she presented him with a Butler Trust certificate at Lambeth Palace in 1977. He is delighted that she has remembered him. She has a phenomenal memory and hardly ever forgets a face or occasion.

In the education wing the Princess meets Butler Trust workers who are helping to mount an anti-drink and drug abuse programme. Here young inmates are being given the opportunity to learn new skills and Her Royal Highness meets several who are cooking in an up-to-date kitchen. One of the local detectives who has been assigned to guard the Princess is taking his job too literally. He is constantly at her shoulder and Shân Legge-Bourke sharply reminds one of his colleagues, 'He does not need to be as close as that all the time. This is supposed to be a secure area.' Some of the police officers in the party are chatting with the inmates like old friends. It is explained that they know one another well because in some cases these very policemen were responsible for putting the prisoners behind bars.

In the young offenders' wing the inmates are playing table-tennis and pool on the landings. There is a library and one of the prisoners has carved a beautiful wooden chess set which he offers to the Princess. This is an unscheduled part of the programme. Normally no gifts are accepted unless it has been previously agreed with the Palace. However, the Princess is touched by the gesture and she accepts the set on behalf of the Save the Children Fund, saying, 'I know exactly where this can go.' Finally, she is shown what prison life is really all about, the inside of a cell. It is tiny, claustrophobic, containing three bunks, a table with plastic knives, forks and spoons and a bucket for each occupant. Pin-ups have been removed before the Princess's visit in a totally unnecessary clean-up. There is one window high in the wall and everything is spotlessly clean. The cell is completely soulless and if the rest of the prison gives an impression that life here is easy and relaxed, a few minutes in this small area quickly alters that opinion.

The prison staff say the royal visit has given a tremendous lift to everyone, staff and inmates. The inmates agree, but for different reasons. They say anything that interferes with the dull routine of normal, everyday prison life is welcome, no matter what the reason.

After the tour of inspection the party moves to the administration block where even the offices of the civilian workers have windows with iron bars. Tea is served in the conference room and the Princess Royal is joined by a succession of local Butler Trust workers and members of the Prison Review Board, whose job it is to interview prospective parolees. The visit is over-running, but only by ten minutes, so Jeff Fuller and Shân Legge-Bourke are not panicking yet. 'When it gets to three-quarters of an hour we start to get a bit anxious.' The Princess seems in no hurry to leave. She is in excellent form, laughing and joking and making easy conversation with a number of people she has never met before and probably never will again. Eventually she realizes it is time to leave and makes her way out. After saying goodbye to the Governor and his colleagues, the police convoy sweeps her out of the prison gates and back to the heliport. Behind her they are all saying how easy she is to talk to and how different from her public image.

There are few formalities at the heliport. A quick word with Susan Williams, who reminds the Princess that they will be meeting again in a couple of weeks when she returns to Cardiff to inspect a gypsy encampment. The policeman remembers to retrieve the pennant from the official car, a quick wave and they are away.

For the people in Cardiff it is the end of a very successful day. For the Princess, there is more to come. Back at Gatcombe there is barely time to see daughter Zara for a few minutes before changing once more and setting out on the next job. She left Cardiff at 4.15 P.M. By 5 o'clock the Princess, at the wheel of her own car once more, sets out from Gatcombe for the ninety-mile drive to Heathrow Airport, from where she is to fly to Switzerland. The lady-in-waiting has changed. Shân Legge-Bourke has driven off for a few days' shooting in Yorkshire; Jane Holderness-Roddam, like the Princess a former Olympic horsewoman, has arrived from her home in Wiltshire to take over. Jeff Fuller has come to the end of his stint as royal bodyguard and the fourth member of the team, Barry Wilkinson, is waiting at Gatcombe to relieve him.

As the Princess drives through the evening traffic to London she listens to a couple of music tapes on her car stereo system. Tonight she feels like pop but she has a wide taste in music so it could be anything from classical to rock 'n' roll. At the airport she is greeted by another group of officials and escorted to British Airways flight BA 720, which leaves on time at five to seven. The destination is Zürich from where they will drive to Berne. The reason for the visit is to attend meetings of the Fédération Équestre Internationale (FEI) which she will chair as President. When she arrives in Switzerland she will meet more officials and have to spend some time doing her 'homework' before tomorrow's sessions begin. Since leaving Buckingham Palace this morning she has driven over two hundred miles, made two trips in a helicopter, ridden out for an hour and a half, carried out an exhausting two-hour prison visit during which time she didn't sit down once, and flown six hundred miles at the end of it. It's all in a day's work.

♦

CHAPTER TWO

EARLY DAYS

Wednesday 15 August 1950 dawned clear and sunny and promised to be a true English summer's day. There were thousands of visitors in London seeing the sights, and England were playing the West Indies at the Oval, that elegant cricket ground which forms part of the Kennington Estate owned by the Duke of Cornwall (also known these days as the Prince of Wales).

Crowds had already begun to gather outside Clarence House, the home of Princess Elizabeth and her husband, the Duke of Edinburgh. They knew through the news bulletins and the comings and goings at Clarence House that the King's elder daughter was about to give birth to her second child, and with that uncanny intuition of crowds everywhere instinctively realized that today would be the day. They were right. Ten minutes before the clock on the tower of St James's Palace struck the hour of twelve noon, a baby girl was born. She weighed exactly 6 lb.

Within minutes a bulletin was issued which said:

> Her Royal Highness the Princess Elizabeth, Duchess of Edinburgh, was safely delivered of a Princess at 11.50 A.M. today. Her Royal Highness and her daughter are doing well.

> (signed) WILLIAM GILLIATT
> JOHN H. PEEL
> VERNON F. HALL
> JOHN WEIR

The infant princess was the first child to be born in Clarence House since the major alterations by John Nash in 1825, and within minutes of her birth the Automobile Association announced that she was its one millionth member, a distinction she was to recall eighteen years later when she had passed her driving test and taken to the road.

Prince Philip was the proudest father and he had double cause for celebration. On the day of his daughter's birth he learned that he had been promoted to the rank of Lieutenant Commander in the Royal Navy. However, he had not attended the birth. In those days it was not the custom for a husband to be with his wife as their baby was born, so he waited near his wife's bedroom with his mother-in-law, the Queen (now Elizabeth the Queen Mother). She was determined to be near her daughter for the birth and had not accompanied her husband George VI to Scotland for their usual summer holiday. He had gone alone – or as alone as one can be with an entourage of seventy-five – and was out shooting when the news was conveyed to him by an aide. Another person who was not present at the birth was the Home Secretary, Mr Chuter Ede. Until the birth of Prince Charles, two years earlier, it had been a requirement for a Government minister to be in attendance in the delivery room at every royal birth. This was to ensure that there was no substitution for the royal child. George VI realized that there was no likelihood of such an occurrence in the mid-twentieth century, so shortly before Prince Charles was born in 1948, he sensibly decided that it was no longer necessary for a Minister of the Crown to be present at royal births.

It was also at this time that the King issued a decree which was published in the *London Gazette*. It said:

> The children of Princess Elizabeth and the Duke of
> Edinburgh are to enjoy the style and titular dignity
> of Prince or Princess before their Christian names.

If His Majesty had not issued this decree the baby daughter of Princess Elizabeth would have been known as Lady Anne Mountbatten, at least until her mother acceded to the throne in 1952.

The birth of a royal child in 1950 was a momentous occasion.

Royal salutes were fired in Hyde Park and at the Tower of London. The Lord Mayor of London was informed officially, as were the Governors General of the Dominions and all foreign ambassadors. Letters were despatched to the Scottish capital to tell the Lord Provost of Edinburgh, the Lord President of the Court of Session, the Lord Advocate and the Lord Justice Clerk of the royal birth. This was an ancient custom dating back hundreds of years to the days when it was considered of vital importance that high officials in Scotland should be kept informed of matters of national interest.

Prince Philip's mother, Princess Andrew, was staying at Kensington Palace and her son telephoned her there to give her the good news. She did not use the telephone very often because she was deaf, but she made a special effort on this very special day. Queen Mary the Queen Mother was another who did not favour the instrument as a means of communication; in fact she never once spoke on it during her long life and made no exceptions. So the news was given to her at Sandringham by a lady-in-waiting.

Affection for the royal family was at its zenith in 1950. The King and Queen had seen their people through a terrible world war. Peace had brought a new glamour to royalty with the wedding of Princess Elizabeth to her sailor prince in 1947; Princess Margaret was the epitome of a romantic fairytale princess and the birth of Prince Charles in 1948 had secured the succession for the foreseeable future. So the news of the birth of Princess Anne (even though her name had not then been revealed) became just the excuse that was needed for a wild celebration. Thousands of messages were sent to Clarence House and hundreds of bouquets of flowers delivered, so many that most of them had to be distributed to hospitals throughout London. The same thing happened with the toys and baby clothes that well-wishers gave to Princess Elizabeth for her baby daughter.

The names of the child were announced two weeks later. She was to be called Anne Elizabeth Alice Louise, all names which had long been in use by the royal family, though Anne had been out of favour for some time because George V, the little princess's great-grandfather, had not cared for it. When Princess Margaret was born in 1930, her mother, the then Duchess of York, wanted to call her Ann because she thought 'Ann of York sounded pretty'. But the King would not give his approval and that was the end of the matter. Elizabeth, of course, came from the child's own mother and grandmother; Alice was chosen as a tribute to Prince Philip's mother and Louise was the Christian name of a former Princess Royal, Edward VII's eldest daughter, later the Duchess of Fife.

Four days after the birth, on 19 August 1950, Prince Philip invited Mr D. A. Boreham, Registrar of Births and Deaths for the Sub-District of Westminster North East, to call at Clarence House to register the birth. The baby was registered as Her Royal Highness, Princess Anne Elizabeth Alice Louise of Edinburgh, and her father signed the register simply 'Philip'. There were a number of other formalities to be completed on that day, including allocating an identity card for the infant – the number is MAPM/396 – and a green ration book, which meant that she was entitled to an allowance of bread, milk, eggs, sugar, butter, margarine and meat. She was also given the usual baby's allowance of one bottle of orange juice and one of codliver oil. The Second World War may have been over for five years but food rationing was still very much in force in Britain, for everyone from the King to the humblest citizen. Princess Anne was third in line of succession to the Throne after her mother, the Heiress Presumptive, and her brother Prince Charles. Two months after the birth, on 21 October 1950, the christening took place in the Music Room at Buckingham Palace, used because the Chapel had been destroyed by German bombs in 1942.

Five godparents, or sponsors as they are called at royal christenings, were chosen. The first was the Queen herself, which was unusual in that until the christening of Prince Charles in 1948, sovereigns and their consorts never acted as sponsors. It was George VI who broke with tradition by suggesting himself as a sponsor to his grandson and the Queen followed his example with her granddaughter. The other sponsors were Princess Anne's paternal grandmother Princess Andrew of Greece, who was abroad at the time so was represented by Princess Alice; Princess Margarita of Hohenlohe-Langenburg, Prince Philip's elder sister; Earl Mountbatten of Burma, his uncle; and the Hon. Andrew Elphinstone, first cousin to Princess Elizabeth. The ceremony was performed by Dr Garbett, Archbishop of York, standing in for the Archbishop of Canterbury who was also abroad – in Australia. It was a formal occasion attended only by the families of both parents. The days when royal godparents would be chosen from the ranks of former flatmates of the mother, and guests would come from show business, the arts and sport were at least twenty-five years away.

Within weeks of the birth, Princess Elizabeth returned to her royal duties. Her father was in poor health and needed to rest, so his elder daughter bore the brunt of the investitures, official visits and affairs of State that he would normally have carried out himself. For the infant Princess Anne it was the start of a childhood in which long absences by her parents would be normal.

Less than two years later, on 6 February 1952, George VI died in his sleep at Sandringham. Princess Elizabeth, who was a week into a long Commonwealth Tour, returned to Britain as Queen Elizabeth II. At the age of eighteen months, Princess Anne became second in line of succession to the throne and, as daughter of the sovereign, she also became entitled to use the distinctive definite article before her name. In formal usage she became Her Royal Highness The Princess Anne – not that it made a great deal of difference to her, of course.

In June 1953 her mother's coronation took place. Anne was not yet three years old and considered too young to attend the long ceremony, so she remained at Buckingham Palace until her parents returned. The only thing she remembers vaguely about the day is being taken on to the balcony of the Palace and instructed to 'wave to the people'.

If Princess Anne was ever affected by the long absences of her parents when she was very young, she never gave any sign of it, which is perhaps why her own children have been brought up to regard it as perfectly normal for their parents to be away from home for long periods. And if the first two years of Princess Anne's life had been marked by her mother's increased attention to public duties, then the change when she became Queen meant that even less of her time could be devoted to her children. Affairs of State took up most of her time as she grappled with the many problems of the business of monarchy in the early days of her reign – and of course she was one of our youngest sovereigns for centuries. She was only twenty-five when she succeeded.

The domestic life of the children was left in the capable Scottish

hands of their nanny Helen Lightbody and her assistant Mabel
Anderson, who had previously worked for the Gloucesters, looking
after Prince William and Prince Richard. The children saw their
parents for half an hour in the morning and then again in the
evening before they went to bed.

Anne may have been two years younger than her brother but
even at tender ages they showed the characteristics which have
shaped their lives ever since. Charles was the quieter, more easygoing of the two. His sister was pushy, boisterous and clearly the
dominating personality. When they acquired their first pony, a
strawberry roan named William, as a joint present, it was Anne
who demanded to be lifted into the saddle at every opportunity.
Charles, who is a natural horseman, and has been since almost
before he could walk, always allowed his sister the lion's share of
their allotted time on the pony. She could never get enough. Helen
Lightbody once remarked, 'Anne will never walk if she can run,'
and when on horseback, even as a child, she would never trot when
she could gallop.

Both the Queen and her sister Princess Margaret were educated
privately at home. They never went to school. But the Duke of
Edinburgh had been educated at Gordonstoun public school in
Scotland and he was determined that his children would follow his
example and receive most of their schooling outside the Palace. It
was a decision that subsequently proved to be the right one for all
of them. But the initial lessons for Charles and Anne were held in
the Palace schoolroom, in what is now the Princess's suite. Miss
Catherine Peebles was engaged as governess to Prince Charles and,
as Princess Anne has said since, 'I just tagged along.' Little love
was lost between the Princess and Miss Peebles, simply because
the Scottish teacher was besotted with Prince Charles and had not
much time for anyone else. When he was sent away to his preparatory school at the age of seven, Miss Peebles was heartbroken.
She continued to teach Princess Anne, and two other little girls,
Susan (Sukie) Babington-Smith and Caroline Hamilton, grand-
daughters of senior courtiers who had been brought into the Palace
to keep the Princess company, but her heart was never fully in
it. When she was discovered dead in her room at the Palace some
years later, Charles was inconsolable. Princess Anne felt only

a sense of guilt because she could not grieve as sincerely as her brother.

The Palace schoolroom functioned until Princess Anne was twelve years old. She and the other two little girls were treated exactly alike. No favouritism was shown to the royal pupil and Sukie Babington-Smith (now Mrs John Hemming) says, 'It was lovely when the Queen was going to open Parliament or there was a State Visit. We would be taken into the Courtyard to see the procession leaving, and if the Queen saw us she would always wave.' I asked Mrs Hemming if she and Caroline Hamilton realized, even at that early age, that Princess Anne was any different. 'Of course we knew that she was royal. Not by anything she consciously did or said, it was simply something about her that made us realize she was different. The Palace was somewhere we went every day, but at the end of the afternoon we went home and she, of course, remained. I can never remember a single occasion when she was treated any differently from us in the schoolroom, apart from the odd time when Miss Peebles would be stricter with her than she was with us. One would see the Queen quite a lot around the Palace but she never came to the schoolroom. If she wanted to know how we were getting on she would send for our notebooks.'

One of the advantages of having their lessons with a member of the royal family was the outings they enjoyed. Sukie Hemming remembers several occasions. 'As we got older we were all keen on tennis and we were taken several times to Wimbledon where of course we were given the best seats ... then we had a craze on ice-skating so we were given individual tuition at Richmond Ice Rink. We took it all for granted, thinking everyone got the same treatment as we did. It wasn't until we each went our separate ways that I began to learn how to do things for myself.'

When the time came for Princess Anne to go to school it was decided that she would go to Benenden in Kent and the other two girls to different schools. They had been together for seven years, constant companions who shared everything. Now they were to be separated and Sukie Hemming believes it was quite deliberate. 'I'm quite sure it was laid down by the Queen and her advisers that we should be split up, and I'm equally sure it was the right thing to do, even though at the time it seemed rather brutal. We never wrote to each other after leaving the Palace; we didn't even have a farewell party; there was no contact.' There still has not been.

Starting a new life at boarding school is difficult enough for anyone at the age of thirteen. For someone who has been brought up in a palace with servants at your beck and call, and adults who either bow or curtsey whenever they meet you, it could have been a traumatic experience. For Princess Anne it was a relief. She was longing to get away from the Palace schoolroom and meet more girls of her own age, from different walks of life. Even so she went through the 'first-night' nerves of any newcomer. The royal car carrying her and the Queen to Benenden was late arriving, the reason being that the Princess had been sick *en route*. Princess Anne had not been required to sit the normal entrance examination. Her then headmistress, Elizabeth Clarke, who is now retired, explained. 'I had been invited to lunch at Windsor Castle and, realizing it could not have been because of my scintillating conversation or sparkling personality, I guessed it was something to do with education. Several days later I received a personal telephone call from the Queen informing me that it had been decided to send Princess Anne to Benenden, if she was acceptable.' This latter part of the message referred to the Princess's educational standards. 'It was important,' says Miss Clarke, 'because if she had not been at the same level as the other girls coming in it would have been unfair to the school, and we would not have been doing her any favours by making an exception.' Anyway the problem did not arise because Miss Clarke spoke to the Princess's tutors at the Palace and they satisfied her that her newest student would be up to the required academic level. There were 300 pupils and 40 staff at Benenden on 20 September 1963, the day Princess Anne started, and the yearly fees were £525.

Some years after she had left the school Princess Anne told me what her first impressions were: 'The continuous noise and the fact that everywhere you turned there were so many people.' She also mentioned that even today the smell of cabbage or polish brings back immediate and evocative memories of schooldays in Kent. She also said that her parents did ask her if she wanted to go away to school and she agreed, which was just as well as 'It wouldn't have made any difference no matter what I said.'

The Princess adapted to the routine of school life remarkably quickly, considering her upbringing and the fact that she was having to live and work with hundreds of other girls for the first time. It was also her first experience of sharing a room – hers was in Guldeford House, one of the six at Benenden, where her dormitory, Magnolia, contained four beds. The three girls she shared with were not specially chosen, and the Headmistress, quickly realizing that it might be possible for someone to try to exploit a relationship with the Princess, nipped any such possibility in the bud by making sure every girl in the house sat next to Princess Anne by rotation. So no one could claim that 'special relationship' either at the time or later. Indeed, as Princess Anne herself said some years afterwards, 'Fortunately, children aren't so stupid. They accept people for what they are rather quicker than adults do. They have no preconceived ideas, because how could they have? They accepted people for what they were and had other things to do so they weren't bothered.'

Elizabeth Clarke was determined that her royal pupil should be treated no differently from any of the other girls, and the Queen fully supported her in this view. If there was a special occasion when Her Majesty thought the Princess should attend some royal event, she would telephone Miss Clarke herself to ask permission for Anne to be absent from school. This permission was not always given. There were several occasions when the Headmistress thought it more important for Princess Anne to remain at school than to join her parents at Buckingham Palace, and said so. The Queen never demurred and always listened to the advice of Miss Clarke. Her Majesty took an intense interest in her daughter's education and frequently rang Miss Clarke to discuss her progress. 'Once one got over the initial shock of realizing that it really was the Queen on the telephone, the conversation became very informal and relaxed,' she says.

The Queen and Prince Philip also visited the school whenever they could. They tried to make their visits informal but the strict protocol and security arrangements which surround every royal journey, no matter how short or private, meant that police forces in the counties through which they drove were always on the alert, the routes cleared and the staff at the school warned in advance. Elizabeth Clarke recalled one conversation she had with the Queen on a quiet Sunday evening. They had been talking about the examination system in force at the time, something with which most parents would have been familiar. The Queen, however, gently interrupted Miss Clarke, saying, 'You'll have to explain that a little more fully. Remember, I never went to school.'

The five years at Benenden passed fairly uneventfully with the Princess making friendships which have lasted ever since. She continued her riding lessons at the stables of Mrs Hatton-Hall (formerly Cherry Kendall, a highly successful Three Day Eventer in the 1950s) at nearby Moat House, and played tennis and lacrosse for the school teams. Benenden did not have a brilliant academic record and Princess Anne turned out to be an average scholar. She excelled in three subjects: English, History and Geography, because, as one of her teachers explained, she liked them. Those she did not care for, such as mathematics, she did badly in, simply because if she had no interest in a subject she made little effort. Another reason might be that her teachers did not push her as hard as perhaps they would have one of the other girls. The relationship between the Princess and the staff at Benenden was friendly but formal. They called her Princess Anne; all the other girls at the school called her just Anne.

In her final term in the sixth form at Benenden the Princess took her 'A' level examinations. She did not do brilliantly but she did manage two passes – in History and Geography – which were enough to have taken her on to university if she had so wished. Miss Clarke said later, 'If you look at the acceptance levels for university entrance in 1968, I think you'll find that she could easily have gone if she had wanted to. The fact that she didn't apply was her own decision as far as I am aware, but I believe that academically she could have gained a place on her own merits.' A short while ago I discussed the question of a university education with Princess Anne. She said, 'You must remember that girls did not have as many career opportunities in those days as they do today, and in my case there were added difficulties obviously, so I believe I was right in deciding not to apply for university at the time. But I think it might be nice now if the time could be found, to go and study something like Geology perhaps.' However, with upwards of 500 engagements a year and that number increasing all the time, it is highly unlikely that the time could be found – tempting as the prospect sounds.

When the time came for the Princess to leave Benenden she did so with a certain amount of regret but, ever a realist, in the knowledge that there was another chapter waiting to be written – and enjoyed.

The school was sorry to see her go. Her presence had sent Benenden to the top of the fashionable league in girls' public schools and brought the name of the school into great prominence. But there were also a few disadvantages, such as the unwelcome press attention all year round. Elizabeth Clarke enjoyed having Princess Anne as a pupil and found her a confident and mature student. She summed up the overall feeling of Benenden when the five years were up. 'She made a definite contribution to the school and I think we all felt that in spite of the press and television attention, which we could have done without, the benefits of having her here outweighed any disadvantages. I hope we, in our turn, contributed something to her training for her future role in public life.'

They had also tried to teach her something of the economics of life with what they thought considerable success. Each girl was allowed £2 a term pocket money and this was normally spent long before the end of term. Princess Anne was the exception; she always had something left over. Miss Clarke thought it must be either because she was not used to handling her own money or because the school was teaching her to be frugal. The Princess explains it differently, saying, 'I was brought up by a canny Scottish nanny so I've always been mean with money.'

CHAPTER
THREE

♦

LOVE AND MARRIAGE

The Court Circular published on 30 May 1973 read:

> It is with great pleasure that The Queen and the
> Duke of Edinburgh announce the betrothal of their
> beloved daughter The Princess Anne to Lieutenant
> Mark Phillips The Queen's Dragoon Guards, son
> of Major and Mrs Peter Phillips.

So ended months of speculation, rumours and denials about the
relationship between the Queen's only daughter and the Olympic
medal winning army officer she had been seeing secretly for over
a year.

It also meant an end to the practically non-stop worldwide interest
in who the Princess was going to marry. From the moment she left
Benenden School she had only to be seen in the company of any
eligible young man for his name to be added to the growing list of
prospective bridegrooms. According to the world's press, Princess
Anne was going to marry Prince Carl Gustav of Sweden, in spite
of the facts that at the time of the reports she was still a schoolgirl
of fourteen and he was just four years older and the only time they
had met was as guests at the wedding of King Constantine of the
Hellenes. When she was eighteen the Princess went with a party
of friends on a skiing holiday in the French Alps. One of the group
was David Penn, a former Page of Honour to the Queen. By the

time they had returned to England they were practically engaged – at least that was the story which appeared in several newspapers. Brian Alexander, whose father, Field Marshal Earl Alexander of Tunis, was one of Britain's most gallant soldiers of the Second World War, was another apparent contender for the royal hand, and any friend of Prince Charles who happened to be invited to Buckingham Palace or Windsor Castle was immediately added to the list of would-be suitors. Two of them were members of the Prince's polo team: Sandy Harper and Andrew Parker Bowles. They often found themselves on the guest list at private royal functions and, as Andrew Parker Bowles was a serving officer in the Household Cavalry (of which regiment he is now Commanding Officer), he came into regular contact with Princess Anne – and all the other members of the royal family. Colonel Parker Bowles is now married, to the former Camilla Shand whose name was at one time romantically linked with the Prince of Wales, and both he and his wife have remained close friends of both Prince Charles and Princess Anne – and their respective spouses. Sandy Harper is a polo player of repute and when he was one of Princess Anne's escorts he took her to some of the liveliest nightclubs and discos in London. The press had a field day when they went to see the nude musical *Hair* and Princess Anne, wearing a purple trouser suit, got up on stage and danced with the cast. Sandy Harper eventually married an actress, Suzy Kendall.

Then there were the bachelor sons of various members of the Royal Household who were often invited to join houseparties at the royal residences. These were young men who were regarded by the Queen and Prince Philip as suitable 'escorts' for their daughter as opposed to being 'boyfriends' in the accepted sense of the term. Princess Anne was never particularly involved with any of them, but she was attracted by one or two of her dates, in the same way as any healthy young woman of her age would have been.

When the time came for her to be married – and there was no rush as she was only twenty-three on her wedding day, the supply of eligible foreign royalty was running a bit thin. The royal houses of Europe were of course well known to her parents and there was no prince they felt strongly enough about to suggest as a husband for their daughter.

Anyway, Princess Anne had already made her feelings on the subject quite clear some years before, when she said, 'They'll have a job marrying me off to someone I don't want. I'll marry the man I choose no matter who he is or what he does.' In fact there was never any question of an arranged marriage. There was no need. The days of the offspring of royal houses being paired off for political reasons had long gone. Even so the Queen had to hold a special meeting of the Privy Council at Buckingham Palace in order to give formal consent to her daughter's union. The Royal Marriage Act of 1772 does not allow any member of the royal family to be legally married without the consent of the sovereign 'under the Great Seal declared in Council and entered into the Privy Council books'.

Mark Phillips was the second prominent horseman to whom the Princess became attracted. The first was a Welshman, twelve years her senior, Richard Meade. He is a treble Olympic Gold Medallist who has won just about every major title the equestrian world has to offer. At the time when Princess Anne came into the competitive world of Three Day Eventing, Meade was at the height of his career. In addition he was slim, good looking and came from Monmouthshire where his family had farmed for generations. He was, and remains, one of the most popular figures in the sport and it is not difficult to see why he became so attractive to the young and, at that time, aspiring royal competitor. Perhaps the biggest obstacle to his being taken seriously as a suitor was his age. He was thirty-two when the Princess was twenty and a number of royal observers felt the gap was too large. Perhaps he was a father figure. Princess Anne had always loved and admired her own father both as a parent and as a fierce competitor. Whatever the reasons, Meade went the way of all the other so-called prospective husbands, and once Mark Phillips came on the scene, no one else had a look in.

In 1968 Mark had been chosen to represent Britain at the Olympic Games in Mexico. Through no fault of his own he ended up as a reserve rider but still qualified for a team gold medal. On their return to London the entire team was given a reception by Whitbread, the brewers, at their historic cellars in the City. Queen Elizabeth the Queen Mother was invited to join them and, knowing of her granddaughter's passion for horses, asked if she might bring her along. The organizers were of course delighted and Anne found herself sitting next to the young army officer who was to become her husband five years later.

Apparently it was not love at first sight for either of them but there was a certain 'chemistry' as each became aware of the other. After the reception Mark was invited to join a small dinner party at a London club at which the host was Lieutenant Colonel Sir John Miller, the Crown Equerry, and the man who had first introduced Princess Anne to eventing. Mark didn't know the way to the club so decided to follow the official car in his old banger, but he got stuck at traffic lights, became thoroughly lost and eventually turned up so late that Princess Anne thought he had decided not to bother.

After that initial meeting things went a little more smoothly as they met frequently at horse trials up and down the country. They soon found they had many mutual friends and it wasn't hard to arrange to be included in the same house parties. On one occasion Princess Anne was staying with Lady Fitzalan-Howard, eldest daughter of the Duke of Norfolk, at her home in Yorkshire. Among the houses on the estate was one occupied by a relative who had a nephew staying at the same time. His name? Mark Phillips of course.

This sort of 'coincidence' was to occur time and time again; but the press didn't get wind of the story until the end of 1970. The equestrian world is very close and no one gave the newspapers the tip-off about the friendship which was developing into love. Considering the attention that had been given to most of Princess Anne's other boyfriends, it's amazing that they didn't catch on sooner.

It was in 1971 that the media started to notice how frequently the couple were to be seen together. In April of that year they both competed at the Badminton Horse Trials. Mark was the winner, an achievement that must have raised his prospects considerably in the eyes of the Princess, who came a creditable fifth. She got her own back in September at Burghley, when she won the Raleigh Trophy and the individual gold medal at the European Three Day Event Championships. She was on top of the world. Winning the European Championship at twenty-one meant, in effect, that she was the best in the world. A month later they were both at the Cirencester Horse

Trials – he was taking part, she was supporting him. It was while they were there that the most significant sign to date was given that Mark was something more than just another boyfriend. He was invited to Buckingham Palace to attend the Silver Wedding Anniversary celebrations of the Queen and the Duke of Edinburgh. Four weeks later Princess Anne made her first visit to the Phillipses' family home at Great Somerford in Wiltshire. Mark himself tells the story of how he telephoned his mother to ask if he could invite a friend for the weekend. He told his mother it was a girlfriend but forgot to mention her name. 'I was about to put the phone down when Mother asked, "What's her name?" When I said, "Princess Anne", there was a deathly pause at the other end.

'"You must be joking," she stammered.

'"No, I'm absolutely serious," I replied.

'"When did you say you were coming?"

'"It will take us about an hour and a half."'

Anybody who knows Mark will understand how this could have happened. He is casual to a degree in the way he conducts his life and, since he never gets flustered himself he cannot understand why anyone else should make a fuss.

After this first visit the Princess became a frequent caller at Great Somerford, driving herself down the M4 accompanied only by her detective. Mark was a serving officer in 1st the Queen's Dragoon Guards based at Bergen-Belsen in Germany, where his brother officers soon realized that he was serious about his latest girlfriend because he refused to join them on their forays into town to make new conquests among the local ladies. Previously he had enjoyed something of a reputation as a successful lady killer in the Mess, and 'Noddy' Holdsworth and Eric Grounds (who was to be his best man) were let into the secret and sworn to secrecy.

Princess Anne spent Christmas as she always had with her family at Windsor, but when the royal family moved to Sandringham for the New Year festivities, Mark was invited to join the house party. He remained at Sandringham for three days, undergoing what can only be described as a 'looking over', and then Princess Anne drove him to Harwich where he was to catch the boat to the Hook of Holland *en route* to Germany. As they said their farewells in the public car park, the Princess kissed Mark goodbye. It was their first kiss in public and a watchful car park attendant was the only person to witness it. He quickly told a number of reporters what he had seen and from that moment the royal 'rat-pack' knew that they had been right all along. Anne and Mark were an item!

As Princess Anne was the first of the Queen's children to have a serious romantic entanglement the press went wild. Now that their suspicions were confirmed the royal watchers of the national newspapers gave the young couple no respite. Every public appearance by the Princess was recorded by photographers and reporters. And as she was in the middle of a strenuous eventing season it was easy for them to find out where she was going to appear and to be there in force. Stories appeared speculating on when the marriage would take place, where they would live and what title Mark would be offered when he became a member of the royal family. At the time it was considered unthinkable that any husband of Princess Anne would remain without a title, particularly as Antony Armstrong-Jones had been created Earl of Snowdon on his marriage to Princess Margaret.

Yet in spite of all the press speculation and attendant publicity the couple themselves insisted that there was no romantic attachment and that rumours of an engagement were 'absolute nonsense'. Of course nobody believed them. Especially when the Princess drove herself ninety miles down the motorway, immediately after a gruelling eight-hour flight from Ethiopia, just to be with Mark at his Wiltshire home. This was in February 1973 and the Princess's visit to Ethiopia, on behalf of the Save the Children Fund, had been marked by an unusually large press party. They weren't interested in the reason for her trip. All they wanted to know was, 'Are you getting engaged and if so when?' Princess Anne actually issued a denial during the visit, saying, 'We are not engaged and there is no prospect of an engagement.' Back in England the couple tried to carry on as normal; Princess Anne with her public duties and Mark, when he was on leave from his regiment, training his horses.

It seemed that the more the press wanted them to announce their engagement the more determined they became not to. The 'will they – won't they?' stories went on for months, with the Buckingham Palace press office officially denying that there was to be an announcement or at least saying that it knew nothing of such an

Right: Four generations of royal ladies present as Princess Anne is nursed by her mother in the Music Room at Buckingham Palace. Watching are her proud grandmother (now Queen Elizabeth the Queen Mother) and her great-grandmother, Queen Mary (widow of King George V).

Below: 2 June 1953 – Coronation Day. The Princess Royal says the only thing she can vaguely remember about it is being taken on to the balcony at Buckingham Palace and told to 'wave to the people'.

Above: Princess Anne was five when she attended her first Highland Games at Braemar. Here she poses for photographers with her older brother Prince Charles, both wearing the kilt.

Right: Susan (Sukie) Babington-Smith (left) and Caroline Hamilton, the two girls who were chosen to join Princess Anne in the Palace schoolroom. Here they are arriving at Wimbledon in 1960 to watch the Wightman Cup tennis between Great Britain and the United States.

Below: The thirteen-year-old Princess Anne being welcomed to Benenden by the school's headmistress, Miss Elizabeth Clarke, at the start of her first term.

Above: This formal study of the Princess was released on her sixteenth birthday, 15 August 1966. She was then a sixth-former at Benenden.

Right: The seventeen-year-old Princess with her nineteen-year-old brother Charles. This was a formal occasion at the Royal Opera House when they were in the audience to watch Rudolph Nureyev in *The Nutcracker*.

Left: Her first car. The Princess started driving in the grounds at Windsor Castle. Here she goes through her paces under the watchful eyes of her royal instructor – her father, the Duke of Edinburgh – at the polo ground in Windsor Great Park.

announcement, which was quite true at the time. The press office did not know anything because no one had told them. This is not unusual at Buckingham Palace. If the royal family wants to keep something absolutely private for a time, they simply do not inform the press office. In that way the Press Secretary can truthfully claim that he knows nothing about a particular story without having to tell a deliberate lie. The press office does not lie but there are occasions when it prefers not to know. In fact the only official denial about the engagement came from the Queen's Press Secretary Robin Ludlow at the end of January 1973. He told John Knight of the *Sunday Mirror* that an engagement was not expected at this time – which was the literal truth from his point of view. This was ten weeks before the official announcement, by which time Ludlow had left the Royal Household to be replaced by Ronald Allison, who was at pains to point out that *he* never issued a denial. The *Sunday Mirror* printed the story as told to John Knight and were justifiably angry when the eventual truth came out.

It was during this period that the Princess also told another reporter that there was to be no engagement. While riding at Warfield near Sandhurst Her Royal Highness spied a reporter and photographer on a public footpath. She rode over to them and asked what they wanted. On being told that it was because of the speculation about a romance between her and Lieutenant Phillips the Princess replied: 'There is no romance between us and there are no grounds for these rumours of a romance between us. We are finding it difficult to train properly with so many press photographers surrounding us all the time. I can't understand why there has been all this interest in us riding together. Lieutenant Phillips has been coming here solely to exercise the horse he is riding at Badminton, which is stabled here and belongs to the Queen.'

Badminton was to prove an important milestone in both their lives. In equestrian terms it was a disaster. After winning twice Mark was unplaced this year when both his horses failed. Great Ovation retired lame and his other mount, Columbus, owned by the Queen, was unplaced. Princess Anne did a little better but had to be content with eighth place. On the final Sunday evening, when competition had ended, they went for a walk together in the countryside near Mark's home. It was then that Mark proposed and was immediately accepted. He later said it was not a preplanned proposal, it was done literally on the spur of the moment. Perhaps they were both so fed up with their performances during the week that they needed each other badly at that moment. At any rate it was exactly the right time – for them both. Much later the Princess said that it was 'the first time he'd thought of it'. But she admitted that she had considered the matter for some time and had already decided that if he asked her she would say 'yes'.

There was still some time between the private acceptance of the Princess and the public announcement of the engagement. Protocol demanded that before an official announcement could be made all the Commonwealth Heads of State had to be informed as well as certain members of the British Government, the Archbishop of Canterbury and immediate relatives of the Princess and Lieutenant Phillips. Also, as a serving officer, Mark had to have the permission of his Commanding Officer, Lieutenant Colonel Maurice Johnston, before he could get married. Once the announcement was made Colonel Johnston said that he was 'relieved that the secret was out. I was completely in the picture from the beginning. It has certainly been a well kept secret. Now it's official the regiment can share all the joy and pride I have felt all these weeks.'

By one of those happy coincidences of simply being in the right place at the right time I was present when the official announcement of Princess Anne's engagement took place. I was working as a reporter at BBC Television News in London. It was the Spring Bank Holiday and a very quiet news day. The weather was perfect and we were looking for stories. The duty editor told me that he had a feeling something was going on up at Balmoral, the Queen's Scottish home. Normally the Queen uses it only during the long summer holiday but for some reason she and some of her family were there on this particular weekend. I was ordered to fly up to Scotland with a camera crew to find out what was going on. There had after all been tremendous speculation about Princess Anne and Mark Phillips for months so anything we could find out about them would have been worthwhile. Anyway, when I eventually arrived at the gates of Balmoral Castle there was quite a crowd gathered. It was a warm May and the tourists had started to arrive early that year. I sent my name in via the lodgekeeper and after a great deal of telephoning between lodge and somewhere inside was invited to drive through the grounds, past the castle itself to Craigowan House (which is now used by the Prince and Princess of Wales and their family when they are in residence). There I met Squadron Leader (now Sir) David Checketts, the Prince of Wales's Private Secretary, whom I had known for some years, since the Prince had lived for a while in Aberystwyth, West Wales.

David told me who was present at that time. The Prince of Wales, who was serving in the Royal Navy, had flown 16,000 miles from his base in the West Indies, just for the weekend. His Equerry, Captain Nicholas Soames, was also present, with Princess Anne and Lieutenant Mark Phillips. The Queen and Prince Philip were also staying on the estate but were not in the house at the time. I was also informed that as nobody from the press office was in attendance there was little chance of an announcement being made from Balmoral. It would have to come from Buckingham Palace.

I was given permission to film a report giving these details and also one, which was to be embargoed, saying that an engagement would take place. Then I was told privately that such an announcement would be made that evening by the Buckingham Palace press office. The films were rushed to the nearest BBC studios in Aberdeen with the strict instruction that only the first one was to be used unless the official announcement had been made. This came shortly before six o'clock and we were able to transmit a world exclusive report of the occasion from Balmoral. I then received a telephone call from Balmoral telling me that the Princess and her fiancé would be leaving Aberdeen on the overnight royal train for London. The news had of course got around like wildfire and hundreds of well-wishers were waiting for the first glimpse of the couple – and the engagement ring. Princess Anne, dressed in a tweed suit, happily obliged the public and the press by showing off her ring for the first time. It was a solitary sapphire set in diamonds on a band of Welsh gold. They had chosen it together from a selection sent to them by Garrard, the Crown jewellers.

Mark had driven himself to Balmoral in his red BMW. Because of the security that now surrounded him he could not drive back to London and, as he was now practically a member of the family, he was allowed to travel on the royal train.

Events moved fairly swiftly after that. Reporters are not invited to travel with royalty so we had to make our own arrangements for getting back to London. I was required to present myself at Buckingham Palace at eleven o'clock the following morning to conduct the official engagement interview with the happy couple. I made it by the skin of my teeth and entered the forecourt just as the Band of the Welsh Guards were striking up one of the hit tunes of the day – 'Congratulations'.

The television interview was filmed on the rear terrace of the Palace with Princess Anne bearing the brunt of the questions. She was totally in control, answering questions readily and fluently. Mark was a little hesitant at first – I believe it was his first experience of television – but gradually he relaxed and told me about his formal interview with Prince Philip when he arrived to ask for the Princess's hand. He said he was 'petrified – but he was very good to me'. Princess Anne confirmed that they had both realized that their relationship was serious after the Badminton Trials in April and that 'It has been very difficult to keep it secret for six weeks.'

After a private luncheon at the Palace – it was the first time Major and Mrs Phillips met their future daughter-in-law's parents – Princess Anne went off to fulfil a longstanding engagement for Riding for the Disabled and Mark returned to his unit where they held a mess party at which he was toasted as 'the Princess's own'.

During the six months between the announcement of the engagement and the wedding in November the Princess had a full list of commitments on behalf of Save the Children and Riding for the Disabled and she was also in the middle of the eventing season. Meanwhile Mark was given leave from his regiment to help prepare for his new role as a member of the royal family which involved a crash course in how to handle himself on television. To this day he is not comfortable when confronted by cameras and microphones but, contrary to what some observers claim, he is not tongue-tied when talking on his own subject. He is a naturally shy person with a hesitant manner at first but when he gets to know someone well the reserve drops. The problem in those early days was that he was totally unprepared for the kind of media attention he attracted once he became associated with Princess Anne. She had grown up in the full glare of the spotlight and has always been able to handle the press on her own terms. Her 'naff-off' remarks to intrusive photographers have become part of Fleet Street folklore; and even today, when her relations with the media are better than at any time in the past, she can be a little prickly if she feels she is being manoeuvred into a position that is to her disadvantage. But back in the early seventies, when Mark's exposure to the press had previously been confined in the main to the attentions of the equestrian writers, most of whom were old friends anyway, he found it an uncomfortable experience to be pounced upon by microphone wielding reporters whenever he put his nose outside his barracks. A lot of effort was put in by a number of people to try and make him more at ease with the media. None, however, was very successful. His natural reserve made him appear self-conscious and unsure of himself, so when he appeared in public with his fiancée, she always answered most of the questions, responding to those she wanted to with wit and refreshing candour and ignoring those she didn't care for.

The wedding was set for 14 November 1973, a day for double celebration as it is also Prince Charles's birthday. Westminster Abbey was the obvious choice – it was where the bride's mother and grandmother had been married – and 1,800 guests were invited.

One of the problems with a royal wedding is that even though it is officially regarded as a private affair, as opposed to a state occasion, certain matters of protocol have to be observed. One of these affects the selection of guests. If the 1,800 guests had been chosen from among the families and friends of the bride and groom, as happens at most weddings, it would have been easy to accommodate them all. But of course this was no ordinary wedding and before Anne and Mark could decide whom they would ask, there were those official guests who had to be invited. Representatives of British and foreign governments and every Commonwealth country to start with. Then there were the foreign royalty and members of local authorities in the United Kingdom, followed by representatives of the armed forces, especially the units with which the Princess was associated, army, navy and air force, and all those organizations of which she was a patron, president or member. By the time the official guest list had been worked out less than a hundred places were left to be filled by friends of Anne and Mark.

Fortunately for Mark's family as parents of the bride the Queen and the Duke paid for the ceremony, as they did for the weddings of their sons, the Prince of Wales and the Duke of York. Her Majesty knows it would place an intolerable burden on the parents of her children's spouses if they had to pay for a ceremony in which they play but a small part themselves, so she assumes this responsibility on their behalf. It is a thoughtful and much appreciated gesture, as Major Ronald Ferguson, the Duchess of York's father, admitted in 1987.

Any wedding of a member of the royal family is organized by the Lord Chamberlain on behalf of the Queen. She pays for the ceremony, the wedding breakfast and the reception that follows, with the government paying for police who are on duty, the transport costs of the servicemen who line the wedding route, the building of public viewing stands, and decorations in the Mall. If it had been a state occasion, i.e. the wedding of the sovereign, the country would have paid for everything.

From all over the world gifts began to pour into Buckingham Palace. An official had rashly said that the young couple 'were starting from scratch and need everything'. Soon they had everything from coat-hangers to carpets, diamonds to dressing gowns: one thousand five hundred and twenty-four gifts in all, including a wedding garter from a Mrs E. J. Dore which the Princess refused either to confirm or deny she wore during the ceremony. The presents completely filled one of the State Apartments in St James's Palace where they were put on display, the receipts going to charity, and the gift list ran to a hundred and one pages. Three ladies were brought into the Princess's office to deal with the flood of congratulations, cards and presents, and every single donor received a personal letter of thanks within two weeks of the great day.

The 'wedding of the decade' attracted television crews from all over the world, the Americans in particular being highly indignant that they were not allowed to take their cameras inside Buckingham Palace to interview the bride and her mother. In Japan, all scheduled television programmes were scrapped on the day of the wedding so that the entire output could be devoted to covering the run-up, the ceremony itself and the aftermath. In Canada and Australia it was the same story with millions of people watching the events as they happened despite the fact that, because of the time difference, they had to stay up all night.

In Britain, colour television was still very much in its infancy and the leaders of the television industry had much cause to thank Princess Anne and her husband to be. The wedding did more for the sale of colour television sets than any other single event – in precisely the same way that the wedding of Princess Elizabeth in 1947 had accelerated interest in the old monochrome sets.

The 'Anne and Mark' souvenir industry boomed as everything from toilet rolls to tea cloths, all bearing the supposed likeness of the couple, were sold in their thousands. You could get a pair of silver plaques with the bride and groom in profile for £1,250 or a box of matches wishing the couple 'Health and Happiness' for a halfpenny. The world and his wife were determined to enjoy what promised to be a splendid occasion, and if some enterprising entrepreneurs made small fortunes out of it, what harm in that? Just before the wedding day Anne and Mark gave what subsequently became the regulation television interview. It was a joint interview with the BBC and ITV and was painful both to watch and to listen to. Andrew Gardner and Alastair Burnet were the interviewers, and from the start it was obvious that neither they nor their interviewees were comfortable. The questions had been submitted beforehand and vetted by the Palace press office so there was no spontaneity or sparkle. In addition, both the television men were years older than Anne and Mark and their attempts to get on the same wavelength made for an embarrassing programme which must have left all concerned most unhappy.

It is easy to understand why the Palace feels they must give joint interviews. It is in order to give the impression that they are being impartial. But the interviewers, who are always experienced reporters, are intimidated by the presence of each other, and the resulting programme is always stilted, uncomfortable and frustrating for both participants and viewers. Exactly the same format with precisely the same results has been used for the pre-wedding interviews with the Prince and Princess of Wales and the Duke and Duchess of York. All it would take to put things right would be to allow each television company a few minutes alone with the subjects and everyone, including, I suspect, the Palace press office, would be happy.

Princess Anne did not have a hen party with any of her old friends before the wedding. She spent the eve of her wedding day in her rooms at Buckingham Palace watching television. Mark, however, had come over from Germany a couple of days earlier to get ready for the big day. His fellow officers in 1st the Queen's Dragoon Guards had given him a right royal send off, and when he and his best man, Eric Grounds – the regiment's adjutant – arrived at the Guards Club in Piccadilly where they were to spend the two nights prior to the wedding, they immediately contacted more of their cronies to set up the stag night to end all stag nights. There was no way that Mark Phillips was going to be allowed to give up bachelorhood quietly. As the champagne flowed throughout the night Mark and his friends remembered many occasions which were best left unreported. Suffice it to say that until his marriage into the royal family Mark had enjoyed life to the full, as only a young, healthy, good looking cavalry officer can.

The night before the wedding was bitterly cold and very wet. In spite of this, thousands of onlookers camped out on the streets of London to make sure they would be in a good viewing position when the festivities began. Luckily, the morning of 14 November 1973 dawned bright, sunny and dry as the crowds thronged into The Mall. By eight o'clock it was estimated that more than 50,000 were lining the processional route and the television and radio stations opened up for more than six hours' continuous coverage. The distinction of being the first person interviewed went to Mrs Gwen Henderson. She was the lady with the responsibility for vacuum cleaning the carpets in front of the High Altar in Westminster Abbey and in honour of the occasion she wore a new overall and a hat complete with feather.

The Abbey itself had been closed for nine days before the wedding day so that extra carpenters could be brought in to build additional seating for the press – which they had to pay for at the rate of £23 a time on the Sanctuary Stand (as opposed to £5 when Princess Alexandra had been married in 1963). Electricians supplied special spotlights which were carefully placed where they would add the kindest glow to the bride's hair and complexion. Plenty of overtime was worked and the wedding provided useful profits for many of those involved with the service. Members of the choir each earned around £200 as their share of the royalties on the many recordings from radio, television and films. Eight years later their colleagues at St Paul's would receive much more, when the wedding of the Prince and Princess of Wales was seen and heard by nearly a thousand million people and video cassettes of the ceremony sold by the hundred thousand. Even Princess Anne received a bonus on her wedding day. Her Civil List allowance was increased by £15,000 to £35,000. However, she didn't see any of it. It all went on salary increases for members of her Household.

Long before the guests were allowed to enter the Abbey, a team of police officers with dogs specially trained to sniff out explosives inspected every inch of the thousand-year-old church, and when the first guests entered at 10 o'clock they had to submit to the indignity of having their handbags searched; such was the atmosphere at all public events at the time because of activities of terrorists throughout the world.

The ceremony was not due to start until 11.30 but most of the guests arrived up to an hour and a half early. Old hands at the Royal Wedding game had come fully prepared with Thermos flasks and sandwiches which were surreptitiously consumed during the long wait. The biggest problem was that no lavatories had been provided inside the Abbey, and once inside it was impossible to leave, so bladders with the consistency of cast iron tanks were needed.

Mark's family, including his maternal grandmother Tiarks, who had confessed it was 'a feather in the family's cap to have a royal', sat together facing the royal family. The Queen, Queen Elizabeth the Queen Mother, the Prince of Wales and Prince Andrew were there together with Princess Margaret and other members of the family. Princess Anne had decided that she did not want any bridesmaids or pages, just two nine-year-old attendants, her youngest brother Prince Edward and her cousin Lady Sarah Armstrong-Jones, the daughter of Princess Margaret.

The outstanding guest among the foreign royalty was undoubtedly the late Princess Grace of Monaco, who looked elegant and stylish in a white outfit – the only woman apart from the bride to wear white.

At twelve minutes past eleven the bride's procession left Buckingham Palace. It was the first glimpse for the millions watching on television and the thousands lining the route of the wedding dress. Within an hour 'sweat-shops' throughout London's East End were busy producing copies of the new 'Princess Line' with high collar and flared sleeves, which were on sale later that same day at £16 each. For the next few months brides up and down the country were married wearing replicas of the Princess's dress. The fifteen-minute drive to Westminster Abbey was taken in the traditional Glass Coach used by all royal brides, with Princess Anne accompanied by her father in full dress uniform of an Admiral of the Fleet. She appeared to be slightly nervous but when Prince Philip asked if she was, replied, 'No, of course not.'

Although the ceremony was televised live and seen by an audience approaching six hundred million, the actual moment of the exchange of vows was not seen on the screen. The Queen and the Princess had insisted that the moment of consecration, when Mark placed the ring on the Princess's finger, should be kept private, and no cameras were allowed in front of the couple. Only about sixty people, out of the 1,800 in the Abbey, could see what was happening – both families, close friends and those taking part in the service.

Anne and Mark both gave their responses in clear voices with no hesitation; and when they went into the Chapel of Edward the Confessor to sign the marriage registers, the Archbishop of Canterbury, Dr Ramsey, told them of his own cause for celebration that day – it was his birthday. Mark was to say afterwards that he had to pinch himself when he saw his parents' signatures alongside those of the royal family. Three registers had to be signed: the Royal Marriage Register, which is kept in the custody of the Lord Chamberlain, and two Abbey registers, plus the distinguished visitor's book. The marriage certificate itself must be one of the most signed of all public documents, containing as it does the names of the Queen, the Duke of Edinburgh, Queen Elizabeth the Queen Mother, Prince Andrew and Prince Edward, the Archbishop of Canterbury, the Dean of Westminster, Lady Sarah Armstrong-

Jones, Major and Mrs Peter Phillips and Captain Eric Grounds, the best man.

Throughout the ceremony and during the long walk back through the Abbey to the waiting crowds outside, it was obvious that Princess Anne had been helping Mark to stand the strain. Her quiet encouragement as they turned to bow and curtsey to the Queen in the Sacrarium and the steady flow of whispered conversation was witnessed by lip readers in the television audience. Apparently she asked him a number of times if he was all right, and when they reached the West Door of the Abbey, she said, 'Be ready to acknowledge the crowds on the way back.' The Princess had thoroughly enjoyed her wedding day; Mark was glad the ceremonial side was nearly over.

Of the 1,800 guests who had been invited to Westminster Abbey only 120 were asked back to Buckingham Palace for the wedding breakfast; the others had to make their own arrangements. It is traditional at royal weddings that only those close to the bride and groom, plus visiting royalty, are invited to join the royal family. The meal was served in the State Ballroom where the guests sat at twelve tables – ten to each. The menu was scrambled eggs, lobster, shrimps and tomato in mayonnaise, followed by a main course of partridge (from the royal estates) with fresh mushrooms, peas, cauliflower and new potatoes (all from the kitchen garden at Windsor) and, as a dessert, peppermint ice-cream filled with grated chocolate.

When Mark had asked his old friend and colleague Eric Grounds to be his best man, Captain Grounds had hesitated slightly before agreeing. This was because he was petrified at the thought of having to make the traditional best man's speech in front of the Queen and all her family. As he put it, 'I'm never very good at standing up in public and speaking. The thought of doing it in front of the Queen terrified me.' He need not have worried. The best man does not have to make a speech at royal weddings. The only person who did so was the bride's father, the Duke of Edinburgh, who began with the words, 'Unaccustomed as I am' . . . with a long pause for laughter . . . before continuing 'to speaking at breakfast.'

The honeymoon started at Thatched House Lodge, Princess Alexandra's house in Richmond Park, which had been loaned to the couple for their wedding night; and the following day they flew to Barbados to join the Royal Yacht *Britannia* which the Queen had put at their disposal. The yacht was already on its way to New Zealand, where it was to be used during the State Visit by the Queen and Prince Philip in the new year, so it had only to make a slight detour to collect the Princess and her husband in the Caribbean.

What they had not reckoned with was the unpredictable weather in that part of the world in November. For the first week at least there were gale force winds and twenty-foot waves, so instead of the romantic interlude they had planned, they spent the first few days suffering the agonies of sea-sickness.

When the storms subsided and they recovered, a new game was invented. It was called 'lose the pressmen'. Dozens of reporters and photographers had found out that they were in the West Indies, and hired every speed boat and helicopter available to see if they could catch up with the young couple. Island hopping became the name of the game as *Britannia* played hide-and-seek with its fleet of assorted following craft. It was all carried out with reasonably good humour, the press getting a few decent pictures to satisfy their editors back in London, and Princess Anne and Mark Phillips being able to spend most of the time in privacy.

After two weeks on board *Britannia* it was back to work. Royalty rarely gets the opportunity to have a vacation without any public duties and the honeymoon was no exception. The Foreign Office had arranged a crowded programme of events which meant an exhausting tour of Ecuador, Colombia, Antigua, Jamaica and Montserrat. It was Mark's first introduction to the royal round of official duties and he came through his baptism of fire unscathed. If he felt nervous about taking his place in the limelight, it certainly didn't show. True, the Princess bore the brunt of the pressure, but she had by now had five years as part of the 'Royal Firm' and was well used to handling large crowds and civic dignitaries. Mark proved to be a welcome and sturdy support to his new wife. He did not put a foot wrong, and when they returned to a cold and wintry Britain on 16 December – just in time to join the rest of the royal family for Christmas – the press were honest enough to admit that, in spite of their predictions, he had made a useful contribution to the royal round of duties. As an initiation, it was fairly painless, but it obviously did not give him a taste for public life and since then he has kept as much in the background as he can decently do without offending the Queen.

There was a large house party at Windsor Castle for Christmas 1973: the Queen and all her immediate family with cousins, aunts, nieces and nephews; and, for the first time, Mark's parents and his sister Sarah were invited to join the group. For the Phillipses it was a fairytale ending to a magical year. They had seen their only son marry the Queen's only daughter and, instead of a quiet family Christmas at home in Wiltshire, were spending the holiday at the largest castle in Europe as part of the most famous family in the world.

Princess Anne had acquired a new husband and would shortly also have a new home – the first she could call her own. After twenty-three years of living in palaces and castles she was about to become mistress of Oak Grove House, married quarters provided by the army; fit for a colonel, but shortly to become home to a very lucky captain!

CHAPTER
FOUR

♦

WIFE AND MOTHER

1974 began as excitingly as the previous year had ended. The Queen invited her daughter and son-in-law to accompany her and Prince Philip on their state visit to New Zealand, Australia and the Pacific islands. It was an opportunity for Her Majesty to show off the latest member of the family and for the couple themselves it meant an extension to their honeymoon, even if they would have to 'sing for their supper' during the exhausting official round of duties. *En route* to New Zealand, Princess Anne and Mark flew to Canada for a brief, three-day visit. They stayed in Government House in Ottawa, from where they flew to Quebec for a short visit – the first by any member of the royal family to that touchy, separatist province since the extremist elements had started their campaign of violence against the Canadian government. From Canada they flew to Christchurch on the South Island of New Zealand where the Queen was to open the Commonwealth Games. Her Majesty had appointed Mark to be an aide-de-camp, and the state visit gave him a chance to see the business of monarchy at work, and the Queen an opportunity to see how her son-in-law shaped up under the pressure of an extended royal tour.

Mark couldn't believe how difficult it was to stand around all day, making small talk with people he had never met before and trying to look interested in everything he was being shown. He said later that it made him realize just how professional the royal family is. They can make the most boring event appear to be one they have always wanted to attend and – even more importantly – give their hosts the feeling that they have enjoyed every moment. It is a neat trick that takes years of training to acquire. The Queen is a past master in the art of making everything seem interesting, so is Princess Anne. The Duke of Edinburgh is slightly less so.

Sitting in the drawing room at Gatcombe Park I once asked the Princess if she didn't find some of the things she was asked to do absolutely stultifying. Her reply was a classic in royal understatement: 'I don't find any of them boring, but obviously some are less interesting than others.'

One incident which was anything but boring occurred shortly after they returned from New Zealand. They had moved into their new house, provided for them by the army at the Royal Military College at Sandhurst in Surrey. Mark had been promoted to captain shortly before the wedding and posted to Sandhurst as an instructor. It was a compromise posting. As a normal serving officer's wife Princess Anne could have been asked to go and join him at the regiment's headquarters in Germany – or wherever he might be stationed throughout his career. But of course she was not a normal officer's wife. However she might wish to be regarded, she was still the Queen's only daughter and fourth in line of succession to the throne, so the whole question of how she could fit in with her husband's duties had to be resolved. Security was a constant problem. Outside Britain it could have been a nightmare; within the United Kingdom it was believed possible to provide suitable accommodation which was reasonably secure and from where the Princess could continue to carry out her public engagements.

Oak Grove House in the grounds of Sandhurst was the answer to the problem. It had five bedrooms; there was a degree of privacy, and once the authorities had closed a public footpath which ran close to the house there was not much chance of anyone being able to look into the downstairs rooms. As a captain, Mark did not qualify for a house of this size, but because any married quarters he could have had would have been unsuitable for a member of the royal family, he was granted the tenancy. The annual rent was £400 a year (the same as he would have paid in a normal captain's quarters). Just before they moved in a great deal of fuss was caused by newspaper reports that the army had spent a further £25,000 on 'doing the place up'. In fact the army or, more correctly, the Department of the Environment, which has responsibility for maintaining service property, spent only £5,000. And this was on essential repairs which they would have been required to carry out whoever was going to live in Oak Grove House. The extra money for redecoration and certain internal alterations came from Princess Anne's own pocket. In common with all her brothers she has a trust fund which was set up by her mother and from which she is able to draw money at the discretion of the trustees. One of them is the Earl of Carnarvon, the Queen's racing manager, and he keeps a pretty close eye on the Princess's finances. The house was furnished mainly by the gifts they had received at their wedding and the wallpaper came from Buckingham Palace where a large stock is kept for the family's own needs. The dining room was furnished by the Royal Warrant Holders' Association, the drawing room by the Lords Lieutenant of all the counties of England and Wales. There was a magnificent 200-year-old grandfather clock given by the City of Westminster and the carpet was a wedding present from the Prime Minister of Iran. Even the coat hangers they used were wedding presents. Princess Margaretha had given them eight dozen as a very practical start to their married life together.

Sandhurst is particularly well off for stables and Mark had six allocated for his and the Princess's use, so they were able to take all their horses with them apart from the Queen's horse Columbus, which was kept at Alison Oliver's stables at nearby Warfield.

Five weeks after they moved in the incident occurred which was to change their lives and the security which surrounded every member of the royal family. On Wednesday, 20 March 1974 the Princess and her husband were staying in London at Buckingham Palace. They had agreed to attend a special showing of a film entitled *Riding Towards Freedom*. It was made on behalf of the Riding for the Disabled Association of which Princess Anne was Patron at the time, and they both featured in a number of scenes. The film was shown at Sudbury House near Ludgate Circus in the City of London and after seeing the film and meeting officials of the Association they left to return to the Palace. It was just after 7.30 in the evening. They were being driven in an official limousine by Mr Alexander Callendar, one of the Royal Mews' most experienced

Right: The Princess and Mark Phillips at the Chatsworth Horse Trials less than six months before they became engaged. At this time they were still denying there was any romance between them.

Below: The Royal Wedding – 14 November 1973 at Westminster Abbey. The bride and groom stand in front of Dr Ramsey, Archbishop of Canterbury, who conducted the ceremony. The wedding was seen by a worldwide television audience of 500 million.

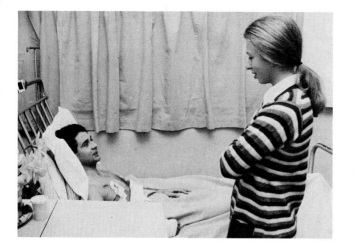

Right: 'When I'm approaching a water jump with thousands of spectators and hundreds of photographers waiting, the horse is just about the only one who doesn't know I'm royal!'

Below: The Montreal Olympic Games, 1976. Although both Anne and Mark were selected for the British team, Mark ended up as reserve rider. He gave tremendous support to his wife and the other members of the team. Here he is with Anne shortly before the cross-country phase at Bromont.

Top: March 1974 and Princess Anne visits her detective, Inspector James Beaton, who was shot three times during the attempt to kidnap her. He is now the Queen's personal bodyguard and was awarded the George Cross for his bravery.

Above: Anthony Andrews and his wife Georgina have been friends with the Princess Royal and Mark Phillips for many years. Here Mark is seen with Anthony and Georgina at a charity function held at the family store – Simpson's in Piccadilly, London, April 1989.

Right: The Princess Royal has been associated with the Riding for the Disabled Association for nearly twenty years. She regularly visits branches to meet workers and riders. Here she is at one of the Norfolk groups.

Below: As Patron of The Butler Trust, the Princess Royal visits prisons throughout Britain. Here she is at Cardiff Prison accompanied by the Governor, Shân Legge-Bourke (Lady-in-Waiting), the author, and Jeff Fuller, her bodyguard.

Below: As President of Missions to Seamen, Her Royal Highness likes nothing better than sharing a joke with sailors in many parts of the world. Here she is enjoying the company of seafarers in the China Coast Bar, which is run by the Missions to Seamen, in Hong Kong.

chauffeurs who had been in royal service for more than twenty years. It had been an enjoyable evening and the Princess and her husband were in a relaxed mood as they chatted to Princess Anne's lady-in-waiting Rowena Brassey (now Mrs Andrew Feilden). The other occupant of the car was the royal detective, Inspector James Beaton, who is now the senior member of the Royalty Protection Department at Buckingham Palace as the Queen's personal police officer.

It was only a fifteen-minute journey from the City back to Buckingham Palace and at that time of night traffic in The Mall was not particularly heavy. They were less than four hundred yards from the Palace, just past the turning for St James's Palace, when a light coloured Ford Escort swerved sharply in front of the royal limousine forcing it to stop. Before anyone could do anything, the driver leapt out of the Ford and fired a gun at the royal car. Jim Beaton got out of the car and ran around to the rear offside where the Princess was sitting – when being driven she always sits immediately behind the driver. The assailant promptly shot Inspector Beaton in the chest. Beaton had drawn his own gun and he fired once, missing the gunman through his injury which was agonizing, and the second time he fired his gun jammed. Meanwhile the would-be assassin or kidnapper (at this time nobody knew just what he was) had managed to open the Princess's door and, grabbing her by the hand, tried to pull her out, saying – with extraordinary politeness considering the circumstances – 'Please get out of the car.' Princess Anne recalled later that she replied 'with equal politeness because I thought it would be silly to be too rude at that stage, that I didn't want to'. What followed appears in retrospect to have been a slapstick scene from a pantomime. Ian Ball, for this was the name of the gunman, had hold of one of Princess Anne's arms and Mark Phillips had hold of the other. Each was pulling as hard as he could with the poor Princess see-sawing to and fro. Mark won the tug-of-war and managed to drag her back inside the vehicle and slam the door shut. Princess Anne was wearing a blue velvet dress and in the struggle it was torn and the sleeve practically ripped out.

Rowena Brassey had by now managed to open the car door on her side and crawled out to lie face down in the gutter. Ball then threatened to shoot the Princess if Inspector Beaton didn't throw down his gun. Beaton did as he was ordered because he knew his weapon was useless anyway as it had jammed. Ball then produced a second gun, a .22 calibre pistol, and as he raised it Beaton put his hand in front of the muzzle. The gun was fired and Beaton was wounded a second time but he still didn't give up. He made another attempt to grapple with Ball and was hit yet again, this time in the stomach, the bullet passing through the intestines and pelvis before lodging in the tissues at the back.

While all this was going on the Princess had remained calm even though underneath she was badly shaken. She spoke in a quiet soothing voice to Ball, asking what he wanted. He replied, 'I'll get a couple of million.' Inspector Beaton had by now managed to crawl on to the pavement, and the chauffeur, who had kept the engine running all this time, was ordered to switch it off. He disobeyed and started to get out of the car. Whereupon Ball shot him in the chest at point-blank range. The inside of the car was beginning to look like a battlefield. Princess Anne had been given a bouquet of yellow roses at the film première and these were scattered all over the back of the car. She was half lying on the floor with Mark trying to shield her.

Rowena Brassey told me later that she didn't realize at first what was going on: 'The funny thing was it didn't sound like shooting. It wasn't a bit like the noise guns make when you hear them on television. When Mr Callendar was shot he didn't realize it for a few seconds, then all of a sudden he said, "Good God, I've been shot."'

The shooting had not ended. A young policeman was on duty at St James's Palace when he heard the shots and ran across the road to see what was happening. As soon as he recognized the royal car he realized what was taking place and grabbed the gunman by the arm. Ball immediately turned and shot him through the stomach causing serious injury. In spite of the pain and the fact that he was losing a lot of blood the police officer managed to activate his personal radio and call for help. The first person on the scene, even before the police cars had been summoned, was a well-known Fleet Street journalist, Brian McConnell, who was about to get the scoop of his life. He had been travelling in a taxi just behind the royal car and when he saw the various bodies lying around he jumped out of his taxi and walked up to the gunman, saying, 'Look, old man, these are friends of mine. Give me the gun.' What he got for his pains was a bullet in the chest.

All this had happened within the space of a few minutes and by now police cars had arrived with reinforcements. Ball ran into nearby St James's Park trying to escape, chased by an unarmed detective, Peter Edwards, who brought him down with a flying rugby tackle. Ball was overpowered and arrested. From start to finish the entire incident had taken less than ten minutes. Four people had been shot, the amazing thing is that no one was killed. Bullets had been flying around inside the royal car and Rowena Brassey said she was surprised that Mark Phillips had not been hit. He remained inside the car all the time.

Jim Beaton and the other injured men were taken to hospital where they all underwent emergency surgery and Princess Anne and Mark were driven the few hundred yards to Buckingham Palace where they gave statements to the police. The Princess then telephoned her parents who were in Indonesia on a state visit. It was five o'clock in the morning and Prince Philip was woken up to take the call. Once he had been reassured that Princess Anne was safe and well he told the Queen about the incident. The Princess then telephoned her brother the Prince of Wales, who was on board his ship HMS *Jupiter* in San Diego, California. She knew that the international news services would make headlines of the story and wanted to tell her family what had happened in her own words before they could read about it in the morning newspapers or hear it on the radio. There was one more call to make before Princess Anne could leave to drive back to Sandhurst. Her best friend was Alison Oliver, who was also her trainer. Mrs Oliver and her husband had been out for the evening and had heard the news on the radio as they drove home. When they reached Warfield they heard the telephone ringing. Mrs Oliver rushed to answer and heard a calm voice at the other end saying, 'It's me. I'm all right.'

Mrs Oliver told me later that she had never been so glad to get a phone call in her life and, 'It was typically thoughtful of Anne to think of others at such a moment of stress.'

Many years later I talked about the incident with the Princess sitting in her comfortable room at Buckingham Palace. Even ten years after she remembered clearly every moment. 'My first reaction was anger. I was furious at this man who was having a tug-of-war with me. He ripped my dress which was a favourite blue one I had made specially to wear away on honeymoon, but of course our main concern was for the people who had tried to save us and who had been shot. They were very brave and looking back on it now their actions seem even more courageous when you think about them in the cold light of day.'

Inspector Beaton was the worst injured of the four men who had been shot. He needed surgery to his chest, stomach and hand and he spent weeks in hospital where he was visited several times by Princess Anne and Mark. Beaton hadn't been in the job very long. In fact he was appointed Princess Anne's detective on the day she was married. The Queen, when she returned to England, realized the full extent of the kidnapping attempt and also the bravery of those who had tried to protect her daughter. When they were all off the danger list they were invited with their families to a reception at Buckingham Palace, which followed a private investiture. Jim Beaton received the highest award possible for gallantry in civilian life, the George Cross. Police constable Michael Hills, the man who had been on duty at St James's Palace, and Mr Ronald Russel, a businessman who had also tackled the gunman, were awarded the George Medal. Another policeman, Peter Edwards, the journalist Brian McConnell, and the chauffeur Alexander Callander, were all given the Queen's Gallantry Medal. Princess Anne herself was made a Dame Grand Cross of the Royal Victorian Order for her behaviour during the incident, with Mark Phillips being created a Commander in recognition of his efforts. Rowena Brassey became a Member of the Royal Victorian Order, the sovereign's personal order of chivalry to which membership is only offered for services which are considered to be of great value to the Queen herself.

The gunman, Ian Ball, a twenty-six-year-old Englishman, was ordered to be detained for life after a trial at which it was revealed that he had planned to hold the Princess for three million pounds' ransom. The bizarre ransom note was found in his possession. It was addressed to the Queen and said:

Your daughter has been kidnapped – the following conditions to be fulfilled for her release. A ransom of £3 million is to be paid in £5 notes. They are to be used, unmarked, not sprayed with any chemical substance and not consecutively numbered. The money is to be packed in 30 unlocked suitcases clearly marked on the outside. The following documents are to be prepared: a free pardon to cover the kidnapping, and anything connected with it i.e. the possession of firearms or the murder of any police officer; a free pardon for any offences committed by myself from parking to murder. As the money is to be banked abroad, I shall be asking for a free pardon to run indefinitely for being in contravention of the Exchange Control Act. Documents are to be prepared for a civilian action to be taken against the police if they disclose my true identity with damages of not less than £1 million. A civilian action to be taken against you or your consorts if you reveal my true identity. No excuses will be accepted for failing to compile these documents. If they cannot be drawn up under existing laws, the laws must be changed.

Then followed a series of even more outrageous instructions on how the money was to be paid and by whom. The ransom was to be carried to Ball by one of his own solicitors and no one else: 'No one else will be acceptable. If he is ill, I want him brought to me on a stretcher. If he is dead, I want his body dug up and brought to the plane.' The Queen herself was to be involved in the transaction. Ball wanted her to come and see him in Switzerland and give him a sample signature so that he could be really sure she was the Queen. The demands went on and on. His preparations for the kidnapping had been made with care and meticulous attention to detail. All his personal documents had been burnt; his savings had been withdrawn from the bank and all the labels removed from his clothing. He had rented a house near Sandhurst and hired a car and a typewriter, paying cash for each. It was obviously no spur of the moment decision.

When Ball appeared in court on 22 May 1974 he pleaded guilty to the charges of attempted kidnapping, attempted murder and wounding. He was ordered to be detained in a special hospital under the Mental Health Act without limit of time. He is still there.

The kidnapping attempt brought sharply into focus the security arrangements of the royal family. Until then the protection of the Queen and her family had been fairly low key. There had never been a serious attempt on the life of any of them and the personal police officers were there mainly to act as buffers between the public and press and their royal charges. In 1981 I talked to Princess Anne about the role of her detective in the early days when she was at school. She said, 'I didn't see much of him. You don't judge things as they are today; the detective was there really only for travelling purposes and he didn't live on the premises, he lived just out of the school grounds . . . he was seen occasionally wandering about, but nobody really bothered about him.'

After March 1974 things changed dramatically. Every member of the royal family was allocated a team of detectives to work around the clock guarding them. They are all armed and experts in unarmed combat, which they are taught by the Special Air Service at their headquarters in Hereford, where they return regularly for refresher courses. The SAS also have detailed plans of the internal arrangements at each royal residence: where the furniture is placed, how many windows, where the doors are, open fireplaces and so on. This is why the rooms in royal homes are never rearranged without the knowledge of the security forces. If they ever found themselves dealing with a hostage situation they would need to know exactly where everything is in any particular room. All the royal cars are fitted with electronic homing devices so that if one deviates from its scheduled route the change can be instantly noted back in the special branch headquarters which monitors all royal journeys. The security authorities have done as much as is humanly possible to make the royal family safe, within the limits imposed by the Queen herself. Her Majesty will not entertain the idea of living in a bullet proof cage. She is determined that she and her family will lead as normal a life as possible under the circumstances and realistically they all know that, if someone is determined enough, an attack would be virtually impossible to prevent.

After the incident in The Mall Princess Anne and her husband returned to their home at Sandhurst where they joined in the normal mess life of the Academy. A few senior officers who were die-hard traditionalists tried to impose their rigid code of behaviour on their royal companion, but the Princess soon let them know that as far as she was concerned she was the wife of one of their junior officers and that was how she wanted to be treated. For the first few months it was a difficult time. Nobody quite knew what to do. Should they curtsey every time she came into a room? Would it be in order to approach her and start a conversation or should they wait until she spoke to them first? Princess Anne soon put everybody at their ease. She was, and remains, first and foremost the Queen's daughter, and she is fully aware of what that entails. But she is also a strictly no-nonsense type of person to whom the overdoing of protocol is as bad as none at all. Once she had become acquainted with Mark's fellow officers and their families, life settled down to a pleasant, easygoing routine. They attended mess functions and parties in other people's homes and gave a number of dinners in their own quarters where the Princess frequently ended up sitting on the floor in her own drawing room – simply because they didn't have enough chairs to go round.

One of their friends at Sandhurst was a young officer in the Argyll and Sutherland Highlanders, Malcolm McVittie. He had first met the Princess four years earlier when he was on duty at Balmoral Castle during the royal family's summer holiday. The following year he was invited to Princess Anne's twenty-first birthday party which was held on board *Britannia* in the Naval Dockyard at Portsmouth. Their friendship continued over the years; he meanwhile got married and he and his wife Wendy found themselves on the guest list to the royal wedding. So it was a happy coincidence that when Princess Anne and Mark took up residence at Sandhurst they found at least one old friend already there. McVittie recalls that 'Princess Anne and Mark set out deliberately to join the normal mess life of the college and they refused point-blank to give dinner parties exclusively for the senior officers. When they entertained at home it was usually an informal gathering for the younger men and their wives or girlfriends, and when she dropped in to one of their homes the Princess had no objection to sitting around the kitchen table.'

The Princess's official duties were beginning to take up rather more of her time. Sandhurst was ideally placed geographically, being only fifty-three miles from the centre of London. It meant that she could exercise her horses in the early morning, leave for Buckingham Palace shortly after nine, do a full day's work and then still be home in time for dinner. She rarely stayed away overnight; she still doesn't if she can help it. The next couple of years passed in this pleasant if occasionally demanding manner, with both the Princess and her husband aiming for the same goal – a place in the British team to compete at the Olympic Games in Montreal in 1976. They both made it – at least both were selected for the squad; but when the time came for the actual competing team to be chosen, Anne was in and Mark was selected as reserve.

Shortly before they left with the rest of the team for Canada, Malcolm McVittie's wife had given birth to their first child, a girl. Somewhat tentatively the Princess was asked if she would consider being a godmother to the baby. The McVitties were not too sure of the protocol about making such a request to a member of the royal family, but there was no hesitation on the part of Princess Anne. She said yes and the ceremony took place in the chapel at Sandhurst on the day after she arrived home from Canada, feeling no doubt both jet-lagged and still suffering the after-effects of a horrendous fall on the cross country section of her event, which had left her badly concussed. The baby was named Alice Louise, two of Princess Anne's names, and Her Royal Highness still takes her responsibilities as a spiritual parent very seriously. They have kept in regular contact since then with the Princess sending birthday and Christmas cards every year and receiving in return handwritten reports of school progress from her goddaughter. Malcolm McVittie and his wife remain friends with Princess Anne and Mark Phillips even if these days they do not see them as often as they used to. Their separate careers have taken them to different parts of the world and today their paths rarely cross. But as McVittie says, 'Ours is not a friendship that relies on seeing one another constantly. We may even go a year or two without meeting, but if we are in Gloucestershire and we know they are at home we always call. Princess Anne leads such a busy life with so many calls on her time that it seems presumptuous to assume one would be welcome, but when she says "if you want to see me, drop in" she means it – and we do.'

In the beginning of 1975 the Princess and her husband found they had to make a number of serious decisions. Mark had come to the end of his posting at Sandhurst, which meant they had to find a new home, and it would have to be one where they could not only keep and train their horses but also make the safe base for raising a young family.

Mark's new posting was to the Ministry of Defence in London as an administrative officer in army training. It was the kiss of death to the young and ambitious cavalry officer. His regiment was serving in Northern Ireland on anti-terrorist duties and Mark wanted to join them. He had hoped to continue as a full-time career officer, perhaps ending up in command. However, to do that would have meant going wherever the regiment went, and as he was now considered to be a member of the royal family, the army thought it unwise for him to go to Northern Ireland. He himself would have been a prime target and the regiment itself would have been placed in an impossible position trying to keep him in one piece. London, and a desk job, was their answer to the problem; it wasn't his. He tried to cope with the mountain of paper work that never seemed to get any smaller, but his heart wasn't in it, and he soon began to feel a sense of frustration and failure. When the Princess told him that she was expecting their first child the news convinced him that he should get out of the army and try to find somewhere different to live and a new career.

He said later that the options were fairly small. Apart from his military training the only job he was equipped for was something to do with horses. He was then at the height of his sporting career with a worldwide reputation as a rider and he wanted to use this expertise and knowledge to make some money.

Princess Anne was totally supportive when he told her of his decision. She knew how much he had given up when he married her and she realized how important it was for him to do something that would allow him to retain his independence. Which was all very well in theory, but the trouble was that he could not afford to buy a house or set himself up in business on his own money. His salary as a captain was £4,500 a year which of course he would lose as soon as he left the army. Even if they found a house that was within Mark's limit he could not have obtained a mortgage without a regular income. Happily the Queen came to the rescue. She told the couple to look for a house and when they had found it to let her know how much it was going to cost. The Princess told me that at first they looked for 'a reasonably sized house with about fifty acres so that we could accommodate the horses'. The difficulty was that as soon as estate agents realized who the prospective buyers were, the prices shot up. Princess Anne and her husband were innocents in the property buying market and actually went to look for houses themselves rather than employing someone to check up beforehand. So it soon became obvious that the Queen's daughter was looking for a property – hence the sudden rise in price!

When they decided to look further afield, in the counties of Gloucestershire and Wiltshire, more suitable properties became available, one of which was Highgrove House at Tetbury, now the home of the Prince and Princess of Wales. It was turned down for a number of reasons, including the price, and the fact that the house was a security risk being close to the main road.

Not too far away from Highgrove House another property was brought to their attention, Gatcombe Park on the outskirts of the village of Minchinhampton. It had been the family home of the Courtauld family for nearly forty years, and Lord Butler, the Master of Trinity College, Cambridge, an old friend of the Prince of Wales, and a member by marriage of the Courtauld family, suggested to Princess Anne that she might like to go and see it.

The house was practically a wreck. It had not been lived in for more than ten years. There was damp everywhere, the roof needed repairs and the entire building was in dire need of new plumbing and rewiring. In addition an arable farm with 500 acres was attached to the property. Princess Anne said later that Gatcombe had none of the things they were looking for. It was far too big and the fact that there was a farm meant that they had to revise their plans. The price was also something of an obstacle. Although it was the Queen who was paying, Princess Anne did not want to abuse her mother's generosity by buying something she would not have thought of in her own right. The royal family never discloses how much it pays for anything so the actual cost of Gatcombe remains a secret known only to very few people. But similar properties in the county at the time were fetching around half a million pounds so the price was probably slightly less than that. Today the estate is worth in excess of three million pounds. The purchase of the house brought its own share of controversy with the most public statement from a leading figure being pronounced by Neil Kinnock, the future Leader of the Labour Party. He said, 'I don't know which is worse – the Queen for being wealthy enough to give it to them, or them for having the neck to take it.'

Having bought the house, the first problem to be resolved was how to get it into a reasonable condition. So much needed doing it was difficult to know where to start. And, as they didn't want to ask the Queen for any more money, the couple had to raise the finance for the repairs and alterations themselves. Princess Anne provided most of it from her trust fund. Mark raised the rest by getting a mortgage, using the house as security. It was a substantial amount. Later he caused a storm of derisive comment when he claimed that he and the Princess were 'just like any other young couple with a mortgage', but he was speaking the truth. The amount of interest on his loan was probably more than the average couple were paying for buying their home. Whatever the amount was – and again it is all pure conjecture because of the royal family's reluctance to discuss private financial transactions – it was raised, and the work was put in hand.

Gatcombe looks like a very large country house from the outside. Inside it is surprisingly compact. On the ground floor are a dining room, drawing room, Captain Phillips' study and a sitting room which Princess Anne uses as an office, with eight bedrooms on the first floor, and the nursery on top. Behind the kitchen downstairs is a sitting room for the police officers, one of whom is on duty at all times, and the usual domestic offices. The impression of size comes from the superb conservatory which was added to the west front in 1829.

The house was built in 1770 by Edward Sheppard, a wealthy sheep breeder and wool merchant. It had passed through a number of hands before being bought in 1940 by Samuel Courtauld, a textile millionaire and the father-in-law of Rab Butler, a prominent Conservative Member of Parliament and Cabinet Minister.

Perhaps it is just as well that royalty do not appear to mind discomfort, because when the Princess first saw Gatcombe it was in a terrible state. There were no rooms which were habitable; upstairs the bathrooms had been built in the front of the house, where the best views are, with the bedrooms all overlooking a jumble of broken down sheds and outbuildings at the back, and the kitchen looked as if it hadn't had a thing done to it since before the Second World War.

Anne and Mark however saw only what they wanted to see: a house that was perfect for what they had in mind. There was plenty of space for the horses, the house could be repaired and above all it offered total privacy. You cannot see Gatcombe from the road. A gatehouse guards a long, curving drive at the end of which there is now a permanent police post manned by members of the Gloucestershire constabulary, and which has been cleverly designed to merge in with the surrounding foliage. From the first moment they saw it they both knew that Gatcombe was the place for them. Mark later recalled: 'We stood on the front steps and looked out at the view; it was quiet, it was secluded, it was peaceful with woods down each side of a long valley. I thought to myself – well, whatever is inside we can change, given time. But this we can never change. This is just what we have been looking for.' They were in total agreement and the Princess has never had cause to regret that instant decision. Today, after living there for twelve years, she loves it more than ever and for her it is a home for life.

The repairs and alterations that were needed took eleven months to complete and even then compromises were made. The original interior design, by David Hicks, a cousin by marriage through his wife, Lady Pamela Mountbatten, proved to be far too expensive. So only part was incorporated in the downstairs rooms; the rest was dictated by how much money they had available. Throughout the period when the restoration of the house was taking place, Princess Anne was still carrying out her public duties in between dashing down to Gatcombe to see how the work was progressing; all the while getting larger as the birth of her baby grew closer. In the end

Anne and Mark officially took over the house on 29 September 1976. Less than two months later the Princess gave birth to their first child and he brought them back to Gatcombe for the first time.

On the evening of 14 November 1977 Princess Anne and Mark joined the Queen for a private celebration dinner at Buckingham Palace. It was the couple's fourth wedding anniversary. It was a quiet but pleasant occasion and around midnight Anne and Mark retired. Shortly after four o'clock the following morning Anne woke her husband to tell him that she was starting to have the baby. A car was on standby for the short drive through Hyde Park to St Mary's Hospital, Paddington, where a suite in the private Lindo Wing (now known as the Royal Wing) had been made ready. Mr George Pinker, the Queen's gynaecologist, had been summoned. He was a consultant at St Mary's and knew that all the trained staff and equipment he might need in an emergency were readily available. The Princess went into labour almost as soon as she entered the hospital and six hours later – at 10.46 A.M. precisely – she was delivered of a healthy baby son weighing in at 7lbs 9 oz. Mark had stayed with his wife during the birth and was present at the delivery.

A special telephone link had been established from the suite direct to Buckingham Palace and within minutes Mark had phoned the Queen to give her the good news that she now had a grandson. The Duke of Edinburgh was on an official visit to Germany and the Queen rang him immediately. All of which meant that for the first and only time in her life she was late for an engagement. An Investiture was due to start in the State Ballroom at 11 o'clock and as the minutes ticked by the waiting recipients and their friends and families began muttering among themselves. Royal engagements always run to time. Eventually, some ten minutes late, the Queen entered the Ballroom and apologized to the people waiting with the words, 'I apologize for being late, but I have just had a message from the hospital. My daughter has just given birth to a son.' There was a stunned silence for a moment and then, encouraged by a gesture from Lord Maclean, the Lord Chamberlain, spontaneous applause broke out. It was the first time applause had been heard at an Investiture – and the Queen was delighted. And Mark, with a nice line in self-deprecating humour, told reporters, 'It's good to know I can do something right sometimes.'

The new baby – his names were to be Peter Mark Andrew – was fifth in line of succession to the throne, and the College of Arms revealed that he was also the first royal grandchild in 500 years to be born a commoner. His parents wished him to remain so in spite of the fact that the Queen had it in her power to give him a title in his own right if she so desired. Princess Anne was as determined as ever not to allow her child to be ennobled simply because of the position of his grandmother, particularly since his father was without a title. Mark's decision not to accept an earldom on his marriage was due not just to stubbornness on his part, but a genuine reluctance because he had neither inherited the title nor done anything to earn it himself. He is not against the hereditary system as such, and if his father had been titled, Mark would have accepted whatever, in time, had come his way.

There were no complications with the birth and a few days later Mark turned up to collect his new family and drive them back to Gatcombe. He immediately ran into trouble. When Princess Anne left the hospital carrying baby Peter she got into the front seat of the car, thereby arousing the wrath of the car-safety lobby who felt that she should have known better and set a good example by sitting in the back. They were right of course, even though this was before the days when seat belts were compulsory in Britain, but it was perfectly understandable for the Princess to want to sit beside her husband. There was another sour note. This time, totally predictable, from the Scottish Member of Parliament who was well known for his anti-royalist leanings, Willie Hamilton. He said when the news of the birth was announced, 'How charming – another one on the payroll.' Anyway, Mark drove his family down to Gloucestershire where they were to start their new life together. A new baby, a new home and, for him, a new career.

The christening was held in the Music Room at Buckingham Palace, where Princess Anne herself had been baptized, and the godparents were: the Prince of Wales and Prince Andrew, a fellow eventer Jane Holderness-Roddam (now a lady-in-waiting), another old friend, Lady Cecil Cameron, Captain Hamish Lochure and a cousin of Mark's, the Reverend Geoffrey Tiarks, one of whose ecclesiastical ancestors had been chaplain to the mother of Queen Victoria.

Back at Gatcombe Anne and Mark settled down to become a farming couple. Mark resigned his commission in April 1978, ending ten years of military service. He was sorry to leave the regiment and Princess Anne sympathized, saying, 'It was a pity, but it was more or less forced on him. If he had been able to do what he wanted to, which was basically stay to command a squadron and then possibly the regiment, I would have been very happy, though I don't suppose I would have made a very good colonel's wife . . .'

If Mark has had cause to regret his decision he has never allowed it to be known and once he had left the army he threw himself wholeheartedly into being a farmer and trainer of horses. He knew a great deal of the latter, practically nothing of the former, so he enrolled on an intensive farming course at the Royal Agricultural College at Cirencester for three months. These days his business interests take him away from Gatcombe for a large part of the year so a manager and three full-time employees run the farm when Mark is away. The Princess has always enjoyed country life and when her royal duties allow lends a hand on the farm, driving tractors at harvest time when several other members of the family are also recruited as voluntary labour.

The arrival on the scene of Master Peter Phillips meant only a slight change in the routine of the Phillips household. A nanny was brought in to look after him on the top nursery floor and, in common with most other well-to-do families, he was seen only in the mornings and evenings by his parents, though the Princess did occasionally bath him herself if she was at home. Princess Anne had said a number of times before the birth of her first child that she was not a particularly maternal sort of woman, and Peter's arrival did not seem to make much difference to her outlook. With no immediate change of heart on her part friends felt that as Peter grew older he grew closer to his father. As soon as he was able to walk Mark would take him around the estate with him, often perched on his shoulders, and on the few occasions that photographs were taken of the family it was usually Mark who was holding the boy's hand.

Three years later things were to change. Princess Anne again found she was pregnant and was reported as saying that this was '... an occupational hazard if you're a wife'. She moved from Gatcombe to Windsor shortly before the birth and then returned to the same suite in the Lindo Wing at St Mary's Hospital. Mark remained in Gloucestershire working until he was told that his wife had been taken to hospital and the birth was imminent. He had been present at the birth of his son, but it was not an experience he was desperate to repeat. Nevertheless when Brenda Hodgson, the Princess's personal secretary, telephoned Mark at Gatcombe he drove straight to St Mary's, where, as luck would have it, he was in plenty of time to witness the birth of his daughter. He said afterwards that he was glad he had been present.

Princess Anne's daughter was born at precisely 8.15 P.M. on 15 May 1981, three months to the day before her mother's thirty-first birthday. Four days later Mark came to collect them and drove them back to Gatcombe and three weeks later the child's name was announced. It was Zara Anne Elizabeth. Zara is a Greek biblical name meaning 'bright as the dawn' and it took every member of the royal family, except the Prince of Wales, by surprise. The reason Prince Charles wasn't surprised was that he had chosen it. Princess Anne explained to me that, 'The baby had made a somewhat positive arrival and my brother thought that Zara was an appropriate name.' An unusual name certainly but not, it appears, unique. 'I heard from just about every other Zara in Britain at the time and I promise you there are quite a few,' said the Princess. Including, one might add, someone who is fairly close to her: the daughter of one of her ladies-in-waiting, Shân Legge-Bourke.

If Princess Anne's claim to be 'not very maternal' had been true in the past, it certainly changed completely once her daughter was born. Around this time I was spending quite a lot of time in her company making a television film of her working life, and a few weeks after Zara was born I had to go to Gatcombe to discuss a number of future engagements. The Princess looked superb; she has always enjoyed excellent health and she keeps extremely fit, so the birth of her daughter was a mere hiccup as far as her working life was concerned. Once we had finished our programme meeting, she asked me if I would like to see the baby. We walked into the conservatory where Zara was sleeping in the kind of big old fashioned pram still favoured by the royal family. It was obvious that the Princess was thrilled with her new daughter and I left with a deep impression of the pride and pleasure she took in the child. Since then I have seen them together many times and, even though Zara can be a handful sometimes, she is still very much her mother's daughter and the day she leaves to go away to school will be a sad one for Princess Anne. She loves to have Zara with her whenever she can, and in the same way that Mark is rarely seen around Gatcombe without Peter in tow, when he is home from school, Zara is never far away when Princess Anne is at home.

Gatcombe is the sort of house where no rooms are sacred. It has a lived in look about it and the children have the run of the place; they are not restricted to the nursery floor and never have been. The entrance hall is littered with toys, wellington boots, a rather splendid if now somewhat scruffy looking rocking horse and a table covered in copies of magazines such as *Horse and Hound* and *Farming Today*. A bowl of water lies in readiness for whichever of the family's dogs happens to be first in through the door. At the present time there is only one dog which lives in the house. He is a corgi called Apollo who is there purely because of his sex. As the Princess explains, 'He is a refugee from the Queen's collection of corgis. He is a dog and she only has bitches.' So he was removed from Buckingham Palace and given a home at Gatcombe. Until fairly recently there were a number of other dogs including a lurcher and a foxhound. But these have died and so far not been replaced. The gundogs remain outside the house, living in kennels on the estate. There is a sweeping staircase to the first floor and the pictures on the walls are sporting prints. When Princess Anne and Mark moved into Gatcombe they were offered a selection of very expensive paintings from the Royal Collection. They declined the offer, choosing instead pictures by lesser known artists but all with a theme they both felt they could live with.

The drawing room is the nicest room in the house, leading immediately off the hall – to the left as you go in. It is furnished in typically country house style: deep armchairs and sofas with chintz covers, the focal point being the fireplace where they burn logs from the estate. And if you happen to be a visitor in the winter a huge fire is always burning. When the log basket needs to be replenished the Princess does not bother to call a servant, she does it herself. Similarly, if you arrive at coffee time, the tray is placed on a low table in front of the fire but it is the Princess herself who pours. Formality is not the order of the day at Gatcombe. The one thing that distinguishes the drawing room at Gatcombe from that in any other country house is the collection of photographs around the room. They are nearly all of members of royal families, either British or foreign, and all inscribed personally by the subjects to Anne and Mark. This is the room where Princess Anne receives official guests when she is not at Buckingham Palace. If the commanding officer of a nearby military installation is leaving his post (the Princess is Honorary Air Commodore of RAF Lyneham) he will call to make his farewells and to introduce his successor. This is another case of the Princess doing what comes naturally instead of going by the book. She knows that her visitors have come from just around the corner so it would be highly inconvenient for them to pay an official call on her at Buckingham Palace, when Gatcombe is only a couple of miles' drive away. It is a thoughtful gesture on her part and one that is very much appreciated by those with a busy schedule. It also gives them a chance to see her at home in her own surroundings, which is much more pleasant than the formality of the Palace.

The Princess's sitting-room leads off the drawing room and it is here that she spends much of her time when she is in the house, doing her homework. If she is going to an engagement direct from Gatcombe, her Private Secretary will send all the relevant information by bag from the Palace. Her Royal Highness will spend a couple of hours preparing, and if she is to make a speech, it is in this room that it is written – at the desk which is placed near the box windows overlooking the terrace. It is also in this sitting-room that Anne has lunch when she is at home. It is usually served on a tray and they eat while watching television, though television is a luxury not often enjoyed by the Princess. As she once told me, 'I see so little television there's not much point in starting to watch a serial.' Mark, on the other hand, is a self-confessed addict. He loves to watch any kind of sport and he has a massive collection of old movies on video tape in his own quarters, waiting, as he says, 'for the day when I can settle down to watch them'.

Life at Gatcombe for the Princess is divided into the days when she is on royal duty – and that can mean upwards of fifty engagements a month these days – and those 'non-royal' days when she reverts to being a country woman and the mother of two young children. When there isn't an official car waiting outside the front door or a helicopter of the Queen's Flight standing by in one of the upper fields, the Princess likes to drive Zara to her local school where she starts at nine o'clock. If Princess Anne isn't available one of the detectives will take Zara to school. Then it's back to the house to change into riding clothes for the early business of the day, which is horses. The Princess's horses take up most of her so-called off duty hours. Caring for high-class horses requires constant time and attention and, with just a couple of grooms at Gatcombe and around a dozen horses, there's plenty of work for everyone. Mark deals with the business side of running the farm; Princess Anne has nothing to do with that. But they share the work that is needed to get their horses in top form for the competition season, which is perhaps why they are both in such superb condition themselves. Three or four hours every day in the saddle make sure there is not an ounce of surplus fat on either of them. When she isn't working her own horses the Princess rides out for David Nicholson, one of the most successful trainers of race horses in Britain. His stables are just 45 minutes' drive from Gatcombe, and while he is glad of the extra pair of hands to help with his string, she in turn has developed an interest in racing which is turning into another successful adjunct to her equestrian career.

Working with horses doesn't leave Princess Anne much time for anything else, particularly if you include the two or three days hunting she likes to get in during the winter. Many of her closest friends live near Gatcombe and they know they are welcome to drop in if the Princess is at home. They have only to look in the Court Circular in *The Times* in the morning to find out whether she has an engagement that day. If she hasn't, they usually telephone first to see if she is at home, or just drive over for an hour or so. Princess Anne spends quite a lot of time on the telephone and her private number at Gatcombe is changed frequently because enterprising members of the press have a habit of finding it out and ringing up trying to get a quote on any number of topics. Those who need to know are given the right number to get through to Mark or the Princess. There is also an office number at Gatcombe which Mark's personal secretary, Margaret Hammond, guards against unwelcome callers.

Other members of the royal family are not regular visitors to Gatcombe Park even though the Prince and Princess of Wales live just a few miles away at Highgrove House. It's even nearer across the fields by helicopter. Prince and Princess Michael of Kent are also near neighbours, completing the 'Royal Triangle' in this part of Gloucestershire, but no one can remember when they were last seen at Gatcombe. The Duke of Edinburgh, however, is someone who is welcome at any time. His daughter would love it if he could call more often than he does – father and daughter are the closest of friends. The Queen has of course been to Gatcombe a number of times and she and the Princess speak frequently on the telephone. There is a direct link between Gatcombe and Buckingham Palace, as there is between all the royal residences and the Palace. This is not just to make private calls easier but also for the more important reasons of security.

Prince Edward is close to his sister and his niece and nephew. One of the things he enjoys is lending a hand with the harvest. At least he used to like this before he became employed by the Really Useful Theatre Company in London. These days he does not have so much free time on his hands.

As a wife and mother Princess Anne has had to cope with what has on occasions been unrelenting pressure from the world's press. Many years ago she was first reported as saying that she didn't care for children very much, and more recently in her longest ever television interview – with Brian Walden – she again repeated: 'I don't like children very much.' She was referring to her role as President of the Save the Children Fund and the fact that she is able to carry out her duties more effectively because she does not become emotionally involved. But of course, a remark like that means just one thing to the general public: she does not like children. The majority of women think it is unnatural for another woman to feel that way. Surely, they say, the maternal instinct is the strongest of all female characteristics? Perhaps it is with most women, but when one is honest enough to say out loud what one feels inside, should it inevitably lead to general condemnation? And the fact that Princess Anne has revealed her own feelings about children generally, does not mean that she does not love her own children, of course. She is a devoted mother to Peter and Zara and when she is at home spends a lot of time with them.

True, the Princess spends longer periods away from home than most parents but, as she explains: 'They have grown up knowing that I have a job to do which means being away for part of the time and they are used to my comings and goings.' The same applies to her relationship with her husband. When he married into the royal family Mark knew that he would have to take second place to his wife on all public occasions – in the same way that Prince Philip had to accept his secondary role to the Queen. Mark also knew that if he was to keep any semblance of individuality it was important for him to establish an independent role from that of being merely consort to the Queen's daughter. In any case, there was never any question of Mark taking on royal duties. Constitutionally there is no role for the husband of a female member of the royal family, whether she be Princess or Queen. Mark did not want to merely 'tag along' behind Princess Anne as she went about her various engagements. There would have been a public outcry if he had. So he used the skills and talents he had acquired in the army and as an international horseman to set himself up as a professional competitor, trainer and entrepreneur. His management company IMG (International Management Group), which is owned by Mark McCormack, the world's leading sports agent (his clients include Jack Nicklaus, Boris Becker and Martina Navratilova), arranges highly lucrative appearances for him all over the world. This means he spends around three months of the year travelling, but it also brings him in an annual income not far short of half a million pounds. Almost as important as the money itself is the fact that by being able to earn such sums he can contribute to the upkeep of Gatcombe and help to keep his wife in something approaching the style to which she is accustomed.

Because the Queen bought Gatcombe Park for Anne and Mark it is sometimes assumed that Her Majesty also pays all the bills.

This is certainly not the case. They look after the maintenance themselves. Gatcombe is a private residence and not a 'Grace and Favour' home owned by the Crown and therefore the responsibility of the Department of the Environment. If Gatcombe had been retained as an official royal residence all the costs would have been met from the public exchequer; but, even though the house is registered in the Princess Royal's name (not her husband's), they can only claim from the Civil List that part of the house which is used by the Princess for her royal duties. To the outsider this might seem to be a slightly ridiculous state of affairs and one which could easily be abused. But the Princess is fastidious about her use of public funds and so, at the beginning of every financial year, a member of her personal staff will go to Gatcombe accompanied by a surveyor from the Department of the Environment, and between them they will decide the priorities as far as repairs and decoration are concerned. Budget control is tight and overspending is simply not an option. The Princess sees all the accounts and every penny is watched at Gatcombe Park. Mark may not have enjoyed always having to take second place to his wife in public, but he does enjoy the responsibilities of parenthood. He is an easygoing father who finds it difficult to be stern with his children; Princess Anne has no problems in disciplining the youngsters. But it is to Mark that they turn when they need something, and not just because they think he is a 'soft touch'. He has a quiet authority and they know when they have gone far enough. However, they also know he is fair and slow to anger, so they often turn to him when the need arises.

In much the same way, but for different reasons, Princess Anne and her brothers still discuss any problems they might have with their father. Once a year, in the weeks just before Christmas, Prince Philip invites his children to Balmoral, where they enjoy a private get-together far away from the prying eyes of the press and the public. It is an opportunity for a family holiday (although the Queen is never present). They stay at Craigowan House in the hills above the Castle and only Prince Philip, the Prince of Wales, the Duke of York, Prince Edward and the Princess Royal are there – spouses are not invited. It is a tradition that was started by Prince Philip many years ago and has continued, unbroken, even though three of the children are now married and parents themselves. None of the participants has ever spoken about what goes on at these gatherings and, equally, none has ever missed a year. At home, Prince Philip is very much head of his own family and with his children Mark Phillips occupies a similar position.

Gatcombe Park today is a large country estate with a very comfortable house and more than a thousand acres. The extra land was acquired when Mark approached one of his neighbours, Captain Vaisey Davis, to see if he wanted to sell 'a couple of fields'. Captain Davis was the owner of Aston Farm which adjoined Gatcombe. He, in turn, surprised Mark by offering him his entire farm of 533 acres, not just the few fields Mark had been interested in. It was an offer Mark could scarcely turn down as it made such economic sense to join the two estates. But it also meant that he and Princess Anne would have to go further into debt to borrow the money for the purchase. There was no problem about getting the extra cash. Plenty of financial sources were available and the farm was excellent security. Mark began negotiations with a commercial organization but before the deal was signed a 'good fairy' in the form of his mother-in-law came on the scene. Princess Anne and her husband were dining with the Queen one evening and telling her of their plans to raise the money to buy Aston Farm on a 'lease-back' arrangement. This is a very common form of financial transaction whereby an institution buys a property and then leases it back to the person who wants to use it. When Her Majesty heard the details of the scheme, she said, 'Why can't I be the institution? I'll buy it and rent it to you in the same way.' And that is exactly what happened. The Queen bought Aston Farm and rented it back to her daughter and son-in-law, becoming their landlord in the process. It was an ideal solution to the problem and Gatcombe became an economically viable proposition. It was also a very shrewd investment on the part of the Queen as Aston Farm has more than trebled in value since she bought it.

On the outside Gatcombe looks very much as it did on the day Princess Anne and Mark first saw it in 1976. Inside it has changed considerably. The personality of the Princess has been stamped on the house in every room. Unlike most of the other royal homes it has a 'lived-in' look about it. From the moment you walk through the front door you are aware that a family lives here and it's a happy family. There are few clues to the royal status of the lady of the house – until she appears. When she does – whatever she's wearing and however she's feeling – one is never for a moment left in any doubt that here is the Princess Royal.

CHAPTER
FIVE

♦

PUBLIC LIFE

'I think it is fair to say that throughout the world when one thinks of Save the Children, one immediately also thinks of Princess Anne, and in this country, certainly, the reverse is equally true.' Nicholas Hinton, Director General of the Save the Children Fund, was speaking in his office at Mary Datchelor House, the world head-quarters of the Fund, in London's east end.

Nobody would argue with that comment. The Princess has reached a stage in her public life when she has become totally identified with one particular organization – Save the Children. It is not something she has set out to do, and when it is pointed out that she has been president of SCF for almost twenty years it sometimes comes as a surprise. To many people her name became synonymous with the Fund only after her major tour to African countries in 1982. That was when the 'high profile' began with favourable press stories appearing in newspapers and magazines about 'the caring Princess'. But the fact remains that she has been working actively for Save the Children since 1 January 1970, the day she officially took over as president from the late Viscount Boyd of Merton, a former Colonial Secretary.

Nicholas Hinton has been Director General of Save the Children for less than five years. He was brought in to reorganize the charity which had earned a reputation as a worthy but somewhat outdated body which needed revitalizing. His predecessor was a tremen-dously enthusiastic and popular man who had reached the age of retirement, and it was felt that perhaps a younger man, with more recent experience of the outside world, would bring a fresh approach. Saving the children is a multi-million pound business these days and it needs a hard-headed commercial attitude if it is to compete with all the other charities which aim to empty the public pocket.

When Mr Hinton was appointed he was given specific targets to achieve; targets which meant that a number of personnel would be replaced and others would move from comfortable niches to more exposed positions. Since he took over as Director General not one senior manager is doing the same job as when Nicholas Hinton arrived on the scene.

In the early days of his stewardship there was a certain amount of wariness between himself and his president. They had already met a number of times and he knew of her immense reputation as the public image of the Fund; yet he too has been used to a high profile – he is a former parliamentary candidate and was well known in various aspects of public life before he joined the Fund – so there might have been the danger of a conflict between these two highly volatile characters. The fact that there has never been the slightest difficulty is a tribute to his perceptive interpretation of their relation-ship and Her Royal Highness's perfect understanding of the role of a non-executive president. Nicholas Hinton says, 'I have rarely come across anyone who so perfectly understands the difference between being a non-executive president and a chairman. She is kept fully informed of all she needs to know regarding the working of the Fund and yet she has never once stepped into those areas which are my responsibility and mine alone. This is a very important boundary in a voluntary organization – it's rather like that between the shareholders of a commercial company, the nominal owners, and the executives who are employed to run the place. The relationship is rarely written down so there are no specific rules to follow, but if you get them muddled it can be disastrous.'

Because SCF has come to occupy the major part of the Princess's public life there is a great deal of communication between the Fund and the Palace. Nicholas Hinton probably speaks to Colonel Gibbs, the Princess's Private Secretary, at least once every day; no other executive of any of the nearly one hundred organizations with which she is associated is in such close and frequent contact. Yet the relationship between the president and the Director General has not yet developed into the close friendship that existed between the Princess and John Cumber, who was Nicholas Hinton's immediate predecessor. Mr Cumber was of course of a different generation and in his eyes the Princess could do no wrong, while she in turn regarded him as an affectionate 'uncle figure'. With his perfect manners and old world charm he was a throw-back to the days of colonial benevolence and brought to the Fund a missionary zeal rather than a cool, businesslike brain. Nicholas Hinton's relationship with the Princess is totally professional; he is never tempted to try and make it anything else. Unlike David Nicholson and Malcolm Wallace, her equestrian advisers, he never telephones her personally on any occasion – all contact is via Peter Gibbs. Similarly, Her Royal Highness corresponds with him through her Private Secretary. If he has an important decision to make regarding the deployment of staff, at home or abroad, he makes that decision without reference to her. She wouldn't expect him to consult her on matters which lie within his own jurisdiction, and he is the sort of man who would only accept the top job in the Fund on the understanding that he would be left alone to get on with it. He does not view the Princess through rose-tinted spectacles, admitting that 'On long tours there are days when she can be a bit difficult, but so can we all.'

If there is an area where the two do disagree it is in the Princess's attitude to the media. She is going through a comparatively calm period with the press which has lasted several years, but she is still suspicious of reporters and photographers in the main and will not normally go out of her way to help them. Nicholas Hinton knows only too well how important it is to the Fund to get the best possible publicity and this means having the media on your side. He says he cannot persuade the Princess to agree in advance to cooperate with the press and, particularly on overseas tours, when television crews are working to a strict deadline, they need to know if they are going to get that all-important interview at the end of the day. The Princess Royal, in spite of all overtures from the Director General and his public relations staff, still refuses to commit herself in advance. And she finds the presence of the official Buckingham

Palace press secretaries completely unnecessary so never takes one with her on any of her tours.

Nicholas Hinton would like to see a definite arrangement pro-grammed into the schedule at the beginning of the tour, so that he can tell the press that they are going to get an interview, and when. So far the Princess has given interviews at the conclusion of all her major overseas visits, but only at the eleventh hour – which is an ulcer-making situation for those who have to deal with the press. If only she and the Director General could see eye to eye on this one subject he would be a more contented man. However, this is the only bone of contention between them and Nicholas Hinton is honest enough to admit that 'When she does do the interviews in the end she is superb. No one can handle the press as she can and she usually has them eating out of her hand by the time they leave.'

Photo opportunities are rife during these long tours to Africa and Asia, and if the Princess wanted to exploit her position she could guarantee front page exposure every day simply by picking up the most appealing looking infant and being photographed holding it in her arms. That she has consistently refused to do so speaks volumes for her own independence of spirit and her complete lack of interest in self-publicity.

Her own view on publicity is slightly different from that of her Director General. 'It is simply not true that I do not give television interviews during these tours. I believe it's fair to say that I have spoken to the press on every single occasion. What I object to is having microphones stuck in my face as soon as I arrive in a country, before I have had time to look around and form any opinions. I know that journalists have a job to do and they all want to be first, but my rule is that I try to give them all the same chance – at the end of the tour, when at least I have something that is hopefully useful to say.' The Princess goes on to express the opinion that reporters are always pleading that theirs is a special case anyway, when all they really want to do is scoop the opposition.

Having made his point about the Princess and the press, Nicholas Hinton is fully aware of the value of having the Princess Royal as president and readily admits it: 'She can go to places which would normally be closed to the rest of us and of course she can also approach the top people personally on our behalf. We might spend months, even years, trying to reach the right person in one of the Third World countries when we are looking for help with a particular problem. The Princess Royal is able in most cases to speak to whoever she wants, even if it is a head of state. This was the case in Uganda recently. We had been trying without success for many months to obtain permission to go to a certain area. The Princess was visiting the country; she spoke to the President personally and within weeks permission was given. That is the sort of help she can give to us which no one else can do.'

Another example of the more practical benefits she brings to the Fund came during a visit to Hong Kong in 1988. The Princess was in the Far East to attend meetings of the International Olympic Committee at the Olympic Games in Seoul. Just before the opening day she flew to Hong Kong for two days of public engagements. It was suggested that while she was there she should attend a small, formal dinner party being organized on behalf of the Save the Children Fund. There were less than forty guests sitting down, but they were all people of immense stature (and comparable fortunes) in the colony. At the end of the evening the staggering sum of £750,000 had been raised. It was the biggest single fund raising event held by Save the Children and Nicholas Hinton is in no doubt that the only reason so much money was donated that evening was because the Princess Royal was present in person.

She herself finds the public banging of drums slightly embarrassing, saying, 'It is a bit blatant I suppose, but if the Fund benefits that's all that really matters in the end.' Either directly or indirectly the Princess has been responsible for raising millions of pounds in the twenty years she has been president. When she started, the annual income from donations was fifty thousand pounds; today it is heading at a rapid rate towards forty million. And this has happened at a time when so many other equally worthwhile charities are all desperately seeking a slice of the global cake.

The Princess has become totally professional in her attitude to and dealings with the problems of famine relief in Africa and other Third World countries, though she is quick to point out that Save the Children is not primarily and solely a famine relief organization. The Fund's operations span more than 50 countries where over 750,000 children are helped every year, and it is only when the

Princess goes on one of her high profile major overseas tours that the world hears about the work that goes on year in year out. SCF also has an enormous aid programme in the United Kingdom, much of it in the fields of health education for immigrant mothers, many of whom had lacked the most basic knowledge of hygiene and child care until they entered Britain. The Princess is involved in every aspect of the Fund's activities, whether in an inner city area, a gypsy camp or any other context. The Fund workers keep her fully informed and, even though some of them have private views about a system which includes an hereditary monarchy (Nicholas Hinton says he knows of a number of people on the staff, both at home and abroad, who dislike the very idea of a monarchy), there isn't a single man or woman who does not appreciate the efforts of their royal president. As far as the Fund is concerned, she is their president first and a member of the royal family second.

The Princess Royal seems to go out of her way to prove that she is not affected by the sights she sees in some of the poorest areas of the world; countries where one in five children die before they are three years old and where malnutrition makes six year olds look like little old men and women. Her view is that she would not be doing any good by wringing her hands and saying 'How appalling' when confronted by these pathetic little bundles of humanity. She is right of course. Empty emotions are futile and even more so when the field workers are involved. They have to steel their hearts to be able to carry on with their work. But the Princess is vulnerable, and she does care a great deal. When she was in Bangladesh in 1986 she saw a number of heart-rending sights in a children's nutrition centre in Dhaka. Tiny babies who were sick and under-nourished were being cared for in spite of the centres being grossly underfunded. It was explained to her that families with three or four children had less than £1 a month to feed themselves. This was one occasion at least where the 'caring Princess' could not prevent her feelings from showing.

She admits that 'most of the people in the refugee camps don't know who I am, but that doesn't matter as long as the work gets done'. Her Royal Highness also regards herself as 'a natural pessimist', saying, 'I usually expect the worst. But I don't regard the prospects for the Third World in that respect. I think the

problems are solvable. Luckily SCF does not give money to governments where perhaps it might not always be used in the way we
intended. We provide aid direct to those who need it, through our
own field workers, so there's no chance of any abuse.'

One of the difficulties in trying to help under-developed countries
is doing so in a way which will not upset their leaders. 'You have
to remember you are dealing with sovereign states and they have
their pride. They don't want to be overtaken and run by other
people no matter how well meaning they are.'

On many of her overseas tours the Princess is required to meet
the leaders of countries where repression and corruption are the
way of life. She never flinches from these contacts, knowing that if
she did the Fund would suffer. In South East Asia she spent ten
days visiting Korea, Singapore, Thailand, Laos and Burma. The
then acting President of Laos had been accused by the United States
government of being responsible for organizing the bulk of the
world's opium growing. The Chairman of the Burmese Socialist
Party was, according to Amnesty International, personally behind
the execution of hundreds of his country's ethnic minorities. Yet
both these men played host to the Princess Royal. Before she went,
no member of the royal family had ever been to Laos. The Foreign
Office opposed the trip, particularly the Burmese sector, where no
fewer than eight rebel armies were fighting the government forces.
The Princess wanted the visit to go ahead and Nicholas Hinton
supported her. They were right. Afterwards Mr Hinton said, 'We
expected the trip to be fraught with difficulties. Instead, countries
which are considered to be rigidly anti-West not only welcomed
her, but felt honoured to have her as their guest. And they listened
to her ideas and suggestions. Only good can come of it – good for
the children of South East Asia we are trying to help, and good for
the relations between the countries.'

The same sort of situation occurred in Sudan, where the scale of
SCF operations was enormous. Twenty thousand refugees were
being cared for in a huge camp constructed by the Fund, with a
massive immunization and feeding programme going on continu-
ously. The Princess Royal was obliged to go through with the
formal presentations and introductions, but she quickly made it
clear where her priorities lay. She changed into sensible khaki jeans

and desert boots, with her hair protected from the clouds of dust by a bright cotton headscarf and a bush hat. With temperatures never falling below 90 degrees she let her hosts know she was anxious to get on with the job, seeing and learning as much as possible.

Accommodation was basic to say the least. Her Royal Highness spent the nights in the staff compound where no special arrangements had been made, although one of the field workers had given up his hut. There was an iron bedstead complete with mosquito net, and in honour of the royal visit a fresh toilet pit had been dug. There was also a Heath Robinson contraption of a shower which had been constructed out of old piping and two oil cans – but the water was cold.

Nicholas Hinton says it is inevitable that the Princess's visits disrupt the everyday working life of the projects, but no one minds too much. 'It lets them know they are not forgotten back at headquarters.'

The Princess feels this sort of contact is invaluable. It provides her with more information than any number of briefing papers. She is a good listener and asks the right questions. She eats sparingly on these visits, always with the workers in their canteen, and one thing she really enjoys is to talk long into the night – always probing, trying to find the right answers and solutions to the problems which face them all.

And while she has been aware of the situation in Ethiopia and the Sudan for many years (her first overseas visit to famine areas on behalf of Save the Children was to Ethiopia in 1973, over ten years before the television reports which focused world attention on the problem), she welcomes the involvement of people like the pop star Bob Geldof, who has done so much to raise money and provide aid to the starving peoples of Africa. It was Geldof who said in 1985, 'This is the year compassion has come out of the closet.' The Princess believes this 'one-off' campaign has helped to make people think more about the long-term problems: 'In the past, although people have been very generous, it has been perhaps in response to a particular type of natural disaster and has lasted for just a short space of time. What Mr Geldof has done is bring the plight of the refugees in Africa to a wider public.'

Some other agencies felt that because of the attention Bob Geldof was attracting, they might lose out in terms of donations, but the contrary has happened in the case of Save the Children. The Princess Royal says that people have actually given more to SCF since the Geldof campaign, 'probably because they already knew what we were capable of doing through our past record'. She is realistic about the reasons why her Fund is getting so much more money now than before, and she is grateful for it: 'In that first year after Band Aid we moved into a different league in terms of voluntary agency income. It was quite dramatic; we trebled our income and what is even more surprising is that the level of giving has continued at a high rate. It would have been quite understandable if it had dropped back a lot after that first year, but it hasn't, so the level of interest and of the public's rate of giving to relief agencies has been increased almost entirely due to that one great spurt of energy and publicity.' She also puts paid to the myth that the British are not the most generous of people when it comes to giving to charity. 'That's absolute rubbish. As the population of Britain has become more affluent in the past few years they have actively sought ways of giving their money away. The level of donations not only we in the Fund, but all other voluntary agencies, are receiving shows just how generous the British people are. You might expect people to become more selfish the more they have. In Britain the opposite has happened. We have become a nation of givers. There aren't many appeals – from any part of the world – which go unanswered in Britain.'

Nicholas Hinton believes that what Geldof did was to attract contributions from a section of society which had tended not to give to charity in the past, chiefly young people, and those youngsters have stayed 'in the net'. The excitement has died down since the Ethiopia campaign but the level of giving has remained fairly constant with a new generation of regular contributors maintaining the income that is needed if the Fund is to carry on with its work.

Although, as we have seen, the Princess Royal has been president of the Save the Children Fund for longer than any of her predecessors, most people, if asked when she took over, would probably say it was some time in the last seven or eight years. Nicholas

Hinton says this is because the media attention began during the 1982 tour of eight African countries: 'That's when people started associating her with the Fund.' She is now as knowledgeable about its work as anyone who works there, even full-time, and before going on a visit, either at home or abroad, she does her 'homework' thoroughly so that she is fully aware of what is going on and, even more importantly, how the money raised is being spent.

Nicholas Hinton would like to see her talents used in a wider area than just for Save the Children, 'Though in no way do we want to lose her. There is no one who could do the job better than she does and it would be a tremendous task to try and replace her. But her experience, her talents and her energy all combine to make her into a remarkable woman with a unique skill which should be put to use in the world arenas beyond our own Fund.'

As a roving ambassadress for the Save the Children Fund wherever the Princess goes she usually manages to interest her hosts in their projects. President Banda of Malawi and President Kaunda of Zambia have both fallen under her spell and lent their practical support to SCF schemes in their countries. Other members of the royal family are made aware of her involvement and even the Queen has been recruited as an 'unofficial consultant'. During a State Visit to Bangladesh in 1983 Her Majesty was shown around a children's clinic which was in urgent need of help. She promised to bring it to the attention of the Princess Royal when she returned to London. She kept her promise and several months later when the Princess was due to make one of her SCF tours to India she included the hospital in her itinerary and saw to it that sufficient funds were made available to help with their immediate needs. Prince Charles and the Princess of Wales have also helped anonymously with generous cheques when a special project has been brought to their attention, and other members of the family sometimes tell the Princess Royal if they see any needy cases on their travels.

When she began her role in public life Princess Anne was very much a young woman of her time – and in the late 'sixties, early 'seventies, this meant in general not having the strongest of social consciences. It was the age of the 'beautiful people', when hedonism was the fashion and very few young people showed any appreciation of social awareness or the need to help others. Yet it also paradoxically saw the beginnings of the era when young men and women from all walks of life and every level of society began to realize that there was more to life than their own pleasure, and Princess Anne, who enjoyed the good things as much as the next person, showed that she was prepared to sacrifice some of her pleasures to give time and effort in helping others. At the first general assembly of the Save the Children Fund she attended after becoming its president, she said, 'I feel there is still a vast reservoir of youthful enthusiasm for helping good works that remains to be tapped. Young people of my own age group [she was nineteen] must see to it that the Save the Children Fund grows as successfully in the next fifty years as it has in its first half century.'

And in a comment on her own supposed lack of feeling towards children, she says, 'You don't have to like children particularly to want to give them a decent chance in life.'

With so much attention being focused on Save the Children and, to a lesser extent, Riding for the Disabled, it is easy to miss some of the other less glamorous but still highly active involvements of the Princess Royal. She is also president of the Missions to Seamen, a voluntary organization that traces its origins back to the early days of the 19th century. It was in 1835 that a young Anglican clergyman named John Ashley started offering his services to a group of fishing vessels in the Bristol Channel. At first the rough and ready sailors did not know what to make of their young cleric but gradually he built a reputation as someone who was not there simply to preach but also to give practical help with their everyday problems. From these humble beginnings came the worldwide organization which today boasts 80 Flying Angel clubs where sailors can find food and accommodation at reasonable prices and staff who are genuinely concerned for their welfare. The Society is also represented in over 260 ports throughout the world by honorary chaplains and clergy who work on a part-time basis.

Since 1968 the headquarters of the Missions to Seamen has been located at St Michael Paternoster Royal, a magnificent church in the City of London designed by Christopher Wren. It is also the church in which Dick Whittington worshipped when he was Lord Mayor of London and his house is next door. The General Secretary

or chief executive of the Missions is Canon William Down, known
to all, including the Princess, as Bill. He is an energetic, enthusiastic
priest who combines a true vocation with an honest but shrewd
view of the outside world, as it affects his parishioners on the seven
seas. He is the friendliest of men but one who gives the impression
that he is nobody's fool. He has seen the depths of degradation that
man can sink to in some of the toughest ports of the world and yet
his belief in the innate goodness of people becomes evident in his
everyday conversation. He openly admits that the Princess Royal
is one of his favourite people, and when you talk to her about him
it is equally obvious that the feeling is mutual. He admires her
ability to get things done without any fuss. She likes his friendliness,
which is frank without being impertinent, and his attitude, which
is compassionate without being pious. He also happens to be
chaplain of two of the City Livery Companies of which the Princess
is a member and he has a reputation for making up the most
amusing 'Graces' before their formal lunches. The Princess likes
people who can make her laugh.

When she was asked if she would become President of the
Missions to Seamen she accepted without any hesitation. She had
already met Bill Down on a number of occasions and she knew
about the Missions and what they are trying to achieve. In the short
time she has been with them she has visited over forty Missions
and allowed meetings to be held at Buckingham Palace.

Her Royal Highness has definite views about most things and
the reason why she accepted the offer to become President of
Missions to Seamen is no exception: 'The thing that really attracted
me to it is that it is Christianity working in the most ecumenical
way you will find almost anywhere in the world. It must be unique
in that it takes in anybody regardless of religion, colour, caste or
creed. Sailors are still not treated universally well throughout the
world and the Missions to Seamen tries to remedy those faults.
Another thing is that they don't preach at them, they just set an
example with care and consideration which they don't get elsewhere.
It's a simple philosophy which some people might regard as being
out of date in this day and age, but it works, and from the numbers
we get coming to us in every port, there is obviously still a need.
The original idea was to spread the gospel according to the Anglican

faith and that is still the basic tenet, but no one gets turned away and as the majority of seamen employed today are not Christians you can see how truly ecumenical the movement is.'

The Missions to Seamen are always short of funds – there is no way they can be self-supporting – and from time to time Bill Down is forced to tell the Princess that there is an urgent need for money for a particular project. He says that she has never refused to help and frequently the money has come from a little known organization called Princess Anne's Charities Trust, the name of her own private fund. The Trust was set up in order to accommodate those people who wanted to give money to one of the Princess's charities, but asked her to say which one. It is an organization she takes the deepest interest in herself and when she is on one of her tours she will often see something which she believes could benefit from her fund. It might be a hostel in the Australian outback which needs a new roof, or a Mission Hall in any one of a dozen ports which could do with a couple of extra beds. If she thinks the need is genuine (the Princess does not hand over money without first of all finding out how it is going to be spent – and where) she will instruct the Trustees to issue a cheque to cover the amount needed. Only one condition is attached to the gifts – no publicity of any kind is permitted.

Another example of the practical way she is able to help the Missions to Seamen came about in 1988. For ten years they had been trying without success to obtain dock passes for the main port in Mozambique. The government had tried initially to close down their premises. Eventually they were allowed to carry on but were refused permission to go onto the docks themselves, which meant of course that they could not reach the ships or speak to the seamen. This situation had prevailed since 1978. In 1988 the Princess went to see the country's President; she told him about the problem and within two weeks the docks pass was issued. And that is what Bill Down regards as the main benefit of having someone like the Princess Royal as their President. 'She can go anywhere and ask anyone for anything.'

The Princess Royal's public activities encompass such a wide variety of organizations it would be relatively easy to simply list them in order to illustrate their diversity. She is Patron of the Butler Trust, which looks into conditions in the prison service;

Commandant-in-Chief, St John Ambulance and Nursing Cadets; Chancellor of London University; President of the British Academy of Film and Television Arts (BAFTA); Patron of Jersey (CI) Wildlife Preservation Fund; Patron of the National Townswomen's Guild; President of the British Olympic Association; Chief Commandant of the Women's Royal Naval Service (WRNS); Honorary Air Commodore RAF Lyneham; Honorary Life Member of the Flying Doctor Society of Africa; Patron of the British School of Osteopathy. The list goes on and on, running to nearly a hundred public appointments all told.

As one can see not all are charitable works. One which the Princess works hard for is the British Knitting and Clothing Export Council (BKCEC), which is anything but a charity. It is in fact a trade association which represents most of the leading manufacturers of British clothes, whose main business is to operate as a marketing organization to maximize the export potential of the apparel industry. They have five hundred members ranging from top fashion designers like Jean Muir and Bruce Oldfield (both of whom make clothes for members of the royal family) to old established traditional businesses such as Austin Reed and Aquascutum. The Princess Royal became involved with the Council shortly after attending a fashion show in Japan as a guest of George Young, the head of Jaeger. She liked what she saw and realized the importance to the country of having a healthy export trade, so when it was pointed out to her that she could do something to help, she agreed to become president.

Peter Valpy is Director General of the Council and he is convinced of her value to the industry. 'Everything she does enhances the work and stature of the British clothing industry. Since she took over the pace of our activities has speeded up enormously.' And he is honest enough to admit that her presence has endowed the clothing industry with an authority it had not previously enjoyed. 'Let's be frank about it. Having the Princess Royal on our team has given a cloak of respectability to what is after all "the rag trade".' It is an industry which employs some 250,000 people throughout the country, and the Princess knows she is doing something positive to help an important part of British industrial life. In the past year she has undertaken twenty-four engagements on behalf of the

Council, a very high figure when one considers the other calls on her time. Peter Valpy thinks that part of the attraction of the Council for the Princess is that 'She is able to help the export drive in a positive manner and also that she likes to think she belongs to an organization.' He bases this last opinion on the fact that she was brought up in a fairly secluded atmosphere which he believes has since given her a sense of isolation. There has never been any evidence of a feeling of isolation on the part of Her Royal Highness but it is a purely personal theory which of course Mr Valpy is perfectly entitled to hold. Others in the council feel that she likes to be involved in a dynamic, commercial organization which is completely different from any of the voluntary bodies for which she works. The Princess travels overseas for the Council and, with her fluent command of French, is perfectly comfortable in European countries where much of the current activity is taking place in the months leading up to the Single European Act of 1992.

As with most of her other activities, the Princess tries to arrange her work for the Council to fit in with other aspects of her official programme. If there is the remotest possibility of visiting one of her charitable projects or picking up a cheque on their behalf she always aims to combine the two purposes. When she was in Hong Kong prior to the Olympic Games she visited the new Marks and Spencer store in the colony. This was on behalf of the BKCEC. It was of course a tremendous bonus for the company; it's very rare for a member of the royal family to be so closely connected with what is so obviously a commercial occasion. The bonus as far as the Princess is concerned is that whenever she visits a shop or factory she is usually presented with a handsome cheque for one of her charities – normally either Save the Children or Riding for the Disabled – as was the case on this occasion, so everybody benefited.

In her years as president of the Save the Children Fund the Princess has managed not only to combine her own roles in her other activities but the organizations themselves. The Townswomen's Guild – another of her organizations – launched an appeal for £750,000 to build a new children's nutrition unit for the Save the Children Fund in Dacca, Bangladesh. They achieved their target and the CNU is now built, open and operating. The Townswomen's

Guild would not have even heard of the project and its needs if the Princess had not brought it to their attention.

Wherever she goes there is a practical element to her visit. When she and Mark went to the Dubai Horse Show, she accepted a cheque for £20,000 for the SCF: not an overlarge amount from a country where there is said to be one Rolls–Royce for every eight inhabitants, but very welcome nonetheless. This was an occasion when she combined the sporting side of her life with the professional role and also that of being a member of the royal family. The visit included three banquets, to one of which the Princess Royal wore a full length Maureen Baker gown in pale blue satin with a tiara in her hair. Roses had been flown in from Paris specially for the evening and whole sides of spicy lamb were roasted – the Princess drank Coca-Cola.

Next morning it was business as usual; this time royal business. An official courtesy call on the President of the United Arab Emirates to whom the Princess handed a letter of goodwill from the Queen. Then it was back to her role as an ambassadress for the Save the Children Fund: a visit to a school for physically handicapped children where she marvelled at a little girl with a walking frame who managed a determined if shaky curtsey. On then to the local Missions to Seamen building, competing, on borrowed horses, at the Dubai Horse Show and finally squeezing in a little personal Christmas shopping with Mark before they left for home. When the Princess Royal goes shopping she does not usually handle money herself. Her detective is always with her and he pays, being reimbursed when they get back to London, after the Princess has been billed. Similarly, on overseas trips Her Royal Highness, although she has a passport and needs visas in the same way as everyone else, does not fill out immigration forms herself. Peter Gibbs does it for her and signs his own name on her behalf. The baggage of the Princess and the team is not normally inspected by Customs officers either. A form is sent to Buckingham Palace shortly after they return home and this is completed by everyone including the Princess. All gifts are declared, and the duty paid. Health regulations are adhered to rigidly, the Princess having her inoculations either at the Palace or from a doctor who lives near Gatcombe.

DOUBLET.

BORN - 9.5.63.

DIED - 13.5.74.

EUROPEAN
CHAMPION
- 1971 -

This is the shot all the photographers have been hoping for – the Princess Royal going into the water at Badminton. In fact, she has fallen in the lake only three times in nearly twenty years and she has completed the course five times.

Inset: When Doublet had to be put down after breaking a leg at Windsor in May 1974, Princess Anne described it as one of the most traumatic events of her life.

Above: During this visit to Africa on behalf of the Save the Children Fund, everyone lent a hand in pulling the ferry across the river Gambia. Princess Anne joined in together with her bodyguard, Philip Robinson.

Left: Her Royal Highness eats sparingly at the best of times. Nobody is quite sure what she made of this sumptuous feast held in her honour in Dubai in 1984.

Above right: There aren't many tourists who do their shopping accompanied by armed guards, but here they were taking no chances with their royal guest as she toured the local souk in 1984.

Right: Anne and Mark were delighted to take part in the Dubai Horse Show in 1984, when the ruler made them promise to return as soon as possible. He also presented the Princess with a handsome cheque for the Save the Children Fund.

Below: A moving tribute to Princess Anne in 1984 from the slum dwellers of Bangladesh, some of whom had less than £1 a month to feed a family of four.

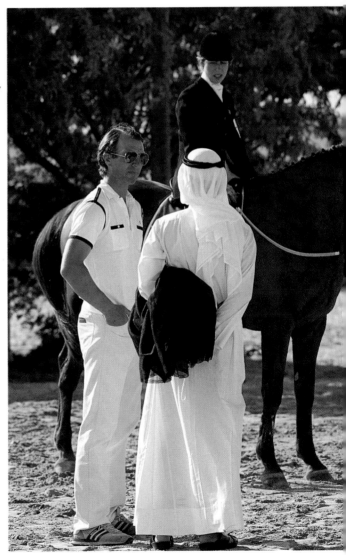

Below: A rare picture of the Princess Royal holding the hand of an African boy in a refugee camp in the Sudan (1985). Behind her are Philip Robinson, her longest-serving detective, and Lt-Col. Peter Gibbs, her Private Secretary.

Right: The Princess says she doesn't mind in the least if people do not know who she is on her overseas tours 'as long as the work gets done'. This lady looks rather sceptical as her royal visitor leaves her hut.

Far right: A reflective study of the Princess Royal during a Save the Children Fund visit to the Sudan in 1985. She says the sights do not get her down; in fact she is optimistic about the problems the relief agencies face in the Third World.

Above far left: In North Yemen the Princess learned of some of the problems facing young mothers when she toured a clinic in the company of a heavily veiled guide wearing traditional dress.

Above left: An important part of every official overseas visit is the exchange of gifts. A signed photograph of herself is greatly treasured by all the Princess's hosts. The President of the Sudan admires his personal present at a formal presentation in Khartoum in 1985.

Left: 'She can ride anything on four legs', and here she proves it – camel riding in the desert at Qatar in 1987.

Above: Royal Ascot, and the Princess Royal, accompanied by the Earl of Carnarvon, the Queen's racing manager, follows Queen Elizabeth the Queen Mother as they walk towards the royal box.

Right: The Princess sees the funny side as she tries to pierce the camouflage of these soldiers of the Royal Signals – one of her regiments – during a tour of inspection at Warminster, Wiltshire, in 1985.

As Chancellor of the University of London, the Princess Royal attends nearly every degree ceremony. In 1987 she awarded an honorary doctorate to Bob Geldof with whom she shares a common interest in famine relief.

The travel costs of the Princess Royal are very large, even though she usually travels with a comparatively small entourage. If she is flying with an aircraft of the Queen's Flight, no money changes hands. The entire cost is charged to the Ministry of Defence. When she uses commercial airlines, however, there is a strict division of payment. It all depends on which of her organizations she is representing. For example, if she is travelling on behalf of the Queen – representing her at an independence ceremony perhaps – the Foreign Office foots the bill. For a trip such as the three-week visit to the Far East at the time of the Olympic Games, it becomes more complicated. As a member of the International Olympic Committee her fares and hotel expenses were paid by the IOC – as were the expenses of all the other delegates. Part of the visit was as president of the Fédération Équestre Internationale, so they picked up their share, and the British Olympic Association also helped by paying a proportion of the bill for the Princess and her team. The only people whose expenses are not covered in this way are the police officers. Wherever they go, all their fares and accommodation is paid for by the Metropolitan Police, even when the expenses for the rest of the party are being met by the Foreign Office.

When the Queen or the Prince and Princess of Wales travel abroad, they are accompanied by a great many people and take their own supplies of food and drink. The Princess Royal believes 'small is beautiful', travels with a minimum of fuss and never takes any special food, not even the Malvern water so favoured by her mother. Her dresser is responsible for looking after such basic medical requirements as aspirin and 'tummy-bug' tablets. During the 'recce' the Private Secretary makes sure he knows the name and address of a reliable dentist in every country they visit – but so far they have never had to call on one.

One of the bodies the Princess is involved with but whose activities peak only once every four years is the British Olympic Association. As a former Olympic competitor herself she knows only too well how important it is for the athletes to be supported by an efficient organization. This is why she accepted the job of president when there were those who said that it was 'a can of worms' that anybody with any sense wouldn't touch with a barge pole. The BOA has more than its share of internal politics, with the aims and egos of a wide variety of sports administrators and personalities to cope with. Dick Palmer, the friendly, gregarious Secretary, is one of the most respected figures in world athletics, and he says that the choice of the Princess to be President was brilliant: 'Almost in one move she has managed to instil a sense of unity in the Association. We were a number of separate entities before she came, and obviously not all our problems have been solved overnight; but where she is concerned, everybody is in total agreement. She is the best thing to have happened to British athletics in the last ten years.'

The Princess joins the other members of BOA at their committee meetings at their headquarters in Wandsworth where Dick Palmer says she shows how shrewd she is by the way she gets her views across. 'She is very crafty about finding the best strategic moment to make her contribution. She waits until everybody else has had their say and then puts in her twopenny worth, so she always makes sure she has the last word.'

The president of the British Olympic Association heads the fund-raising appeals which send our teams to the Games; hence the increased activity in the years of, and immediately prior to, an Olympic Games. In between things quieten down a little but at the moment a further goal is exciting the president and her colleagues. The city of Manchester is bidding to stage the 1996 Olympics and so far have raised a total of £1.7 million, all from the private sector, to support the bid.

The Princess helped to launch this bid at a reception held in the Mansion House in London on 20 February 1989. It was a glittering occasion with the Lord Mayor, High Sheriffs and other civic dignitaries on parade in their ceremonial dress. The cream of British sport was present, including Sir Arthur Gold, the newly elected Chairman of the British Olympic Association, of whom the Princess said, 'He has the most encyclopaedic knowledge of all sports I have ever come across.'

The leaders of sports such as bobsleighing, yachting, rowing and wrestling joined with personalities from athletics and swimming to add their support for what promises to be one of the most exciting prospects for British sport since the last time the Games were held in Britain, in London in 1948.

The novelist Jeffrey Archer, himself a former international

sprinter, says the Princess 'is stunning' and compares notes with Ron Pickering, arguably the best athletics commentator in the world. Pickering, who is known for his aggressive style, chats animatedly with the Princess as she works her way around the room canvassing support for the project. Afterwards he says, when asked about her position as president of BOA, 'There's no one better. At last the BOA is getting its act together with the right person in the right place at the right time.'

The evening has gone well and the Princess has obviously stimulated interest from the bankers and stockbrokers who have attended the presentation. She has spoken without notes, in a voice that carries her own undoubted enthusiasm to her appreciative audience. The fact that she hasn't asked for any money – at this stage – has also gone down rather well. 'We would never have got this sort of turn out if the Princess Royal had not been here,' Sir Arthur Gold comments. She will spend a lot of time in the coming months working towards the goal of getting the Games to Manchester. And then in the autumn of 1990, as an elected member of the International Olympic Committee, she will spearhead the attack on the final citadel of the selection committee. If she has anything to do with it – Manchester is home and dry!

This ability to bring a sense of enthusiasm and commitment to every one of her roles is a unique talent that is appreciated by all her organizations, especially the lesser known charities such as the Home Farm Trust which cares for the welfare of handicapped adults. They have never been on the upper rungs of the league table in donations, so when the Princess Royal attends one of their functions they are delighted, and their director says, 'If she turns up, our money is trebled.'

On 1 February 1989, the Princess Royal gave a reception for 118 young people, all under eighteen, in the Music Room at Buckingham Palace (where she had been christened in 1950). It was a delightfully informal occasion with fewer than half a dozen adults to get in the way. The Princess is Commandant-in-Chief of St John Ambulance Cadets and the reception was a thank you from her to some of the outstanding cadets in Britain and Northern Ireland. She was greeted by the Cadet of the Year, a happy sixteen-year-old from Ulster, who remained as her escort throughout the evening. His only regret was that he alone could not be photographed with the Princess or even have his name revealed, because of the possibility of threats to his life from terrorists in his home province.

The Princess Royal, wearing a green dress and dark blue gloves, came into the Music Room from the White Drawing Room next door and immediately began talking to the first group she met. She heard how one youngster from South Shields had been invited because he had spent a thousand hours looking after old people in his area – lighting their fires, cooking their meals and helping with shopping and cleaning around their homes. At each group Her Royal Highness heard similar stories. She even met one young girl whose father had told her to 'spit in the Princess's eye because I can't stand the royal family'. The young lady said afterwards that the Princess had been the easiest person to talk to she had ever met and she was going to tell her father so when she got home.

There was a lot of laughter coming from every group as the liveried footmen carried trays of soft drinks and canapés which were soon finished off by the cadets. They had been brought to the Palace by special coaches, one of which, a cadet said, 'had not managed to negotiate the arch leading to the Grand Entrance.' All the side had been scraped. 'Obviously,' the young man pointed out with exquisite logic, 'the building was designed to cope with carriages not charabancs.'

The reception had been scheduled to last two hours. It overran by forty-five minutes – just because the Princess and her guests were having such a good time. They were treated in exactly the same way as the most senior diplomats at a formal Palace function, with one slight difference. They all wanted a souvenir of Buckingham Palace to take home with them. So a friendly footman advised them to ask to use the lavatory – and take a piece of royal toilet paper away. Towards the end of the evening there was a distinct move towards the cloakrooms, and the following morning the cleaners had to replace just one indispensable item in the royal loos.

The most obvious charity for the Princess to join was the Riding for the Disabled Association. As one of the best known riders in the country it made a lot of sense for her to use her knowledge and contacts to help both physically and mentally handicapped people meet this new challenge.

The RDA has six hundred groups in Britain and today they look after more than twenty thousand children and adults. Marjorie Langford is chairman of the Association and she is always full of praise for the person who began as their royal patron but is now president. 'If you accept that a patron is merely a figurehead who lends her name to the charity, then obviously we got it wrong when we asked Her Royal Highness to become our patron. She has always been much more than that. She has been involved in all our activities and spends as much time visiting the smallest out of the way branch as she does larger ones nearer London. Our former president, Lavinia, Duchess of Norfolk, who was the person who first introduced the Princess to RDA, recognized this fact and they have now reversed their roles – the Princess has become president and the Duchess is patron. Though even that gives the wrong impression because they both work equally hard for the Association.'

The condition of some of the people in the RDA is not very pleasant to see: youngsters with severe physical handicaps which would turn the strongest stomach. The Princess never flinches. Grubby hands clutch her dress and dribbling faces press close to her; nothing seems to put her off. When this point was put to her she said, 'How could you turn away? It wouldn't be the children who would be affected – most of them don't know who I am anyway – but their parents would be very upset and they are the ones you have to consider.'

Fund raising is another major problem for the Riding for the Disabled Association, and if when the Princess Royal visits a factory or shop in one of her other capacities she is asked to accept a gift, she frequently suggests that a donation to RDA would be more appreciated. She is not shy about asking for money where one of her charities is involved.

Being a senior member of the royal family means receiving an extraordinary number of invitations to join this or that association, become president or patron or simply lend one's name. Every organization in the country, commercial and voluntary, knows the value of having royalty associated with their enterprise. In the early days of the Queen's reign, members of the royal family accepted practically every position they were offered, on the grounds that to refuse would be impolite. Today they are much more selective, declining more than they accept. The Princess Royal researches an organization in great detail before she will even consider accepting an invitation. She is not in the least interested in lending her name and then sitting back and doing nothing. If she cannot see the practical advantages she turns it down.

When it was suggested to her that she should succeed her grandmother, Queen Elizabeth the Queen Mother, as Chancellor of London University, she thought long and hard before allowing her name to go forward as a candidate. She knew she would get a bad press because she had not been to university herself.

The Queen Mother had been Chancellor for thirty years and could have stayed for life, but she herself asked to be allowed to stand down and suggested her granddaughter as a successor. The Princess told me: 'It's not very easy to refuse her anything so I agreed to let my name go forward.' But it wasn't simply a question of rubberstamping the Princess's nomination, there was the formality of an election to be got through, and there were two other highly commendable candidates in Nelson Mandela, the jailed African Nationalist leader, and Jack Jones the former leader of the Transport and General Workers Union. So the left wing of the university were sure of massive support. When the votes were counted after a vigorous campaign it was discovered that the Princess had scored a runaway victory, polling more than three times as many votes as her opponents.

She was enrolled as Chancellor on 17 February 1981 and earned the respect of the student body when she politely declined the offer of an honorary degree, saying, 'I think we should wait and see if I do anything to earn one first.' So far she has still not accepted a degree from that or any other university.

The work of a Chancellor is mainly ceremonial and even this has changed in the eight years she has been head of the university with numerous visits to the various colleges, hospitals and other parts of the far-flung university. At degree ceremonies as many as 1800 students pass before her in an afternoon at the Royal Albert Hall; which is something of which she does not entirely approve though she understands the practical reasons. 'I do not even have time to shake hands or hand over their degrees,' she says sadly. 'We now have more than forty thousand students and fifty faculties so it's all we can do to get through a degree ceremony in a day and we have five a year.'

The services play a large part in the lives of the royal family. Almost without exception they have strong connections with every branch of the armed forces, with the Queen, of course, being Commander-in-Chief of the Army, Navy and the Royal Air Force. The Princess Royal has enjoyed a close relationship with all three services ever since she began her role in public life. She is Colonel-in-Chief of twelve regiments, including a number in Canada, Australia and New Zealand, Commandant-in-Chief of the Women's Royal Naval Service (WRNS) – her only uniformed appointment – and Honorary Air Commodore of RAF Lyneham, one of the nearest air force bases to her home at Gatcombe Park.

All service appointments are made by the Queen personally as head of the armed forces, but the choice of which member of the royal family they would prefer as their Colonel-in-Chief or Commandant is left to the regiment or service themselves. The 14th/20th King's Hussars, one of the proudest cavalry regiments in the British army, were very quick off the mark when they were looking for a new Colonel-in-Chief back in 1969. They knew that Princess Anne (as she then was) had just emerged into the royal spotlight and was taking on a limited number of official appointments so they immediately asked Her Majesty if they could invite the Princess to join them. The Queen said yes and so did her daughter when the invitation came.

The commanding officer at the time was Lieutenant Colonel (now Major General) Mike Palmer, who was responsible for inviting the Princess to make her first official visit to the regiment in Germany. It was an instant success. The soldiers enjoyed meeting a young, glamorous princess of their own age and she delighted them by dividing her time equally between the other ranks and their families and the officers. She also joined in with all the old regimental customs, including 'drinking the health of the Emperor' which is done by sipping champagne from a large silver chamber pot captured from King Joseph of Spain's carriage in 1813. The chamber pot had been a gift to the king from his brother the Emperor Napoleon – hence the toast.

Like all cavalry regiments the 14th/20th is now a highly mechanized tank unit and, learning of Princess's fascination with anything to do with transport, they quickly showed her the rudiments of driving a 50-ton Chieftain tank and then let her loose. She enjoyed the experience so much that every year since then when she visits her regiment on manoeuvres, a drive in one of the tracked monsters is always included in the programme. She is kitted out in green denims for the occasion, complete with colonel's pips on the shoulders – the stores claim they should be allowed to display a 'By Appointment' sign over the door. The Princess explains tactfully that she does not issue Royal Warrants.

She pays equal attention to her other regiments and when, for example, she visited the Royal Corps of Signals for the first time, she was given a rapid fifteen-minute course of instruction in the use of their sophisticated technology. The manual said the course should have lasted six weeks; royal commitments meant that the instructor had to try to instil some sort of basic knowledge into his Colonel-in-Chief in less than an hour. He was somewhat surprised later that morning to discover not only that the Princess had digested most of what he had tried to impart, but that she was able to ask intelligent questions also. This is part of the secret of her success. She has an insatiable appetite for knowledge and is able to find something interesting in almost everything she is asked to do.

One of her most recent service appointments was as Colonel-in-Chief to the Royal Scots (The Royal Regiment.) Her great-aunt the late Princess Royal had held the post for more than fifty years. When she died in 1965 the Queen asked the regiment if they would like another member of the royal family to succeed her. They politely but firmly replied that they would be honoured to be led by whoever Her Majesty suggested but would prefer to wait until the person they regarded as the rightful heir should be available. This was their way of saying that, as Princess Anne was only fifteen at the time, they were willing to wait until she became of an age to take over the responsibilities of leading a regiment such as theirs. It was also a subtle hint that they were hoping she would, in time, be created Princess Royal.

In 1983 the regiment indicated that they would be delighted and honoured to have Princess Anne as their Colonel-in-Chief, and she was equally pleased to accept. On the day of her appointment she was presented with the same diamond brooch in the form of the regimental symbol that had been presented to her great-aunt during the First World War. It was a proud day for the Royal Scots, which was only matched four years later when they heard that their Colonel-in-Chief had indeed been given the title they felt she so richly deserved and been created the Princess Royal.

The Princess's attitude to her service units is very similar to that she uses towards her other associations. She is aware that, because she is who she is, certain matters of protocol have to be observed. Just as on a civil visit there are dignitaries and public officials who must be greeted and spoken to in the official line-up, she understands that the requirements of service life dictate that the Queen's only daughter – and one who holds a high honorary rank – must be afforded the respect due to someone of her rank. As a matter of fact she gets on very well with most service officers. As the wife of a former cavalry captain who lived for the first years of her married life in the surroundings of the Royal Military Academy, she knows the form perfectly, and accepts the confines of the military class system as a tradition that is suitable to all ranks. But she will not spend all her time in the company of senior officers who might try to monopolize her if they could get away with it. She insists on meeting the non-commissioned officers and other ranks – and their families. During the course of a conversation we had at Gatcombe some time ago she confided that 'some of the best evenings I've ever enjoyed have been in the sergeants' mess'. And when soldiers of the Royal Corps of Signals were involved in the fighting in the Falkland Islands, suffering many casualties, the Princess drove to their barracks at Tidworth in Hampshire to comfort the wives and families who were waiting for news. One of them said later, 'She was just like one of us. As she had a brother who was on active service out there, she realized what we were going through and she just sat there and listened. That was what we wanted. Someone who could be with us and listen to our worries. The other great thing about having her with us was that she could get all the information from the top brass without having to go through channels like the rest of us. When she speaks people listen.'

The Women's Royal Naval Service (WRNS) is the most glamorous of the three services. With their smart navy blue uniforms and romantic attachment with the sea, they attract the cream of female volunteers, and they are suitably selective in choosing from those who want to join. As the Princess learned to sail at an early age she has always had an affinity with the sea and has said, 'I would have quite liked to become a Wren if it had been possible, though I do get sea-sick every time I go on board a ship for the first few days.' Her appointment as Commandant-in-Chief of the WRNS was welcomed by the Royal Navy as the continuance of an old royal tradition. Her father, grandfather and great-grandfather had all served in the Royal Navy so nothing could have been more appropriate than that she too should take a leading role in the senior service.

At the present time the WRNS has a complement of some 300 officers and nearly three thousand ratings, so it is a compact, thoroughly modern service in the Royal Navy of today. Two of the previous Commandants of the WRNS, Elizabeth Craig McFeeley and Voula McBride, served under the Princess Royal and they have no doubts about the benefits of having her as their Commandant-in-Chief. Miss McBride says, 'She kept us on our toes right from the moment she took command. It was not a case of just having a royal name on our letterheading, but someone who cared about the interests of the service and who wanted to play her part in our welfare.' The Princess is also, by virtue of her appointment, President of the Women's Royal Naval Service Benevolent Trust which provides relief in cases of necessity or distress to anyone, of any rank, who is serving or has served in the WRNS since the outbreak of the Second World War in 1939.

Miss Craig McFeeley, who has now retired, recalls that 'Her Royal Highness has never been content to sit back and accept everything she is told. If she has a query she will ask for specific answers and you cannot fob her off. We were very lucky to get her because she exemplifies exactly the image we want the WRNS to have these days. She is modern, thoroughly professional, intelligent and, as the first member of the royal family to have a separate career – with her riding – she has brought a fresh outlook to the position of Chief Commandant and that is so important in this day and age.' Chief Wren Sue White, who worked in the Princess's private office until a few weeks ago, has been closer to her Chief Commandant than most of her more senior colleagues. She too feels that the WRNS could not have had a better 'boss'. 'As she is roughly the same age as many of those still serving she is able to understand our problems better than many of the other senior officers, and with her high profile it gives the WRNS a much better image.'

Image may be an important facet in these days of media conscious organizations, civil, military, commercial and voluntary, but it is not necessarily the most important single factor. Money is. They all need money to keep going and the presence of a senior member of the royal family at a function is a guarantee of a full house. When the Princess of Wales attends a fashion show, every seat is oversubscribed. When the Duchess of York turns up at a film première, the organizers are sure of massive publicity and the box office takings go up accordingly. The Queen's name on an invitation list means no refusals by any of the other invitees – if it's for a charity, their cheque books will be prominently displayed. The royal family is well aware of its value for fund-raising and makes its decisions about which invitations to accept and decline partly on the understanding that money for the cause will be forthcoming if they attend.

The Princess Royal leads a very busy life. Her public commitments cover a wide variety of organizations, some glamorous such as the British Academy of Film and Television Arts (BAFTA) where she mixes freely with many of the biggest names in the film world; some distinctly unglamorous like the Butler Trust, looking at the sordid world of the penal system, or being President of the Royal School for Daughters of Officers of the Royal Navy and Royal Marines (Haslemere) which doesn't get much publicity, or a Visitor to Strathcarron Hospice in Scotland, where the director Tom Scott says, 'She tries to bring comfort to people who know they are incurable.'

Whatever role she assumes she brings to it a unique understanding which could only have come about through a wide experience of life lived beyond the walls of palaces and castles. She is a princess for her time – pragmatic but compassionate; practical yet caring. With more than five hundred engagements this year the Princess is easily the busiest member of the 'Royal Firm', yet she doesn't think she works particularly hard. 'There are times when it gets a bit much,' she says, 'but generally speaking I don't believe I do any more than anyone else. I do not like the idea of sitting around doing nothing so if there is any space during a day when I have already got some engagements I try to arrange to fill the time. This is very much the case in London which in other ways would be a complete waste of a day for me. I see no point in sitting around doing nothing when perhaps I might be able to make a small contribution by doing something.'

Anyone who has ever had anything to do with the Princess Royal would never accept that she makes only a small contribution. She is a tough, uncompromising woman who expects the best from all around her because that is what she expects and demands of herself. Nothing less will do. Mark Phillips believes his wife does work too hard. When I put the question to him he replied: 'The short answer is yes. Of course she works too hard; she never stops. But there's nothing anyone can do about it, that's the way she is made and that's the way she will go on as long as she lives.'

◆

THE TEAM

'The Princess Royal's office, Peter Gibbs,' is the brisk greeting which answers all telephone enquiries to Her Royal Highness's Private Secretary. Lieutenant Colonel Peter Gibbs, late of the Coldstream Guards, has been guiding the team that organizes the Princess Royal's life for seven years. He is insistent that it is a team and that each member has a vital part to play. It is a very small team: the Private Secretary, Assistant Private Secretary, two full-time secretaries, one of whom is on secondment from the Royal Navy, and a young secretary, Jane Hambling, who helps out under the Youth Training Scheme, which means that she is only allowed to work on a temporary basis. These are the people who administer the timetable of the busiest member of the royal family.

Every one of the hundred or so organizations, both civil and military, with which the Princess is associated works through the private office. As we have seen, some of them, such as the Save the Children Fund, will be in contact with Peter Gibbs every day, either by telephone or letter. Others need to be in touch only on rare occasions; but if the Princess Royal is an officer of their organization she will be sent all the minutes of important meetings, documents to be signed and letters to be read. The amount of paperwork that passes through the office is prodigious. And after a major tour or television appearance, the correspondence increases accordingly. If the Princess has made a controversial statement, such as when she described the disease AIDS as 'a self-inflicted wound', hundreds of letters pour into her office. They all receive an acknowledgement, even those writers whose sole intention is to insult her – and her family.

The office – it is actually three small interconnecting rooms – is located on the second-floor front of Buckingham Palace in what used to be the schoolroom. Colonel Gibbs' office is along the passage from the Princess Royal's sitting room and as he sits at his desk with his back to the window he can hear the band playing each morning as the changing of the guard takes place at 11.30. The room is functional, containing, apart from his desk, a small table which is used by the duty lady-in-waiting, and two leather armchairs. When he has visitors he usually leaves his desk and joins the visitor in the facing chair. Informality is the order of the day among all the Princess Royal's Household.

Next door is the Assistant Private Secretary's office which is really nothing more than a wide corridor. There is a desk, several filing cabinets and a computer. Two small hatches mean that the staff can talk to one another without going into Peter Gibbs' office or to the third office, which is the largest of the three. This is the 'boiler room' where all the clerical work is done on two word processors by the two full-time secretaries and the assistant. The telephones in this office rarely stop ringing throughout the day and there is a facsimile machine which works practically non-stop when an overseas tour is taking place.

And as the Princess Royal's office is the one place in Buckingham Palace where you can guarantee the kettle is always on the boil, a cup of coffee or tea is nearly always available. This is unusual in the Royal Household. In the other Private Secretaries' offices they are always perfectly polite and beautifully mannered, but one is rarely offered any hospitality.

Peter Gibbs joined Princess Anne, as she then was, in 1982 after a distinguished career in the Coldstream Guards, into which he followed his late father who was killed in the Second World War. He lives in the country in Wiltshire, with his wife Sally and their son Evan. During the week he has the use of a Grace and Favour flat in St James's Palace, where his front door opens directly opposite that of Princess Alexandra. If there is one thing you can say about Peter Gibbs it is that he is a large man in every way. He stands well over six feet in height, with a build to match and a voice which has been trained to carry over the parade grounds of Wellington Barracks and the Guards depot at Pirbright. So the Canadian reporter who, having been refused an interview with the Princess Royal, referred to Colonel Gibbs as 'that little pipsqueak' could hardly have been less accurate. Peter Gibbs has the friendly, affable personality of many big men and he is slow to anger. But this does not mean he will put up with any nonsense as several self-important callers have found out to their cost.

Like many senior army officers, he is meticulous in his attention to the smallest detail and he will go over the timetable of a proposed visit again and again, making sure that nothing has been left to chance. The Princess's office has the reputation of being one of the most efficient in the Palace and this is due in no small part to the Colonel's insistence on everybody checking and rechecking.

The Princess Royal calls him by his Christian name, as she does all her staff, but refers to him, when speaking to others, as 'the Colonel'. Theirs is a professional relationship, based on mutual respect, and in the seven years they have been together he has come to recognize the signs which will tell him what sort of mood his employer is in. He is astute enough to know that there are certain times when it would not be advisable to approach her with a particular proposal, so he will bide his time and 'sit on' a letter until the moment is right, and then bring it to her attention. It is difficult to describe the job of Private Secretary to a member of the royal family in precise terms. No two royals are the same and their requirements are vastly different. With the Queen, of course, the Private Secretary is a person of enormous influence in the country. He is the conduit between Her Majesty and the Prime Minister, and also between the Queen and all the leaders of the Commonwealth, and nobody gets to see her without his knowledge and agreement. The Duke of Edinburgh's office is considered to be the most automated in the Palace, and his Private Secretary, Brian McGrath, runs the office like a modern business. Sir John Riddell Bt is Private Secretary to the Prince of Wales (leaving at the end of 1989). At his office in St James's Palace he heads the largest team in the Royal Household. There are fifteen administrators, clerks, treasurers and secretaries to look after the affairs of the Prince and Princess and this is not always thought to make for the most efficient operation. When you ring the Prince of Wales's office you are never quite sure who is going to answer the telephone. If you ring the Princess Royal's office you can be reasonably confident of talking to the person for whom you asked. When Peter Gibbs joined the Royal Household he was not given a job description; very few members are. Instead he was interviewed by the Princess, which was really just an informal chat to see 'what I was like'.

He recalls one of his earliest duties was to attend Her Royal Highness during a State Visit to Buckingham Palace by an overseas Head of State. 'I wasn't sure of the form and when the Comptroller of the Lord Chamberlain's Office prompted me to get on with my job, I didn't know what he was talking about. Then he gently explained that part of my duties was to present the Princess to the visiting Head of State's Household. I muddled my way through somehow, but that's the way things are here. You are expected to make your own way, and if you don't know something – you ask. They will always give you an answer, but you have to know the right question first.'

Since that day Peter Gibbs has rarely put a foot wrong and he is now considered to be among the best Private Secretaries in royal service. He is responsible for every item concerned with the Princess Royal's public life and every request for a visit, either in the United Kingdom or overseas, passes through his hands before it is brought to her attention. He sees every piece of correspondence that arrives in the office and many of the letters addressed to the Princess Royal are answered by him without reference to her. He knows which she will want to see personally, and those she would wish him to handle on her behalf. As the Princess spends most of her time at Gatcombe and he operates exclusively from Buckingham Palace, they talk frequently on the telephone, invariably about some aspect of her programme. There isn't a great deal of time for social 'chit-chat'.

The Princess Royal's diary of engagements is kept by Peter Gibbs and is the 'bible' by which they all work in the office. The programme is planned at least six months in advance, at the twice-yearly meetings which take place in June and December. The Princess, Colonel Gibbs and the two secretaries sit down together in her dining-room at the Palace and study the mass of invitations that have come in and have already been sorted by him. All the available information about the invitations will have been collected in advance: details such as the purpose of the visit, has the Princess been there before, if so when. Are there opportunities for combining a few visits on the same day?

The programme meeting can take up to five hours with the Princess Royal deciding which of the invitations she wants to accept and those she will decline. Her decision is the final one and she never changes her mind. In her view a decision to accept is based on two things: 'Why do they want me and can I do anything for them?' Which is why some prestigious invitations are declined and other seemingly less important ones accepted. 'She will only go if she really believes that by attending she can do something worthwhile for them,' Peter Gibbs confirms.

In the last five years the number of invitations to the Princess Royal has increased fivefold. At the last programme meeting Peter Gibbs handed her twenty-five foolscap pages of requests for visits. When he first joined her Household there were usually less than five sheets to consider.

Once the programme has been agreed, Colonel Gibbs contacts the ladies-in-waiting who decide among themselves which engagements they will attend. The Princess Royal is very relaxed about who accompanies her and allows the ladies to arrange their own rota. So long as she is kept informed she lets them get on with the job in their own way.

Meanwhile Peter Gibbs has started the ball rolling. He writes to the person who has extended the invitation confirming that Her Royal Highness has accepted on the date suggested and asks for a suggested draft programme. Then the transport arrangements are put in hand. If the visit involves the use of a helicopter or aircraft, the Queen's Flight at RAF Benson in Oxfordshire is contacted. The secretary who looks after the bookings checks that an aircraft is available on the required date and then the Queen's Private Secretary is asked to place the request before Her Majesty. There is no question of any member of the royal family booking an aircraft whenever they want. The Queen sees every request and her agreement is not in any way automatic. If she feels the journey could be undertaken less expensively by road and rail, she will refuse to sanction the use of an aircraft with a pointed reminder of the need to be cost conscious.

Once the draft programme has been submitted for Her Royal Highness's comments and approval, the way is clear for a full programme to be made. This involves many hours on the telephone and sometimes dozens of letters. The office will receive queries on all sorts of topics relating to the visit. May the chairman's granddaughter present a bouquet? Yes as long as it is small and unwired (so that the flowers can be used afterwards). Will the Princess accept a gift from the company? This is always a touchy subject because some firms are well aware of the commercial value of a member of the royal family being seen with one of their products, and any form of financial exploitation is frowned on by the Palace authorities. Gifts are usually accepted if they are small and relatively inexpensive, though there have been occasional exceptions which have caused the Princess a little embarrassment simply because they have cost too much. Will the Princess unveil a plaque to commemorate her visit? Yes, but details of the inscription must be sent, and agreed to, in advance. If a meal is included in the schedule the menu must be agreed; the Princess does not eat shellfish but she is not fussy about her food in other respects. Also the meal should not be too elaborate or prolonged. An hour is sufficient for lunch. Her Royal Highness never drinks alcohol but she has no objection to any one else doing so. The same applies to smoking 'as long as no one actually blows smoke in my face'. If she is arriving by car, the hosts need to know on which side of the vehicle she will be sitting. (It is always the rear offside immediately behind the chauffeur, unless, of course, she is driving herself.) Will she sign the distinguished visitors' book? Yes, but a fresh page for her signature only must be presented. If she is attending a religious service, is it permitted to offer her the collection plate? Yes.

How should she be addressed by those to whom she is introduced? Your Royal Highness at the beginning and then Ma'am (rhyming with jam, not smarm). Gentlemen should bow from the neck. (The Princess's great-grandfather King George V said, 'Only headwaiters bow from the waist.') Ladies should curtsey. It is not mandatory for ladies to wear hats or gloves (but in practice most do). The most frequently asked question is, 'What happens if she wants to go to the "loo"?' The answer is that the lady-in-waiting should be advised in advance of the location of the lavatory and, if required, it should be reserved for HRH's exclusive use.

One of the most important aspects of any royal engagement is the 'recce'. This is an advance visit, based on the approved draft programme, to the proposed venue some weeks before the arranged date and is usually carried out by one of the four police officers attached to the Princess Royal. He goes over every step of the itinerary checking with a stop watch the various segments of the visit. He gives advice on the way the programme should be arranged and meets his opposite numbers in the local force to check security. If Her Royal Highness is walking from one area to another any buildings overlooking her route will be examined; if industrial machinery is being demonstrated all safety guards will be inspected. The best positions for the press, radio and television are discussed and many other points of detail. When all the arrangements have been agreed and the police officer is satisfied, he returns to Buckingham Palace for the next stage. This means reporting to Peter Gibbs on the results of the 'recce' and 'fine-tuning' the arrangements so that everything runs smoothly on the day. Finally a full, detailed programme is agreed and copies are sent to everybody concerned.

Individual queries are dealt with at Buckingham Palace by one of the two lady secretaries: Joanna Hockley and Sue White. Jo is a tall, slim brunette with the slightly 'Sloanish' air of many of the younger ladies in the Royal Household. She came to the Princess Royal's office after three years' working in the Lord Chamberlain's Office at St James's Palace. After a preliminary interview with Colonel Gibbs, she was invited to meet the Princess Royal in person. 'She didn't ask me why I wanted to leave the Lord Chamberlain's office because "that would be unfair", and when I said the chance to go abroad was rather appealing, she replied that she couldn't see the necessity for secretaries to travel. Happily we got around that one and I started to work for her.' She has certainly been able to fulfil her hopes as Jo Hockley has been on every overseas tour the Princess has undertaken since she joined. She looks after the applications for visas for the team and makes sure they all have the necessary inoculations and health certificates. It comes as a surprise to some people to learn that all the members of the royal family have passports, with the exception of the Queen.

For a visit within the United Kingdom the Lord Lieutenant of the county being visited has to be contacted so that he can welcome the Princess on the day. But it is when they are planning a major overseas tour that the work load really becomes heavy. Transport has to be booked through the Royal Mews; the embassies of the countries to be visited have to be informed so that their representatives can be at the airport when the Princess leaves. The VIP section at London's Heathrow and Gatwick airports must be told of their royal passenger so that a person of appropriate rank can be there to see her off and greet her on return. Then on the tour itself a mass of paperwork follows them around. As Jo explained, 'I seem to type at the most extraordinary hours – when the Princess gets back from the day's programme we start on the administrative work. Thank you letters have to be typed straight away. If you didn't do them then you would get overtaken and you'd never catch up.'

Also Peter Gibbs has a rule that nothing may be left in the in-tray on his desk overnight. Everything must be cleared even when he is ten thousand miles away. So at the end of every day Sue White, back in Buckingham Palace, sends all the correspondence by facsimile machine to wherever he may be. Jo then types the replies and transmits the answers on her portable facsimile machine so that by the time the office opens the following morning at Buckingham Palace, a stack of new correspondence is ready for typing and posting. It is a proud boast at Buckingham Palace that no letter goes unanswered for more than a couple of days.

In September 1988 the Princess Royal and part of her staff spent three weeks in the Far East during the period of the Olympic Games. When they got back to London Colonel Gibbs' in-tray was empty. They had dealt with everything via the telephone line. One of the main attractions for Jo Hockley in working for the Princess Royal has been the fact that she has been made to feel part of the team. 'I've been given so much more responsibility than I ever had in the Lord Chamberlain's office,' she says. Surprisingly, at this level there is very little contact with the members of the other

Households in the Palace. 'I hardly ever talk to other Households,' Jo comments, 'except perhaps when we are asked by the Queen's Flight if the Princess can share an aircraft with one of the other members of the royal family.'

All the staff in the Princess Royal's office are devotedly loyal and full of admiration for the hard work of their employer saying, 'We're all absolutely exhausted and she never seems to run out of energy.'

The other half of the partnership running the clerical side of the office until very recently was Chief Wren Sue White, who is shortly to leave the WRNS after sixteen years' service. As the Princess Royal has been Chief Commandant of the Women's Royal Naval Service since 1974 it was fitting that, when it was decided that a secretary from one of the three services should join her Household on attachment, it was to the senior service that the honour should go.

When the posting to Buckingham Palace came through, Sue was on the staff of the Commander-in-Chief, Naval Home Command at the Royal Naval Dockyard at Portsmouth, the home port of the Royal Yacht. She was asked if she would like to volunteer for a particular job without being told precisely what it was or who she would be working for. The WRNS, with its customary tact, had conducted its own 'trawl' of all those considered to be possibilities and Sue was the successful candidate. She was only then told who her next boss was going to be. In her own words, 'I was thrown in at the deep end. The first person I met at the Palace was Colonel Gibbs and the second was the Princess Royal. I had never met her before and she put me at my ease from the first moment. Since then I've watched her doing this time and time again. She is magnificent at making you feel you can talk quite naturally to her.' It must also be the only occasion on which the Chief Commandant of the WRNS met one of her Chief Wrens and immediately used her Christian name, but Sue it was and Sue it remained. After coming from a large service establishment to a small, compact unit of just five people, Sue White found a 'tremendous *esprit de corps* which you couldn't have in a larger office'. She felt it devolved from the Princess downwards. Everybody knew his or her job and got on with it, and if the Household was informal, it was because that was the way the Princess has found to be most efficient. 'She prefers to have the people around her on a more relaxed basis because she knows we work better that way,' Sue White said.

The newest member of the Princess Royal's Household is her Assistant Private Secretary, the Hon. Mrs (Madeleine) Louloudis, known to everyone in the Palace as Maddy. Before her marriage early in 1989 she was the Hon. Madeleine Dillon, the youngest daughter of the late Viscount Dillon. She came into the Royal Household through her friendship with Victoria Legge-Bourke, one of the Princess Royal's ladies-in-waiting who moved to America at the beginninng of 1989.

Maddy had been working as social secretary to the late Jack Heinz, a member of the famous Heinz beans family. Around the time he died, she heard from Victoria that there was a job going in London, though in typical royal fashion the actual job was not revealed straight away. When she learnt its nature and who it was for, she said she was interested and was then invited to Buckingham Palace to be interviewed by the Princess Royal herself. She remembers the occasion vividly. 'My first impression, and this has been confirmed by a lot of people who have met the Princess for the first time, is how quickly she put me at my ease. She was very easy to talk to. The job content wasn't discussed at great length; in fact the interview, as a job interview, wasn't in depth at all.' Obviously the Princess Royal was satisfied with what she saw of Miss Dillon (as she then was) and Maddy Dillon was appointed to the position of Assistant Private Secretary as a Member of the Royal Household, which means that she takes her meals in the Household Dining Room and is also invited to state lunches on occasion.

The Assistant Private Secretary acts in all private matters for the Princess Royal, and one of her main responsibilities is the running and maintenance of Gatcombe Park. Mrs Louloudis spends part of her time at Gatcombe, dealing with the domestic staff and matters such as the repair and decoration of the house. With a property as old as Gatcombe, there is always something needing repair, and she, in consultation with the Princess and Captain Phillips, has to decide which has the most urgent priority.

As the house is the Princess Royal's private residence, only part of its upkeep comes from official funds. And that refers only to the house itself. The farm attached is run as a completely separate enterprise, its administration being dealt with by a firm of land surveyors in Cambridge. In addition, anything to do with the stables is the financial responsibility of the Princess and Mark Phillips personally; that does not come out of the Civil List.

The Princess Royal's private expenses are met by her personally from her own bank account. She is able to draw funds from the trust fund set up for her by the Queen. She has a cheque book of her own (her bank is Coutts in common with all the other members of the royal family) which she uses to pay for things such as certain items of clothing. For example her jeans and riding outfits are all personal items which are not used in her official duties so she pays for them herself. Likewise her car, the Reliant Scimitar, is used for purely personal reasons and this too comes out of her own pocket. One of the tiny benefits that comes from being a member of the royal family is that for comparatively small amounts, the cheques are sometimes not presented to the bank, the creditors preferring to keep the precious scrap of paper with the royal signature as a unique souvenir.

Mark has a small office at Gatcombe which is run by his secretary Mrs Margaret Hammond but Maddy Louloudis deals with all the household and private accounts. Technically the accounts have been moved to another department in the Palace, but before anything is paid, it is checked by Mrs Louloudis, even the newsagent's bill. (The *Daily Telegraph* and the *Daily Express* are delivered to Gatcombe every morning.)

The domestic staff at Gatcombe also come under the control of the Assistant Private Secretary. Until a few months ago there was a butler who also doubled as Captain Phillips' valet. But he left and so far no decision has been taken about his replacement or even if there is any need to have a butler at all. The Princess has just engaged a new dresser, who lives in at Gatcombe and travels everywhere, at home and abroad, with her employer. There is also a cook and a nanny – whose only charge now is Zara, with Peter away at boarding school – and two ladies who come in every morning to clean the house. The longest serving member of the staff is the gardener who lives on the estate and spends his days tending the plants in the magnificent conservatory. The grooms for the horses are employed separately and are nothing to do with Buckingham Palace.

There are few women in senior positions in the Royal Household, only one reaching the rank of Private Secretary (Miss Mona Mitchell, Princess Alexandra's Private Secretary). So Mrs Louloudis can be said to have breached what was hitherto a bastion of male privilege. That she has done so with no sign of upsetting any of the other members is a tribute to her own charm and personality and she has easily settled in as an integral part of the Household.

One of the disadvantages of being Assistant Private Secretary is that Maddy does not go on any of the overseas trips with the Princess. Peter Gibbs accompanies her on all foreign visits and does the reconnaisance trips with one of the policemen. Jo Hockley and the dresser make up the rest of the travelling party, while Maddy and Sue White look after things back at the Palace.

With her very full engagement book it has become necessary recently for the Princess Royal to expand both the number of police officers she has to protect her and the number of ladies-in-waiting. Nowadays four policemen work exclusively for Her Royal Highness and nine ladies-in-waiting.

The policemen are headed by Inspector Philip Robinson, a tall, slim figure with a shock of steel grey hair and a permanent tan. He has been with the Princess for eight years, which makes him one of the longest serving officers in the Royalty Protection Department. He and his royal boss (she is not however his employer, that remains the Metropolitan Police) have at least one thing in common: they both profess not to like children very much. So he is not one of those officers who is sometimes photographed carrying one of the children on his shoulders. Philip Robinson is the complete royal police officer. He looks the part and acts it perfectly. When he is with the Princess his eyes are never still, and if he thinks someone he doesn't recognize is getting too close to her, he moves swiftly to move him or her away, with a practised ease that makes you wonder whether he has done anything at all. She is his only responsibility, and her safety and well being are his prime concern. It can be an awesome task in the world today. The policemen do not, however, allow the risks to prey on their minds, realizing that if they thought too much about what could happen they wouldn't be able to do their jobs properly. So even though the knowledge is always there they try to keep it well hidden.

Philip Robinson and his three colleagues (the others are Peter Schmidt, Barry Wilkinson and Jeffrey Fuller) who share the duties of protecting the Princess Royal, spend more time with her than some members of her own family. She is never seen in public without one of them in close attendance, and when travelling to and from an engagement frequently only the two of them are in the car. After eight years it would be reasonable to suppose that some sort of relationship would grow between them but they are all emphatic that never once in all the time they have spent together has any of them ever forgotten who the Princess is. They have an unwritten code of conduct which draws a line separating them from the Princess and they never even try to cross that divide. It's as simple as that. Never for an instant can they forget that she is the Princess Royal. It's a totally professional relationship and it is respected equally by both sides. One of the bonuses, from the Princess's point of view, in having someone like himself around for such a long period is that she is more comfortable with a familiar face, and that is a trait shared by the rest of the Royal Family. Also they know when to talk and, more importantly, when to shut up. If she is particularly quiet on the way to an engagement they know it's probably because she has got something on her mind. Either the speech she is about to make or some other aspect of the job ahead, so they keep quiet. If she wants to talk, she lets them know.

Her policemen find the Princess an easy person to work for in that she has a resigned tolerance to the whole question of security. She realizes what has to be done and accepts that their constant presence is part of the price she has to pay for being royal. There are other members of the family who are not so accommodating and they sometimes humiliate their bodyguards in public and vent their bad temper on them in private.

To the outsider the relationship between the police officers and the Princess Royal may appear rather casual and easy going. Nothing could be further from the truth. It is in fact very strict. They all know just how far they can go and nobody steps over that line. When the Phillipses' children were small the police officers were often photographed holding their hands or carrying them on their shoulders at horse trials, while their parents competed. But again this has given a false impression. As far as the children are concerned they are just like any of the other staff around Gatcombe, and if they weren't around tomorrow it wouldn't make the slightest difference to Peter and Zara. They take the policemen for granted in as much as they have grown up expecting to see different people around the house all the time. They know that if they are not there, someone else will turn up to take their places.

The Princess, though, is very much aware of the disruptive effect on family life that working for her can cause, and she insists on all her police officers bringing their wives to the Christmas lunch she gives every year at Gatcombe. She also arranges for an invitation to one of the Queen's three Garden Parties every summer. It is a pleasant gesture on her part but that is the only benefit the families of the protection department receive. All the wives have long grown out of the feeling that there is something glamorous about being married to someone who works at Buckingham Palace. They have had to arrange lives of their own which are scheduled around their husbands' long absences from home. The wives have to be able to cope without their husbands' help, looking after the domestic arrangements, dealing with pets and children, builders and so on.

With four officers now comprising the team the policemen are able to work a rota which begins every Monday morning when one of them arrives at Gatcombe for an eight-day stint. He lives in the house with his own bedroom cum office, complete with television set and private bathroom. He eats in the kitchen with the rest of the staff and, in theory, after the eight days are finished he should get three weeks off until his next shift begins. In practice he has very little free time. One of the team is usually abroad doing a 'recce' for the next overseas trip; another is on one of the many courses needed to keep up with the latest developments in security work. Then there is the team's usual leave entitlement; so if each man manages to get five days off in a month it is considered to be a good month.

From the security aspect, London is much easier to police than any of the provinces. The Metropolitan police are completely geared up to the needs of the royal family and through years of practice have refined the business of guarding them into a polished but unobtrusive art. They are so used to seeing different members of the family in a variety of roles that they can arrange a royal visit with complete efficiency every time. It is not quite so easy outside the capital. In the first place there are many more people to be presented in the line-up: Lords Lieutenant, High Sheriffs, Mayors and other civic dignitaries, all of whom have to take their rightful place in the correct order of precedence. In addition, when the Princess Royal, or any other member of the royal family, pays a visit to a town, village or factory in the provinces, it is much more of an 'occasion' for the area than the same routine would be in London, and this means the police officers have a more difficult task. When the Princess goes to Cardiff, Bristol or Glasgow the world and his wife want to see her, and the local officials all want the privilege of being in on the act. It's up to her detective to make sure that only those who should be there are close to her, and also to ensure that feelings are not hurt when persons, perhaps of some importance in the region, have to be moved away from the royal presence. In addition they have to deal with their colleagues in the local constabularies, some of whom are senior in rank to them, but must defer to them in matters of royal security. It can be difficult at times and involves combining the tact of the diplomat with the firmness of a schoolteacher. Theirs is among the toughest of all jobs in the Royal Household. They do not get any special privileges in the way of money, apart from a special clothes allowance which enables them to dress the part. They spend between five and six months of every year away from home and family, and if they spend too long in the Royalty Protection Department they could forfeit the chance of quicker promotion within mainstream policing. So what is the attraction? Obviously, they enjoy what they are doing – they are, after all, volunteers – and there's no doubt that a successful stint guarding a member of the royal family cannot harm their career prospects. There is also something new to look forward to almost every day; foreign tours and first-class travel. On top of that they all realize that, no matter how hard they work, the person they are responsible for is working twice as hard.

Apart from the police officers, the Princess's closest companions are her ladies-in-waiting. The number of Her Royal Highness's engagements has increased so much in the past three or four years that she has had to take on three extra ladies so that the total is now nine. Some of these are designated extra ladies-in-waiting, which means that they are supposed to help out only when one of the others is not available. In practice the work is divided fairly evenly beween them all. The nine are: Mrs Mary Carew Pole, Mrs Rowena Feilden, the Hon. Mrs Shân Legge-Bourke, Miss Victoria Legge-Bourke, Mrs Celia Innes, the Countess of Lichfield, Mrs Araminta Ritchie, Mrs Caroline Wallace and Mrs Jane Holderness-Roddam. They share a number of things in common for several of them could be placed in the category of 'high flyer'. Celia Innes runs a successful florists business; Caroline Wallace is a noted sculptress; Jane Holderness-Roddam was one of Britain's most outstanding horsewomen and is currently an equestrian author; Victoria Legge-Bourke combined her duties as lady-in-waiting to the Princess Royal with being social secretary to Mrs Charles Price, the wife of the United States Ambassador to Britain, until earlier this year, and she now works in a public relations capacity in the Price family bank in Kansas City (her position as lady-in-waiting being held in abeyance until she returns); while her sister-in-law Shân Legge-Bourke runs one of the largest private estates in Wales. The most senior of the ladies-in-waiting, Mary Carew Pole, is a magistrate at her home in Cornwall while all the others have jobs and families to look after in addition to their royal duties. The Princess Royal does not admit to choosing any of them because of their outstanding abilities, but it is no coincidence that they each share with her an above average interest in the pursuit of excellence. None of them receives a salary as such but they are reimbursed for all out of pocket expenses plus a small allowance to cover certain clothing costs – extra pairs of tights and shoes (these wear out faster than anything else on royal walkabouts). They are also paid a petrol allowance for the distances they drive getting to and from Gatcombe and Buckingham Palace. There is never very much left over after they have paid their expenses but, as Rowena Feilden has said: 'In the early days I regarded being a lady-in-waiting as my job and I could not have managed without the money.'

Mary Carew Pole (then Mary Dawnay) was the first lady-in-waiting to be appointed by the Princess when she began her public duties in 1970. They met when they were both in the same theatre party and shortly afterwards Mary was asked by Lady Euston (now the Duchess of Grafton, Mistress of the Robes to the Queen) if she would like to join the Household. She had not been connected with the royal family before this but she did not come entirely from the outside, as she knew what was expected from two friends who were ladies-in-waiting to the Queen.

Mrs Carew Pole organizes her life around her family and other public commitments in Cornwall so she tends to join the Princess on those engagements that begin and end at Gatcombe. Even so it can mean a 5 A.M. start to get to Gloucestershire in time to meet the Princess and then not returning home until the early hours of the following morning.

Next to come was Rowena Brassey (now Mrs Feilden) later that same year. Her route to royal service was via the wife of the Governor General of New Zealand. Rowena had been her lady-in-waiting for two years, and it was when Princess Anne visited the country that they met. A telephone call followed and she became the first full-time lady-in-waiting, in much the same way as Anne Beckwith-Smith is to the Princess of Wales today. (Nearly twenty years later the Princess remembered Rowena's connection with New Zealand and invited her to accompany her on a visit to her old stamping ground.) Princess Anne was just starting her round of royal duties so there were not as many engagements then as there are today. Rowena and Mary Dawnay organized their own rota then, each working two weeks on and two weeks off. It was Rowena Feilden, we remember, who shared one of the most dramatic moments of the Princess's life when she was alongside her in 1974 on the evening of the kidnapping attempt. For her efforts during the incident she was made a Member of the Royal Victorian Order, though she feels that perhaps she should have done more than she did.

Shortly after the Princess was married in 1973 it became necessary for a third lady to join them as the diary was filling up rapidly. Princess Anne remembered Victoria Legge-Bourke, who had been at school with her, but a year ahead. They had not been particularly close at school but since then had seen each other a number of times and had skied together in a small party in France. Victoria's brother was also a former page of honour to the Queen so she was not exactly a stranger to the workings of the Palace. Academically she is probably the brightest of all the ladies. When she was at Benenden she shone in most subjects and was one of the first girls at the school to be accepted by Oxford University. She remembers they were all so surprised that the school was given a half holiday to celebrate.

The fourth lady to join the Princess was Celia Innes, who came into the Household in the late 1970s 'quite out of the blue'. She received an invitation to a party at Windsor Castle without, she says, 'the faintest idea why' and a number of other functions followed. Obviously a royal 'looking over' was taking place. Eventually, Victoria Legge-Bourke suggested that she might like to become a lady-in-waiting. That's the usual way for it to happen. The Princess does not generally make the approach herself so that there will be no embarrassment on either side if the lady wishes to refuse. On 1 January this year, Celia's efforts on the Princess's behalf were recognized by the Queen in the New Year's Honours List when she was made a Lieutenant of the Royal Victorian Order.

Because there are two ladies with the name Legge-Bourke on the list of ladies-in-waiting most people assume that one was responsible for bringing the other into the team. What actually happened was that Celia Innes knew Shân Legge-Bourke very well, and when it was decided that yet another name should be added to the growing list, it was Celia who suggested Shân.

The Hon. Mrs Legge-Bourke grew up in the country on the estate of her father, the late Lord Glanusk, in Powys. As his only child she inherited the estate, including a number of farms, some of which are tenanted. She is a Lord of the Manor in a very rural part of Wales and shares a common border on part of her land with the Duke of Beaufort, whose family also has strong links with royalty. Shân is a woman of tremendous energy, dividing her time between Glanusk Park where she and her husband run the farming and forestry operations as a fully commercial enterprise, and her flat in London, which she uses as a base when she is on duty at Buckingham Palace.

The Countess of Lichfield had known the Princess for some years when she was asked to become a lady-in-waiting. Her former husband Patrick, the Earl of Lichfield, is a cousin of the Queen, and they had been frequent guests at royal homes including Gatcombe. The Princess and Mark Phillips had also been shooting on the Lichfield estate in Staffordshire several times. Leonora Lichfield is the sister of the Duke of Westminster, who is said to be the richest man in Britain, but it would be difficult to guess that from her manner. She is one of the most delightful of women, tall, slim and elegant, but with a pleasant, self-deprecating sense of humour. It's also hard to realize when you see her that she is the mother of three children. This is partly why she rarely goes on any of the long overseas trips with the Princess and also why she is usually excused from her duties during the school holidays. The Princess understands only too well how precious the holidays are when you have young children.

Two of the most recent ladies-in-waiting are Araminta Ritchie, who has an enthusiastic and bubbly personality; and Caroline Wallace, who has known the Princess longer than any of the others as she was a groom at Alison Oliver's stables when the Princess started her riding career. She now has a foundry at Swindon where she works as a professional sculptress, her products being sold all over the world. Jane Holderness-Roddam is one of the few exceptions to the rule whereby the Princess does not normally make a direct approach. She was telephoned personally by the Princess one Friday afternoon and asked if she would care to join the team. She was given the weekend to think it over and talk to one of the others about how much time the duties would take up. Jane is one of the most successful riders Britain has ever produced. She won Badminton in 1968 (as Jane Bullen) and again ten years later, as well as riding as a member of the British team in the 1968 Olympic Games in Mexico, so her credentials as a companion to the Princess Royal were well established when she received that personal telephone call. 'I knew her well as a competitor,' she says, 'but you never really get to know someone like her very closely. I was very flattered of course to be asked, but I was glad she gave me some time to think about it as I had no idea what being a lady-in-waiting involved. Fortunately I knew Shân Legge-Bourke so I spoke to her about it and she explained how the system works. The following Monday I telephoned the Princess and said I would be delighted and honoured to accept.'

Mrs Holderness-Roddam lives in a large farmhouse which she and her husband Tim are restoring in one of the prettiest villages in the Cotswolds, about half an hour's drive from Gatcombe. She joined the Princess at about the same time as Her Royal Highness became President of the Fédération Équestre Internationale, and she attends most of the meetings of the FEI with her. She soon got to grips with the requirements of her royal boss after one or two slight hiccups. 'I once moved some papers of hers thinking I was helping, to be told in no uncertain terms that "the papers are left in that way because that's the way I want them left" – it was the last time I moved anything of hers. I also learnt how to recognize the signs when she wanted to be left alone or wanted to talk. She's very easy to work for and very considerate. If she hears that one of us has been ill or had some family mishap she will always ring up herself to see if she can help or send flowers around.'

One thing all the ladies-in-waiting have in common is a highly protective attitude towards the Princess Royal. They know her better than most people outside her own family and they realize how dedicated she is and how hard she works. It is guaranteed to upset them all if they read in the press that she has been sullen or uncooperative, not that that has happened very often in recent years. Celia Innes says, 'Princess Anne has the greatest sense of fun, and some of her comments, particularly when we are driving slowly through a crowd and she can hear what they are saying about her, should be written down for posterity.' Shân Legge-Bourke says, 'Of course she cares about people. She is one of the most compassionate of women. She simply doesn't wear her heart on her sleeve so it's sometimes difficult to know what she's feeling.' Mary Carew Pole continues to be surprised by the Princess's appetite for work. 'She is never bored, and never appears tired; in fact we flag long before she gives the slightest hint of fatigue.'

If the ladies-in-waiting have their views about the Princess she has equally definite ideas about them and what she expects from them. 'What they have to be good at is chatting to people and making them feel comfortable, because that helps me really. It's no good at all if you get somebody turning up in the morning looking like death and furious and ratty about life and uncommunicative. And if, when they go out on a job they just stand in a corner and look glum and bored, that's no help to anyone, least of all to the people at the other end, never mind to me. So it is important that they should be capable of being interested and mixing with the people we meet.'

The fact that the Princess has not had to get rid of any of them and none has been inclined to leave throughout the years they have been together, speaks for itself. There is a feeling of mutual respect between the Princess and her ladies-in-waiting and also, since most of them have to earn a living outside Buckingham Palace, it follows that they are able to keep her in touch with modern life. The days when courtiers, male and female, were drawn from a narrow circle of the aristocracy, have long gone. The requirement these days is for well informed, intelligent and gregarious companions who are equally at ease in a maximum security prison, a football match or a palace. It requires a special blend of charm, diplomacy and commonsense. If the ladies feel they are fortunate in having such a considerate and capable employer, she is equally aware that the good fortune is not entirely one-sided.

One other member of the team who is not a member of the Household but who nevertheless plays an important part in the Princess's public life is her dressmaker Maureen Baker. It is only in recent years that the Princess Royal has appeared in the sort of fashionable clothes other royal ladies have enjoyed. She herself insists she is no slavish follower of fashion, 'But I am getting better and a little more adventuresome as I get older.' The Princess first met Maureen Baker in 1968 when she was working for the fashion company of Susan Small. Princess Alexandra was responsible for making the introduction; Mrs Baker had already been designing clothes for her for some time. Shortly after meeting Princess Anne, Maureen Baker decided to branch out on her own and she opened a tiny showroom behind Oxford Street. From there she still makes dresses and coats for several members of the Royal Family and also the Prime Minister, Margaret Thatcher, and a number of television personalities.

The turning point in her career came in 1973 when she was invited to design Princess Anne's wedding dress. It all came about quite casually during a fitting session. The Princess turned to Maureen and said, 'You had better start thinking about the wedding dress.' The team of seamstresses who worked for weeks were sworn to secrecy, and in spite of all sorts of blandishments from the tabloid press, not a word leaked out about the style or colour. Fittings took place in Buckingham Palace and Maureen Baker became a regular visitor, though even she was stunned during one session to hear the Princess say, 'I want my mother to see this.' Thereupon the Queen walked into the room and, like any other mother, examined the wedding dress in minute detail. It was an anxious moment for Maureen Baker and even more so for the Princess, who was desperately keen to have her mother's approval. When Her Majesty smilingly said she loved the dress, the look on the face of the Princess was, according to Maureen Baker, 'a joy to behold'.

Mrs Baker enjoys designing clothes for the Princess Royal and says there are few women who can claim honestly that they have exactly the same measurements today, after sixteen years of marriage and two children, as on the day they were wed. The Princess Royal can; she still wears a size 10 and, at 5'7", has the right height to show off beautiful clothes to their best advantage. Most of the Princess's outfits are meant to last and when, in Australia some years ago, she heard from someone in the crowd that she was wearing the same dress as the last time she had visited the country, she replied, 'It's a lot older than that.' If she likes something she will wear it for years with Maureen Baker altering the length or some other detail according to the fashion of the day. It is the Princess's proud boast that 'A good suit can go on for ever if it's properly made in the first place and has a classic look about it. I expect my clothes to last me a long time.' In the early days the Princess was prepared to be guided almost totally by Maureen Baker; today she has definite ideas of her own about what she can and cannot wear. Occasionally she will sketch something and show it to Mrs Baker, saying, 'This is roughly what I have in mind.'

The fittings for the dresses are arranged at Buckingham Palace, usually in between engagements so as not to waste too much time. By now Maureen Baker has a pretty good idea of the sort of clothes that will appeal to her royal client and will suggest a range for a particular wardrobe. Sometimes she gets it wrong, however, to be told, 'I'm not wearing that,' and that's the end of it. There is no argument; once Her Royal Highness has made up her mind, she rarely changes it.

The Princess's favourite colours are blues and greens and from time to time she will return from an overseas trip with a bolt of silk or cotton which Maureen Baker will then make up. When the Princess was in Seoul for the 1988 Olympic Games she went to see a little back street tailor in one of the market areas. He was thrilled to have a royal client and made a number of articles for her and also for members of the entourage. They all have an eye for a bargain, not least the Princess, and were delighted, not only with the quality of the clothes but particularly with the price!

If Maureen Baker has any criticism at all of the Princess's style it is her choice of footwear. 'Princess Anne spends so much time on her feet, her shoes are made for comfort,' is the thinly veiled implication that fashion does not figure highly on the Princess's list of priorities when she is buying shoes. Her Royal Highness laughingly agrees, saying, 'I hate spending money on expensive shoes.'

The Princess Royal has a splendid collection of hats, some of which have been acquired in the course of her many overseas tours. The bulk of them though, those which are worn on formal occasions, are made for her by John Boyd at his studio in Knightsbridge. He made his first hat for Princess Anne when she was seventeen and has also designed for the Princess of Wales and for Margaret Thatcher since the day she became Prime Minister. He has a unique talent for spotting what will suit a particular face; and when the Princess is planning an extension to her wardrobe Maureen Baker will show him her preliminary sketches and they will then consult with the Princess before making up the outfit. One thing John Boyd objects to strenuously, no matter who the client is, and that's having someone else add to one of his creations. If the Princess ties a piece of silk or chiffon to a Boyd hat and he sees it, he has no hesitation in letting her know he is not pleased.

In the team that supports the Princess Royal everybody has an important part to play from the most junior typist to the Private Secretary himself. They certainly do not do it for the money. They could all earn much more outside. The hours are long and there are few perks (apart from being able to park easily outside Buckingham

Palace). Yet their loyalty to their employer is total. Her welfare is the sole reason for all their efforts; and if she does like to have the last word in any discussion, they are realistic enough to know that in the final analysis it has to be her decision that is acted upon. In any team there must be a captain. In the Princess Royal's team nobody is ever left in any doubt as to who that captain is.

CHAPTER
SEVEN

◆

THE SPORTING LIFE

'If you are going to have anything to do with horses you have got to give them a hundred per cent of your time, otherwise you might just as well stay at home.' The words are Princess Anne's, when she was asked why she trained so hard. In sport as in everything else she has attempted, the Princess is determined to do it properly and well. So much so that her first trainer, Alison Oliver, said of Princess Anne when she had just started her equestrian career, 'I had never seen anyone who was so single-minded, so determined, so intent on getting to the top.'

Horses were a natural for the Princess; she had grown up with them all around her. Almost before she could walk she was lifted into the saddle. Her mother and father are both excellent riders; her elder brother rides regularly to hounds and is an enthusiastic polo player, so what could be more natural than that she should concentrate on horses as her main occupation in her private life? True there were other attractions which took her fancy for a while. As a young girl she went through the phase of playing little but tennis, because, as she puts it, 'It was considered good for me.' Dan Maskell, who introduced the young Princess to the game and coached her for a time, said that if she had persisted she could have played top class tennis herself, even to Wimbledon standard. She thinks he was being diplomatically kind, saying, 'Temperamentally I am unsuited to tennis.' Anyway it is a game she rarely takes an interest in today; never using the Royal Box at Wimbledon, unlike the Princess of Wales and the Duchess of York who are great enthusiasts. Another childhood opportunity to try something different was ice-skating, but this too did not last, in spite of being given the freedom of the Richmond Ice Rink whenever she and her two palace schoolroom friends paid a visit.

One of her earliest sporting interests, and one which has lasted, is sailing. When she became President of the Royal Yachting Association, she admitted she had not done a great deal of dinghy sailing in her youth though Prince Philip found an avid pupil when he took her out on longer voyages in his ocean-going yawl *Bloodhound* during their annual summer holidays. Sailing is something she still enjoys and she says that perhaps if she had had to give up riding she might have taken up sailing competitively. There has to be an end product with everything she does; not necessarily a prize but at least something to aim for. So if she were going to sail, there would need to be some aim to make the effort worthwhile. Princess Anne also tried angling a couple of times when she was in Scotland as a girl but that never caught her imagination, as it did with her grandmother Queen Elizabeth the Queen Mother, who still likes to fish as she approaches her ninetieth year, or her brother Prince Charles, who spends hours up to his thighs in icy water, for days on end. Perhaps it is the slowness of the pastime that fails to attract the Princess. She is not the most patient of people at the best of times so a sport needs to be fast moving to keep her interest.

Skiing was an occasional childhood sport that has developed into a lifelong enjoyment. She says she only went three times before she was 18 and then not again until she was 35. She is now a more than competent exponent and winter finds her, with her family, on the slopes at the French alpine resort of Morzine or nearby, for a week or so. Mark is also a strong skier and both Peter and Zara are confident on the lower slopes. Skiing is the sort of sport in which one needs to be able to practise a lot. This the Princess is unable to do because of her other commitments; but she is relatively fit, so by the time she reaches the slopes she is able to get down to the serious business of skiing without first having to nurse herself into condition.

Princess Anne was taught to swim when she was a child, in the pool at Buckingham Palace. Her style is conventional and economical. She breathes properly and she can keep going for long periods without getting tired, though she claims to dislike it as a form of exercise, 'unless desperate'. In the summer she and Mark used to spend part of their holiday at Jackie Stewart's home in Switzerland where there is a large pool and they swam every day. Both Zara and Peter were taught to swim from an early age and love the water.

Shooting is another favourite royal sport, the ladies acting as 'pickers up' while the men do the actual shooting. Picking up is a skill that has to be learnt and the Princess is considered an expert. She works her two dogs brilliantly and seems to know exactly where the birds are going to fall. One of her regular guests told me that 'she gets everybody organized', in typical 'brownie pack' fashion.

Mark Phillips is an excellent shot and there is very good shooting at Gatcombe, where Princess Anne often invites friends to join her for a day's outing with the guns.

However, horses have been the main interest of the Princess Royal throughout her life and it seemed perfectly natural that when she decided to go all out to succeed in a sport, that sport should be concerned with horses. While she was of school age the Princess competed irregularly at Pony Club meetings in and around Windsor, with a certain amount of success. When she left Benenden in 1968 she set about making equestrianism almost a full-time career after being encouraged to do so by the then Crown Equerry Lieutenant Colonel Sir John Miller, who retired from royal service in 1988 after more than a quarter of a century in charge of the Royal Mews. He had been a member of the British Team at the 1952 Olympic Games in Helsinki, and was, indeed remains, as President of the British Showjumping Association, a man of considerable influence in equestrian circles. He advised the Princess on the direction her riding career should take by sending her to Alison Oliver.

In 1968 Eventing was a comparatively little known sport, restricted to enthusiasts who were usually the sons and daughters of well-to-do landowners or soldiers, or farmers' offspring who took up 'venting as a natural progression from hunting. There was nothing fashionable about it and very little public knowledge. Even Badminton, then, as now, the leading Three Day Event in the world, would attract only a few thousand dedicated supporters, and there was no television interest in a sport which most people thought, if they thought about it at all, was just for a wealthy élite.

Yet within three years all this would change. Three Day Eventing would become one of the world's most successful spectator sports with more than a quarter of a million people crowding into Badminton and Burghley. Millions more would watch on television throughout the world and riders such as Richard Meade, Mark Phillips, Lucinda Prior-Palmer and Diana 'Tiny' Clapham would become household names. Multi-national companies would fight over the right to sponsor major events and international agents such as Mark McCormack would move into the arena to exploit the commercial possibilities. Up-market companies such as Simpson and Asprey would spend thousands of pounds taking stands in the 'trade villages' which sprang up wherever an event was taking place. Eventually, even Mark Phillips himself would cash in on the popularity of this hitherto little known sporting activity with his own range of exclusive sportswear being marketed through a major mail order company bearing his name.

All this though was in the future when the eighteen-year-old Princess Anne entered the sport. Why did she choose this of all equestrian disciplines? Why not showjumping which was far more fashionable (but in her case rather more time consuming) – and perhaps not quite so difficult for the beginner? It has been claimed that she decided on Three Day Eventing because it is essentially an individual sport and, as the 'loner' of the royal family, it was natural for her to do something on her own, rather than as part of a team. This theory, plausible as it sounds, was destroyed some years later when Her Royal Highness competed successfully as a member of the first all-women team in the European Championships and again in 1976, when she rode for Britain at the Montreal Olympics. On that occasion she suffered severe concussion after a bad fall on the cross country section, but insisted on remounting and finishing the course. Her reason was that 'I was riding as a member of the team so there was no question of quitting.' It has also been said on a number of occasions that she took up this particular sport because this was one way in which she could be number one in her own right.

There is probably some truth in both these theories, but after several conversations with the Princess about her reasons, I believe she chose eventing because if she succeeded in this sport it would be solely through her own ability and not because she was born a royal princess. It is a sport in which it is impossible to show favour; the only way you can win is if your horse is good enough to beat all the others – and you are good enough to stay on!

Princess Anne's observation that horses are no respecters of rank, royal or otherwise, has been proved time and time again. Though perhaps it would be only fair to point out that, contrary to what the press would have us believe, she has been dumped into the lake at Badminton only once, and only four times in fifteen years at other courses. But of course, that single occasion at Badminton was recorded by over a hundred photographers and the spectacular picture appeared in thousands of newspapers and magazines all over the world. Such is the price of being royal.

If horses are no respecters of rank, the same can be said, only more so, of their riders. When Princess Anne entered the tough, competitive world of Three Day Eventing she was not looking for any favours, which was just as well, because the leading riders of the day, Richard Meade, Mark Phillips, Jane Bullen, Chris Collins, were far too intent on their own success to lend a hand to any newcomer, even one who happened to be the Queen's daughter. Mark Phillips was one of those who didn't have much contact with the Princess in the early days. As he puts it: 'I'm rather a shy person so I didn't make any sort of approach. She was just another competitor. I hadn't met her before, socially or in any other way, and, apart from exchanging the usual pleasantries we didn't have a great deal to do with each other.'

Jane Bullen (now Jane Holderness-Roddam) says it was a little difficult at first because 'None of us knew how to treat her. Should we leave her alone in case it looked as if we were trying to ingratiate ourselves with her or should we treat her as one of us? In the end the matter resolved itself and she soon became an accepted part of the scene. She obviously didn't want a fuss made of her and once the initial shyness was overcome – on both sides – she became as friendly as anyone in her position can become.' Indeed, as she progressed through her chosen sport, the Princess welcomed the extreme competitiveness; she still does. Perhaps the greatest rivalry of all on the field is with her own husband. He has beaten her more times than she has beaten him, and he has won Badminton five times while she has yet to win it once. However, it is to her that the greatest individual honours have gone: winning the European Three Day Event Championship at Burghley in 1971 meant that she was virtually world champion. If Princess Anne had been able to beat her husband easily, the thrill would have disappeared immediately. It is the fact that when they ride against each other, they both know the other is trying as hard as possible to win, that makes it all worthwhile. Neither gives any quarter – nor receives any. Mark is generous and chivalrous in his comments about having his wife as a rival: 'I've always enjoyed riding against her and if I wasn't going to win, I can think of no one I would rather be beaten by than her.'

In the early days of her riding career the Princess was coached by Alison Oliver, who was already one of the most successful instructors in Britain when she met Princess Anne for the first time. Sir John Miller knew Mrs Oliver and it was on his recommendation that they got together. However, it was not quite as straightforward as that sounds. In the first place Mrs Oliver was not in the least overawed by the prospect of having her first royal pupil and before she agreed to meet the Princess she wanted to know something about the horses she was going to ride. Sir John was impressed by this because he too felt it was most important that whoever took on the task of coaching Princess Anne should be as strong a personality as the Princess was herself. Otherwise there was the danger of being influenced by the royal 'qualifications' of the rider, which in the long term would not have benefited either of them. Fortunately, Alison Oliver is as independent as the Princess so the problem did not arise.

After an initial meeting at the Oliver stables at Brookfield Farm in Buckinghamshire, Mrs Oliver agreed to take on the Princess's instruction. Princess Anne was under no illusions when she was asked to go to Brookfield. She knew Alison Oliver's reputation and that she did not take pupils simply to obtain a fee. If they weren't good enough they were out. She would not waste her own time or her pupil's if she felt there was no talent to be developed. She wanted to be sure in her own mind that Princess Anne had the will to succeed and, perhaps more importantly, would accept the discipline which would be needed if she was to reach the top. And that was the aim from the very beginning. It wasn't just a case of learning how to be a very good amateur; she was intended to be the best. That was the goal of Alison Oliver right from the start, if not, consciously at any rate, that of her royal pupil. Indeed, the Princess Royal says, 'I was not in the least competitive in those days. I had been brought up not to be. Whereas Mark as a young child had been taken to Badminton by his parents and he had said from the earliest age, "I am going to win here one day," I had no such ambitions. My family had taken me to watch Badminton every year but there was never the slightest idea on my part in those days of even riding the course, never mind winning.'

The training was non-stop and continued day after day. It was a considerable task for the young rider as the association with Alison Oliver coincided with the Princess's introduction as a member of the 'Royal Firm'. It meant that she would leave Buckingham Palace shortly before seven in the morning, drive herself to Brookfield, work for three hours under the supervision of Mrs Oliver and then drive back to London to undertake an official engagement. Then in the late afternoon she would return to the stables for more work and often spend the evenings around the kitchen table, drinking coffee and talking about horses.

One of the early problems to be resolved was how Alison Oliver was to address her royal charge. She told me, 'It would have been impossible for me to keep shouting instructions if I had to remember to say Your Royal Highness every time.' Princess Anne came up with the answer: 'Call me Anne,' she said; 'that's what they did at school.' So Anne it became and Anne it has remained . . . in private at least.

Princess Anne's programme and development were meticulously planned from the start. She had the use of three horses in Sir John Miller's Purple Star and two of the Queen's horses, Doublet, who was to partner the Princess to her greatest triumph at Burghley, and Royal Ocean, a fine Irish thoroughbred, standing at 16.2 hands.

Three Day Events, considered the ultimate test for both horse and rider, are divided into Dressage, Cross Country and Showjumping.

Dressage is designed to test the rider's skill in controlling the horse without any verbal commands, and the horse's sense of obedience and suppleness. The most popular phase, for riders and spectators, is the gruelling speed and endurance test over a cross country circuit of several miles, which has to be covered within a set time limit, while clearing a large number of fixed obstacles of varying degrees of difficulty. And unlike the obstacles in showjumping, which are constructed of light timber which falls down as soon as it is disturbed, those on the cross country section are made of heavier timber which does not give way. If you hit one of them, it is the horse and rider who usually come off worst. Then, on the last day, after a veterinary inspection, comes Showjumping, the final phase. This does not compare in any way with the fences encountered in showjumping proper, but is really a test of the horse's fitness after the previous day's ordeal.

In addition to the actual riding the extra skills of schooling had to be learnt. Princess Anne was already an accomplished rider but had not needed until then to know very much about the other aspects of equestrianism.

Alison Oliver, who now lives in Oxfordshire, recalled her first impressions of her royal pupil: 'I knew there was something there right from the start, but I didn't think, right at the beginning, that she would become a champion as quickly as she did. No one could have foreseen her rapid rise to fame at that time.' Princess Anne also made a favourable impression on the other young riders who were being trained at the Oliver stables at the time. 'Everyone was aware of course of who she was – it was impossible to forget,' says Mrs Oliver, 'but I can't remember a single occasion when she reminded us that she was a princess, or a single occasion when she refused an unpleasant task.'

In the spring of 1969 Alison Oliver decided to test the Princess by entering her, riding Ocean Royal, in the novice class at the Windsor Horse Trials. Among the twenty-seven starters in her section was Mark Phillips. The Princess won the event, her first victory over her husband to be; and so began one of the most successful partnerships in British equestrian history. For the remainder of that year, and the next, Princess Anne and Alison Oliver travelled up and down the country competing with varying degrees of success and all the time edging towards their ultimate goal – Badminton.

The Princess qualified for her first Badminton in 1971 but few expected her to even complete the course. It was said to be the toughest in the world with thirty-one obstacles made up of tree trunks, solid stone walls, cunning traps and, of course, the one place where all the photographers would wait, the Lake. Altogether forty-seven of the best riders in the world had qualified, including the then world champion, Mary Gordon-Watson, who would write her name in the racing history books some years later by becoming the first lady jockey in Britain.

The royal family turned up *en masse* to support Princess Anne and they were well rewarded when she finished fifth in the competition. The winner that year, on Great Ovation, was Lieutenant Mark Phillips. Mrs Oliver and the Princess were delighted with their placing. They had never really expected anything more than to finish, which in itself is an accomplishment fully recognized by the organizers. In 1980 Princess Anne was presented with an Armada Dish for completing Badminton five times.

A month after Badminton it was announced that the Princess had been selected to ride as an individual in the forthcoming European Championships to be held at Burghley in Lincolnshire in September. She was not however chosen a member of the British team. The selectors took the unusual step of justifying her exclusion in a public statement:

> The selectors were greatly impressed by Princess Anne's performance at Badminton. However, since this was the first international competition for both of them, and in view of the very large number of experienced combinations available, it was not thought advisable to include Her Royal Highness in the shortlist from which the team will be chosen. But Great Britain will be allowed to enter approximately twelve individuals, in addition to the team, as the host nation. Princess Anne is being invited to fill one of these vacancies.

Then less than two months before the championships were due to take place, the Princess received what could have been a major setback. She had to have an operation for the removal of an ovarian cyst. Alison Oliver thought that it would mean the end of their European Championship hopes for at least another year; but when she visited the Princess in the King Edward VII Hospital for Officers immediately after the operation she found Princess Anne sitting up and already making plans to return to the saddle. There was no question of the Princess not taking part. She had come too far to give up at this stage, so she went to Balmoral and began taking long walks in the mountains to regain her strength.

A twenty-first birthday party on board the Royal Yacht *Britannia* provided a brief respite; then it was back to training for the big event.

As the date for the European Championships approached tensions started to creep in at the Oliver stables and Princess Anne's nerves began to show. If the day had not gone as she wanted, she lashed out in all directions with her sharp tongue. Mrs Oliver told me, 'I warned everyone to keep out of her way if the signs were ominous and on more than one occasion I led her to a horsebox with instructions to stay there until she had cooled down.' But this did not happen very often and once the row was over it was forgotten. The Princess did not, and still does not, bear grudges. If she has something to say she says it and then it's over and done with. Outwardly Princess Anne gives little sign of nervousness but she admitted that, 'For three nights I didn't sleep much before Burghley.'

In the event the four days of the 1971 European Championships could not have gone better for Princess Anne and Doublet. She went into an immediate lead in the Dressage section with 41.6 penalty points – only one other competitor, Richard Meade leading the official British Team, getting below fifty points. The same thing happened in the Cross Country phase; Princess Anne maintained her lead, beating two other members of the British Team, Debbie West and the reigning world champion Mary Gordon-Watson, into second and third places. So it was a confident princess who rode into the arena on the Sunday afternoon before a capacity crowd which included the Queen and the Duke of Edinburgh. Everybody wanted her to win and as she set out over the first of the twelve fences which stood between her and the title, the crowd grew silent. They willed her over each obstacle until she reached the last, by which time she was unbeatable. Then they went wild. She finished her clear round in a cacophony of sound so loud even the announcer's voice over the public address system was lost. The Queen, smiling broadly, presented her daughter with the Raleigh Trophy, a gold medal and a cheque for £250, and the BBC there and then decided that here was the next sport that would be featured on television.

I was working as a reporter for BBC Television News in those days and had been sent to cover the event simply because Princess Anne was competing. If she had not been there we would have ignored the championships. A few minutes after her victory presentation I interviewed Her Royal Highness and the film of the interview was sent throughout the world. With that single victory, Princess Anne gave Three Day Eventing its biggest ever boost. Suddenly the world became aware of this unknown sport and from then on it would grow in popularity until today it ranks with football and racing as a major crowd puller. The Princess herself deprecates her own part in all this, saying it would have happened anyway. But those who run the sport freely admit that had it not been for Princess Anne's appearances up and down the country and the subsequent press and television coverage, it would probably still be considered a minority interest, confined to the backwaters of the world's sporting stage. Mark Phillips agrees, 'I think it's fair to say that she certainly brought the sport a much higher profile than it had ever had before and it has never looked back.' At the age of twenty-one the Princess had reached the pinnacle of her chosen sport. She had proved that by determination, hard work – and undoubted talent – she could succeed in one of the toughest fields where rank was of no importance, and where, in spite of the satisfactions and disappointments common to all competitors, she was one of the best. It was a heady moment and one which, in retrospect, she feels perhaps happened too soon. A short while ago we spoke about the championship and her feelings looking back. She said, 'Possibly it happened too early in my career. After Burghley there was the danger that I would fall away, because I had reached the top after just three years in the sport, so the incentive might have been missing. I did not really appreciate what we had achieved.' Her husband disagrees vehemently with the Princess's view that it might have been too soon. 'Of course it wasn't. Sport is all about winning and you have to take your chances when they come. Remember most of the successful riders were pretty young at that time. Jane Bullen was only eighteen when she rode in the '68 Olympics.'

This was a vintage year for the Princess. After winning the European title she was voted Sports Woman of the Year, and then received the Sportswriters' award as their personality of 1971. This was particularly satisfying as the writers and reporters had not always taken her seriously as a competitor and the sound of words being eaten must have been music to her ears. The next target was a place in the British team for the 1972 Olympic Games in Munich, but Doublet broke down in training with tendon trouble and that ended their hopes for another four years.

Meanwhile Goodwill, a former show jumper, was bought by the Queen to partner Princess Anne. They were successful in Britain, and in 1973 they travelled to Russia to defend the Princess's European title in Kiev. It was a defence that was to end dramatically at the notorious second fence on the cross country course. It was made up of telegraph poles nailed together over a ditch, and approached downhill on a slippery, winding grass track. The problem for the Princess was that 'I was told to jump it a different way from the way I had walked it – and got it wrong.' She joined a long and distinguished list of casualties at the fence and afterwards described how the fall felt: 'It was like hitting tarmac as far as I was concerned. I had never hit the ground as hard or as fast. The main impact was on the side of my leg and, when I got up, it was numb from the point of my hip to my knee; I couldn't feel a thing. I wasn't, at that stage, aware that there was anything wrong with my shoulder – but I couldn't walk – I could stand on one leg, that was about all. I didn't think I had broken anything, but Goodwill looked completely stunned and I couldn't walk, so I decided there wasn't a great deal of point in going on. I was only riding as an individual, so there didn't seem to be a great deal of honour at stake.' After checking that Goodwill had not suffered any serious injury Princess Anne discovered that she had nearly dislocated her collar bone. A

Above: Gatcombe Park, home of the Princess Royal and Captain Mark Phillips since 1976. The impression of size is given by the magnificent conservatory; otherwise the house is of comparatively modest proportions.

Below: The entrance hall at Gatcombe Park looking very spick and span. Usually it is cluttered with boots, shoes and drinking bowls for the family pets.

Above: The Princess is Colonel-in-Chief of the 14th/20th Hussars, one of the premier cavalry regiments in the British Army. When she visits them on manoeuvres in Germany they always make sure she gets an opportunity of driving one of their 50-ton Chieftain tanks.

Below: When the occasion demands, the Princess Royal can look as glamorous as any of them! Here she is chatting with former Beatle, Ringo Starr, and his wife, actress Barbara Bach, at a charity fashion show held at Simpson's in Piccadilly.

One of the penalties of being royal is having to spend hours sitting (or in this case standing) for official portraits. Livery companies and service units all request pictures, and the Princess tries to accommodate them all. Here the artist is John Ward (1988).

Left: Cnoc Na Cuille, the first horse the Princess rode 'over the jumps' at Kempton Park. The horse was found for her by her trainer David Nicholson and his friend Josh Gifford.

Below: As President of the British Academy of Film and Television Arts (BAFTA) Her Royal Highness enjoys meeting actors and actresses. Here (*above*) she is in conversation with Robert Powell and (*below*) talking to the distinguished English actor Denholm Elliott at a gala tribute to Dirk Bogarde in 1988.

Far left: Her Royal Highness is now recognized as one of the most outstanding amateur jockeys in horse-racing. She rides both in steeplechases and on the flat.

Left: A family affair! The Princess gives an award to her husband as part of the silver-medal-winning British team in the Three-Day Event at the Olympic Games, Seoul, 1988.

Left: Dressed in the country uniform of the typical 'Sloane Ranger'. This photograph was taken in Scotland at a celebrity shoot-out in June 1988.

Below: Every year a celebrity shooting competition is held in Scotland with teams from the royal family, sports personalities and show business stars taking part. Here the Princess and Mark Phillips share a joke with Scottish comedian Billy Connolly.

Inset right: The Princess says she skied only three times before she was 18 and not again until she was 35. At Morzine in France she is making sure Zara gets plenty of practice.

Right: The Princess Royal has been President of the Royal Yachting Association since 30 April 1987. She has sailed most of her life, learning the basics from her father. She says it is one of the healthiest sports she knows.

The Princess Royal at her best – fresh-faced, attractive and elegant. Photograph by Terry O'Neill.

long lasting result of the fall has meant a slight unevenness in her shoulder ever since.

By 1974 Doublet had recovered from his tendon injury to compete once more at Badminton. However, he was retired after a bad fall on the steeplechase phase. It was to be his last competition. The following month Princess Anne suffered the saddest experience of her life when Doublet broke a leg as she was riding him on Smith's Lawn at Windsor and had to be put down. She described the incident as 'quite the most ghastly experience of my entire life', and Lady Susan Hussey, one of the Queen's ladies-in-waiting, says, 'She was inconsolable and completely shattered when I saw her later that day.'

Goodwill now took over as the number one horse in Princess Anne's stable, and in 1975 they were one of the combinations selected as part of the first all-female team to represent Britain at the European Championships at Lumuhlen in West Germany. Their *chef d'équipe* was Colonel Bill Lithgow who, as Commandant of the Royal Military Academy, Sandhurst, had done so much to help Officer Cadet Mark Phillips in the early days of his riding career. Colonel Bill, as his all-girl team always called him, enjoyed having the ladies as a team but recalls, 'One had to remember to moderate one's tone a little.' Perhaps they, in turn, moderated their language when he was around; the people who compete at horse trials – male and female – are renowned for their 'earthy' vocabulary.

The team was one of the most successful ever to represent Britain. Lucinda Prior-Palmer (now Mrs David Green MBE) won the individual Gold Medal, Princess Anne taking the Silver – and in doing so, becoming only the second woman in eventing history to win medals in the European Championships on different horses – while the four ladies together won the Team Silver Medal. It was a brilliant result and one which fully justified the selection of the team in spite of some claims that women were physically unsuited to the rigours of international competition. The Princess's comment that she was not always the most ambitious of competitors was borne out recently when she said, referring to that team success: 'In many ways I regard the Silver medal as a greater achievement than winning Burghley. I was on a different horse and that made it so much more difficult.' So much for the expert opinion that insists that she has to be number one all the time.

The following year saw both Princess Anne and Mark Phillips chosen for the British Team at the Olympic Games in Montreal. It was a five-man shortlist from which only four would ride; the other would be reserve. Anne was chosen to ride; Mark was relegated to the reserve position. He gave a tremendous amount of help to his team mates, any disappointment he may have been feeling hidden as he assisted with their preparations. Of course, he had already won his Gold Medal four years earlier at the Munich Games.

The Montreal Games were not successful for the British Team, with no medals won. Princess Anne fell at the 19th cross country fence, where she was badly concussed, but remounted to finish the course – remembering nothing about it to this day. She was the only British competitor apart from Richard Meade (who came fourth) to complete the course.

When Princess Anne became President of the British Olympic Association in 1983 she said that, for her, 'Being on the short list was an achievement. To get into the squad was another achievement, and to actually ride in the Olympics was really something.' So just getting to Montreal must have been very satisfying. All the same the Games must have been something of a let-down. Today she says that she felt at the time that they could have 'got among the medals' if a third member of the team had completed.

The Princess continued to compete at the highest level for the next five years but did not achieve the same level of success. Two children were born, in 1977 and again in 1981, and nowadays the demands of her royal commitments make it virtually impossible to find the time to prepare and qualify for the major Three Day Events. Also there has never been a successor to Doublet and Goodwill to carry her to the top again. She continues to bring on young horses and still regularly takes part in horse trials; but these days, unless you can afford the very best – and a top eventing horse can cost up to £100,000 – you simply cannot hope to win at the top level. And contrary to what some may imagine, Princess Anne does not have a bottomless purse. She is not able to go out and buy any horse she sees, so is constantly looking for a young, promising horse who will make it worthwhile to devote the hours of attention required. In sport, as in everything else, she refuses to compromise.

If the right horse did materialize the Princess would arrange her programme in such a way as to leave sufficient time to train properly; but she said earlier this year, 'I very much doubt if I will ever again compete in an international event, circumstances being what they are.'

In 1985 Her Royal Highness turned her attention to a branch of equestrianism previously left to her mother and grandmother, racing. The Worshipful Company of Farriers, of which the Princess is a member, had organized a race over the mile and a half Derby course at Epsom, on St George's Day. It was to be for charity and eventually raised some £30,000 for the Riding for the Disabled Association. The Princess was invited to ride and, as with everything else she undertakes, set about making sure she was fully prepared. She rode out three or four times a week at the nearby stables of David Nicholson, believing at first it was only for this one race, and finished in fourth place on Against the Grain. In an interview after the race she said, 'I was immediately conscious that I wasn't going fast enough when I came out of the stalls.' Since then, racing has really got to her and she now trains at David Nicholson's whenever she can, fitting the sessions into her packed programme of official engagements.

She has ridden a number of times both on the flat and in steeplechases, her first winner coming on Gulfland at Redcar in Yorkshire, in her thirteenth race. She said afterwards, 'I've worn number thirteen in competitions and there's always a thirteenth fence so I can't say I'm superstitious about things like that.' She also said, 'You've got so many instructions on your mind as you are riding the race that you don't really appreciate what you've done until quite a long time after. The real pleasure came when I saw the faces of the trainer, the head lad and the girl who looks after the horse.'

David Nicholson trains in the heart of the Cotswolds some forty minutes' drive from Gatcombe. To get there in time for early morning stables, the Princess Royal gets up at 5.30 A.M. and leaves home just after ten past six. The country roads are quiet at that time of the morning and she is able to make good time, arriving at Condicote at ten to seven, ready to start promptly at seven. The exercise lasts until 8.30 when she joins the Nicholsons in their kitchen for breakfast. By nine o'clock she is ready to leave for the drive back to Gatcombe, and the day's programme of official engagements. David Nicholson says she doesn't get any preferential treatment. 'She is exactly like all the other people who ride out here and that's the way she wants it to be. You couldn't run a stable any other way. She gets on well with all the lads and they seem to like her.' He admits that he can sense if she is not feeling in the best form, but goes on to say, 'No matter what mood she is in when she gets here – good or bad – by the time she has ridden out, she has always cheered up. I've never seen her leave here in a bad temper.'

David Nicholson is an old friend as well as the Princess's trainer. He has known her since she joined Alison Oliver in the late sixties when he was riding showjumpers for Mrs Oliver's father-in-law. He and his wife Dinah had already been dinner guests at Gatcombe a number of times when the celebrity race at Epsom was arranged. He offered his help and shortly afterwards the Princess telephoned to ask if she could come and ride out. 'As soon as she started,' Nicholson said, 'she realized that she was going to have to be very much fitter than she had ever been before to ride in a flat race. She started from scratch, riding long canters with shorter stirrups than she had been used to before, and she enjoyed it. Come the day of the race, she rode very well to come in fourth and we were all delighted that it had gone so well. That night a small party of us, including the Princess and Mark and the owner of Against the Grain, went out for dinner and I asked her when she was going to race again. She replied, "I think that's over and out." However, about a month later she telephoned and said she would like to start riding out again and she has been coming ever since.' Later that same year David Nicholson suggested that she should ride in a regular flat race and she immediately agreed. He managed to arrange for her to be issued with a jockey's licence without any publicity so that she could at least make a start without too much attention from the press. They both knew what would happen the moment a reporter got wind of the news that the Queen's daughter was riding in a commercial stakes and kept the secret until a couple of hours before the race in question at Goodwood. 'Then Peter O'Sullevan, the BBC commentator, spotted us walking the course in the pouring rain and of course he twigged. The name of the royal jockey wasn't announced until three-quarters of an hour before the race and of course then everybody wanted to see her and talk to her. To start with, the pressure on her was very heavy, but it's eased off a bit now. It's bad enough for anyone who takes this business seriously, but for her it's twice as bad.' She has now become a well established amateur jockey who has earned the respect of her fellow riders, and David Nicholson feels she is capable of holding her own with any of the amateurs riding today. She listens carefully to his instructions on how he wants her to race, and she has never forgotten his cardinal rule when you are in front: 'Never look round and always make sure you are well past the winning post before you relax.' This explains why when the Princess rode her first winner at Redcar the television cameras showed her apparently riding as hard as ever when she had already won the race.

David Nicholson is a tough, uncompromising trainer who stands no nonsense from anyone. His stables are run with an iron discipline which he applies as much to himself as to those he employs. He is scrupulously fair, and popular with his staff and the rest of the racing fraternity. It's a close-knit world of thorough professionals who are impressed only with performance, whether by horses or people. He is exactly the right sort of trainer for the Princess Royal, handling her in very much the same style as Alison Oliver did all those years ago. He is also a reluctant and recent convert to the idea of lady jockeys, having been totally opposed to the proposal for most of his racing life. He believes the secret of the Princess's success is her determination never to be beaten and her willingness to work as hard as it takes to be that winner. There's nothing very glamorous about racing on a freezing cold January day when you are up to your eyes in mud, but in his view, 'That's when you can see what she's made of.'

After the Princess had had several races on the flat it seemed natural that she should progress towards National Hunt Rules, so Nicholson asked his friend Josh Gifford if he had a suitable horse. He had – Cnoc na Cuille – and the Princess had her first ride over fences at Kempton Park on him, after being allowed to jump six fences at Cheltenham in the company of a vastly experienced jockey,

the Grand National winner Richard Dunwoody. She then rode Cnoc
na Cuille in the Military Gold Cup and the sport of kings had found
a new champion. David Nicholson is convinced that competing in
steeplechases 'gives her a tremendous kick'. Will she ride in the
Grand National? Her trainer knows she is good enough, 'But I don't
think she would enjoy riding around Liverpool in the company of
forty-five other horses and jockeys.' The Princess Royal agrees
with him, 'I still find it terrifying to find myself surrounded by large
numbers of horses and jockeys all going for the same fences at the
same time. The noise is extraordinary and I don't think I'll ever get
used to it. Any number higher than four and I begin to feel hemmed
in. So probably David Nicholson is right in his assessment. I would
not find the prospect of riding around Aintree in such a large group
all that attractive. But I would have quite liked to have had a go at
the course on my own or with another jockey. Perhaps I should
have done it when Mark rode the National course. That was a
missed opportunity.' The opportunity the Princess was referring to
was when Captain Phillips rode the Queen's horse Columbus
around the Aintree course in a solo effort for the benefit of BBC
television cameras. Mark says he would quite like to accompany
his wife around the National course, 'Of course she could do it.
Whether she would enjoy it is another matter. I would quite like
to ride the course with her if somebody came up with the right
vehicles.' Perhaps a pointer here for an enterprising sponsor?

The Princess's remarkable stamina showed itself to good effect
one weekend in 1988. David Nicholson takes up the story:

'The Princess Royal had been invited to ride in a charity race in
Nashville, USA, and Dinah [Mrs Nicholson] and I were lucky
enough to accompany her. We left Heathrow Airport at ten o'clock
in the morning on Concorde and were met at New York's Kennedy
airport by a private jet which took us/on to Nashville. We arrived
at the racecourse at 12.30 local time – and she promptly won the
two o'clock race. The American crowd loved it. They thought they
were going to see just another lady amateur having a bit of fun –
what they actually saw was a jockey who stood out as a professional
among amateurs. After the race we returned to the house where we
were staying and joined the other guests for a dinner party. We
were up very early the next morning, joining Nicky and Diana

Henderson [a very successful British trainer and his wife] to fly from Nashville to Virginia where we landed on the private airfield of Mr Paul Mellon, who is one of the most successful racehorse owners in the world, and also owns one of the most important private sporting art collections. He had flown specially from England to act as a personal guide and his wife had arrived from Paris. There was a timber race meeting in the afternoon, another dinner party in the evening and a special hunt was arranged by the Master of the Piedmont Foxhounds the next morning for just ten of us. We were then taken to Dulles Airport in Washington in time to catch the two o'clock Concorde to London and we were back home by ten o'clock that night. The following morning the Princess Royal, showing no signs of jet lag or any other kind of fatigue, set off on another round of official duties. As far as she was concerned it was just another episode in a crowded diary – for us it was the trip of a lifetime!'

The Princess Royal has proved something of a successful money-winner for her owners. A number have won four-figure prizes, the biggest, £10,000, going to the owner of the horse she rode to win the Queen Mother Cup at York.

When I asked her what is the attraction of racing as opposed to Three Day Eventing her reply was typically practical. 'Racing is so much easier to organize and, in terms of my timetable, it makes good sense. With eventing you have to plan months in advance and then an injury to the horse can upset all your arrangements. With racing, things are so much more "time effective" – the stables are run efficiently, the trainer and owners know which races they are going to enter and, in my case, I can ride in a race and still fit in a couple of other jobs on the same day.'

Malcolm Wallace is Director General of the British Equestrian Federation, responsible for the country's international equestrian effort. His riding pedigree is impeccable. A former Commanding Officer of the King's Troop, Royal Horse Artillery, this lean, forty-one year old has taken part in just about every aspect of riding and training horses. He has ridden in the Grand National (his horse fell); Three Day Events, Flat and National Hunt racing. He hunts, schools race horses, has been *chef d'équipe* to the British Olympic Team and rode some of Princess Anne's horses for her when she was expecting her first child Peter, in 1977. He met his wife Caroline, now one of the Princess's ladies-in-waiting, when she was a groom to the young emerging royal rider in the early seventies. Major Wallace goes everywhere accompanied by his black labrador bitch, which came from Sandringham, and he accepts the legacy of having broken most of the bones in his body as an occupational hazard when one schools race horses as he does.

His relationship with the Princess is close, friendly and also professional – he is a member of the British Olympic Association and the Fédération Équestre Internationale of which she is President. He feels he must always be completely honest and if he has something to say to her, he says it, whatever her views might be. Whilst he is absolutely delighted at her racing success, he admits to being surprised at her love of steeplechasing. 'She is a quiet rider and her horses run for her. Having been eventing for so long and used to riding on her own with great accuracy, it amazes me that she enjoys the hurly-burly of jump racing.' He also expresses some reservations at her continuing to ride for too long. 'I think she would love to ride in the Grand National and I would love to see her do it and then perhaps she should concentrate on the flat. As one gets older, the inevitable falls begin to hurt more and she has started at an age beyond which most pros have given up.'

Malcolm Wallace is full of admiration for what she has achieved, both in eventing and on the racecourse. 'She has won a three-mile 'chase and that's a tremendous achievement – to win the European Championship at twenty-one after only three years in the sport was absolutely marvellous. I believe she is right not to try and ride at advanced level in horse trials now, especially whilst trying to race ride – the two do not always complement each other. Nowadays one has to train full time to be a top Three Day Event rider and many of those who learned their craft in the sixties and seventies are left behind unless they can constantly practise the sport and learn to adapt to the new standards – the Princess simply doesn't have the time.'

She agrees that the attitude to competition has become more 'professional with a small p, and there is more money around now than in my day. But it hasn't really meant an increase in standards. What I really regret is the passing of the day of the gifted amateur, not only in riding but in any sport. I still think essentially that if a sport is no longer fun you shouldn't be doing it anyway. There is still scope for the gifted amateur to make an impression in almost every sport simply because their level of motivation is different.'

I asked Mark if he agrees with the Princess about standards not being higher than in the sixties? 'No, I have to disagree with the Princess here. I think the general standard of competition at international level is much higher than it was in our day.' He also believes she would find it almost impossible to return to competition at the top level. 'Time is against her. With the number of engagements she takes on it would be very difficult to fit a full training programme in.'

David Nicholson disagrees with his old friend Malcolm Wallace about the Princess concentrating on the flat. 'I see no reason why she shouldn't continue to ride under National Hunt Rules,' he says. 'She knows exactly what risks are involved and is more than capable of making her own decisions on retirement – as "Wol" well knows!'

Major Wallace was one of the first people to encourage the Princess when she showed an interest in riding under National Hunt Rules. He took part in her first flat race, but he is the first to admit that no one could have foreseen the success she's enjoyed. He also freely admits that having another member of the royal family taking part in the sport has provided a massive 'shot in the arm'. 'I always wanted to see another of the royals deeply involved in steeplechasing,' he says. 'After all, Queen Elizabeth the Queen Mother is such a splendid patron, and I always hoped it would be the Princess Royal, but who would ever have thought that you could open the *Sporting Life* on a murky January day and look down the card and see a two and a half mile handicap chase at Leicester with the name of the Princess Royal listed among the professional jockeys.'

Racing is a dangerous sport – perhaps that is part of its attraction for the Princess, but it also means that those nearest to her are concerned for her safety when she rides. Mark Phillips says, 'Yes I do worry, but not because of the way *she* rides but because of all the others in the race. It's not always what *you* do in racing, it's what the other jockeys do or don't do that causes the trouble.'

Princess Anne knows that realistically she will never be European

Champion again, but she has a new and even more important role to play as President of the Fédération Équestre Internationale. As Major Wallace says, 'She is a former European Champion who now controls the destiny of other champions, and she has a hell of a job to do. The FEI is going through a difficult period and the Princess Royal has got to sort it out. I cannot think of anyone who is better qualified to do the job than her.'

There are those in international equestrian circles who feel that possibly Prince Philip did not do his daughter any favours when he persuaded her to accept the job of president of the FEI. Prince Philip is a hard act to follow. He ran the Fédération from his office in Buckingham Palace where he would answer every letter personally, often working away on his word processor late into the night. He was a brilliant president for more than twenty years, but the difference between the way he ran the organization and the way his daughter is able to do it, is that he could devote almost all his energies to the considerable task of controlling the fortunes of many disparate talents, while she has hundreds of other duties which demand her attention. One of the problems which might have concerned her was the position of her own competitive career now that she was to become head of the sport's governing body. Was there the danger of any conflict? She didn't think so: 'It's the national associations who run the sport in your own country and I don't have anything to do with that so there's no problem.' And she was in full agreement that there should be a body at the top to supervise the rules of any sport. 'The thing that amazes me about competitors, is that most of them know the rules but some of them choose to take advantage of them in such a way that they don't actually break the letter of the law. Everybody knows what they mean and what they intend, but there's always some silly so-and-so who, because it doesn't actually say you cannot do a certain thing, will always go and do exactly what it doesn't mean. So the rules have to be tightened again and again.'

The Princess was aware when she took over the presidency that there might be problems with some of the long-established figures in the FEI, saying, 'I'm not sure they are going to find a young female all that easy to cope with.' She also had her own way of describing the problems to come: 'Being involved with a professional side of the sport will be interesting as most equestrian sports are amateur, and certainly amateur run, which sometimes makes them rather inflexible.'

Having to follow someone like the Duke of Edinburgh would be difficult enough for anyone, for his daughter it is even more so; inevitably comparisons are made. The Princess says, tongue in cheek, 'He keeps being quoted at me and I've told them that if I hear his name mentioned once more I will go.' The scope of the job has also changed considerably since the Duke's day. As his daughter explains, 'When my father took over as president there were just twenty odd federations throughout the world. He managed their affairs on his own with a part-time secretary. Today we have ninety federations with a full-time staff at our headquarters in Berne, so things are a little different.' She also feels that the FEI has 'grown rather badly, even if some of those involved won't like to hear me say that. In the early days it was possible not to notice the cracks in the organization. It's only now that some of them are becoming apparent. There were a lot of changes that needed to be done but while my father was there nobody minded because he did all the work for them and they were content to let him get on with it. I told them right at the start that I was not going to be the same sort of president as my father had been because I did not have the same amount of time. My life is very different to his.'

Princess Anne inherited a difficult situation and, in typical fashion, she set about sorting it out. Most of the board members are of a different generation from their new president – and it shows. The Princess has a reputation (among a small section of the equestrian world) for not caring too much about the opinions of the 'old and bold', and there is a saying in the British Horse Society and British Showjumping Association: 'If you're over fifty, as far as she is concerned, you're dead!' But Jane Holderness-Roddam, who accompanies the Princess to most FEI meetings, feels this is an unfair generalization. 'If the Princess Royal thinks someone has a valid point, particularly if they have years of experience behind them, she is always pleased to listen to their views, no matter what their age.'

The Princess also feels that the saying is not only unfair but untrue. 'For the first couple of years I was feeling my way and I would have been an idiot if I hadn't listened to some very good advice from people who had been around for much longer than I had been. Age simply doesn't come into it. Some of the most senior members not only talk the most sense but they are uninhibited because they are not out to make names for themselves.'

Many questions were asked when Princess Anne took over the top job at the FEI. Would the older members accept direction from someone who in many cases was twenty years younger than themselves? How would she react to the attitudes of an establishment which had been running things in very much their own way for years? What about her reputation for plain speaking? Was she strong enough to take the decisions, some of which were bound to be unpopular, which were needed if the Fédération was to be run along the lines she wanted?

One of the biggest stumbling blocks was the then Secretary General. He was a man of mature years who had been in the job for longer than most of the members could remember, and there was a general feeling that, in spite of the fact that he had done a splendid job in the past, he should go; but nobody was willing to tell him so. In January this year (1989) the Secretary General retired. There was no public announcement of the reason and no one is prepared to confirm or deny that the Princess forced the issue. Whatever happened, the outcome was the right one and to many of the more progressive members of the FEI it was a sign that their new president was prepared to tackle unpleasant tasks and start the move towards forcing the Fédération to make the decisions which would carry it into the twenty-first century. She has started her presidency in outstanding fashion, and it is significant that, despite her reluctance at first to allow her name to go forward as a candidate for the job, once she had decided, she threw herself into it heart and soul. She was elected unanimously; no one else was even considered; and as a former Olympic horsewoman and European Champion with a vast experience of administration through her many other involvements, she has brought a unique character to the office. She is regarded as very much a working president who takes an active part in every major decision, and unlike most of the other organizations with which she is associated as president or patron, she has an executive role. The Bureau, which is the governing body of the FEI, controls the policy of the Fédération, and as Chairman of the Bureau, Her Royal Highness obviously has a great deal of influence with its members.

One of the difficulties of this latest sporting challenge is that the Princess does not have a great deal in common with some of her fellow members of the executive; and being the person she is, she doesn't 'pull her punches'. This applies not only to the foreign delegates but also to some of the British members. One of the newest members of the Fédération is Richard Meade, the current President of the British Equestrian Federation. Meade of course has even more qualifications as a proven horseman than Princess Anne. He is a treble Olympic Gold Medallist and has been described as one of the finest riders ever. He was also an early friend of the Princess; but today their relationship is correct without being cordial, so diplomacy will have to be used on both sides. It's a question of balancing personal relationships with individual egos.

As President of the FEI the Princess is required to attend a large number of events in the role of spectator, which is sometimes irksome for her. As Malcolm Wallace says, 'She is not a great watcher. Having to go and sit for two and half hours through an FEI competition is not her idea of a great time.' She is even more emphatic, 'One of the things which infuriates me is that the FEI seems to arrange most of its events during the school holidays. I don't have all that much time to spend at home with my children so the school holidays are rather special.' As a rider who still competes regularly, the Princess has found her role as president of the FEI restricting in other fields. 'The demands of the job have curtailed my riding activities quite dramatically in a way that no other organization has, because they always want you at the weekend in the competitive season. I don't mind doing the donkey work, but those "public appearances" are not what I am there for.'

In the early months of her presidency there were a few other minor problems, but she quickly spotted them and managed to resolve them in her own way. For example, Malcolm Wallace tells the story of how, at the first general assembly at which she presided, the British delegate, General Jack Reynolds, who was seventy-one at the time, rose from the body of the hall to express an opinion. It was one with which the Princess disagreed and she said so in no uncertain terms. In fact her apparently brusque manner, which was really just her way of showing that she wanted to move the proceedings along, did not meet with the wholehearted approval of some of those present and she sensed almost immediately that she had lost their goodwill.

The following morning the Princess handled the meeting in a different way and soon had the delegates in the palm of her hand. At the conclusion of events, she received a standing ovation; that night she delighted General Reynolds by inviting him to her private suite for a chat over a drink. It was a perfect example of public relations at its best and also of the Princess's finely tuned antennae warning her that she had perhaps gone just a little too far, too soon, and what she must do to regain the initiative. Major Wallace and others claim these are the true facts of the story. However it is only fair to point out that when I spoke to the Princess about it she said their version is wholly inaccurate – she did not elaborate.

One of her greatest assets as president is that she is so practised, as are all the royal family, in being neutral. So she is able to exert her own considerable influence in a way that does not offend either side. As she puts it, 'I have been a professional fence-sitter all my life.' She describes herself as 'the professional neutralist'. But she does have to be careful when she is chairing the policy-making Bureau meetings. The other members are so nationalistic in their outlook that they cannot imagine anyone could act as chairman without leaning towards his or her own countrymen. As it happens there is no other British member of the Bureau, and hasn't been for many years, which is a particular gripe of the United Kingdom; for the rest of the committee believes, wrongly, that if the chairman is British, then naturally he or she looks after the interests of their own country. What they cannot seem to grasp is that Her Royal Highness is 'stateless' in her roles of chairman and president. As she says, 'If they couldn't trust my father to be independent, I've got no chance.' One of her talents which does endear her to many of her colleagues is the ability to speak French. It always pleases those French speakers in the Fédération when she conducts proceedings in their language and answers questions in their mother tongue.

Shortly after taking on the presidency, the Princess said: 'There is so much scope within the disciplines for getting involved and I shall make a point of being there. Meetings are held in different places and there are federations around the world who would like a visit every now and again. In international sport one must make sure that the sport survives the crossfire of national interests. I hope the various new disciplines will receive the same attention as the old established ones.' It was her public declaration that she intends to be a president in every sense of the word – for all those who take part in equestrian sport, not just the fashionable worlds of showjumping and Three Day Eventing which attract the interest of the big names from commerce and show business, but also the smaller and less well known activities which have perhaps in the past felt submerged by their more glamorous colleagues.

All the same it has to be said that the Princess does feel there are too many disciplines within the FEI today, some of which perhaps would be better served by other umbrella organizations. 'Tent-pegging is one,' she says. 'This is a sport that is practised only by the services and the police and they do not have international competitions, which is one of the rules of eligibility for belonging to the FEI, so they would probably be better off joining the Military Sports Association.'

Another problem the president has to get to grips with is finance. The FEI, like every other sports organization in the world, is short of money. In this case it is because as it has grown the amount of cash needed to service the various federations has also grown accordingly. 'At the moment we are finding it difficult to balance the books,' she says. 'The big boys can look after themselves; it's the smaller federations, who have an equal right to our help, who need assistance and that's where the problem comes in.'

The Ben Johnson affair at the last Olympic Games brought sharply into focus the worldwide problem of the use of drugs in sport, but the problem is by no means confined solely to athletics. The Princess's own sport – equestrianism – is involved in a controversy at the present time over the use of phenylbutazone, known as 'Bute'. This medication is widely used in Three Day Eventing to help reduce inflammation of the joints. 'Bute' has been around for years and in 1980 – under the presidency of the Duke of Edinburgh – the FEI decided to allow its limited use. There were two dissenting votes – Sweden and Libya.

The current problem is that the Swedes are due to stage the next World Championships in 1990 and have threatened to withdraw unless there is a total ban, for Sweden already has a law which prohibits the use of 'Bute' in any circumstances. The Princess Royal handled her first major challenge in masterly fashion. A compromise was reached and the championships will go ahead as planned. The way she handled it gave a clear indication of the sort of president she is going to be.

To the outsider most of the major sporting organizations appear to be 'one-man bands'. The International Olympic Committee is one of them. Its President, the Spaniard Juan Antonio Samaranch, has ruled as a benevolent dictator for many years and nothing that he does not agree with is passed by his colleagues. The Princess Royal is an elected member of the IOC but does not hold any office. She attended IOC meetings in Seoul at the time of the Olympic Games when many of the sporting achievements on the field were overshadowed by the drug scandal involving the fastest man in the world, the Canadian sprinter Ben Johnson. He was found guilty of taking drugs before his event and immediately deprived of his gold medal and sent home in disgrace. Did this cast a blight over the Games as a whole? Not in the Princess's opinion. 'I don't think it cast a blight over the Games at all. I may be splendidly naïve but my attitude to doping in sport is clear cut. Cheating is cheating whatever form it takes. But put the Ben Johnson case into perspective. The actual number of positive testings for drugs in Seoul was one less than in Los Angeles four years earlier. Yet there were a much greater number of competitors taking part. So if you look at the overall figures the Seoul Games was very encouraging. It was very embarrassing for the Canadians who have tried hardest to pre-test their teams before going to the Olympics. The trouble was that Ben Johnson was so much a law unto himself that he just wasn't around to be tested and treated like everybody else. I felt very sorry for the Canadian officials. The statistical evidence is encouraging and when you balance up the performances of those athletes who did not test positive, the Seoul Games did not suffer because of the cheating of one man whose event lasted less than ten seconds anyway.' The Princess also feels that perhaps some good might come out of the spotlight being thrown on this particular athlete. 'The whole business was very sad, but hopefully, it will turn out to be a major deterrent. Perhaps other sportsmen who might be tempted to try drugs will now think again. If Ben Johnson can be thrown out – look out the rest of them.'

The Olympic Games are unique and the Princess recognizes the fact as a former competitor. 'There are some athletes who win medals at Olympic level when they would never win regularly at other events. It's all a question of the highest motivation, which only occurs at this emotional level.'

As a comparatively new member of the IOC the Princess Royal is feeling her way gradually. She has not yet spoken out on any major issues, saying, 'I'm perfectly prepared to bite my tongue until I've learned what the system is all about. Then when I've got something to contribute, they will hear from me.' One of the issues she is prepared to be quoted on at the present time is the way the Olympic Games are being expanded in terms of the number of sports and competitors. She has already expressed her dissatisfaction with this aspect of the IOC's policy. 'What frightens me is that the sheer size of the thing is going to destroy it unless they make some drastic decisions about how many athletes they can cope with. If they carry on in the future as they are right now, no city in the world is going to be able to cope with the numbers that are being talked about and the whole organization could disintegrate.' Her fears are shared by others in the IOC but few are prepared to voice their opinion in the face of fierce opposition from the man who is running the show. As the Princess says, 'The whole principle of the Olympics can be summed up in the feeling in the Games Village. That's where all the competitors and officials mix freely and meet each other every day. If the thing gets so big that they cannot all be accommodated in the same place that easy friendship which is a hallmark of every Olympic Games I've been to will disappear, and that makes me very sad.'

The Princess Royal likes most sports and she can ride anything on four legs: horse, camel or elephant; but one of her lesser known sporting activities is one in which she has to play a spectator role. It is greyhound racing. She hasn't been connected with it for very long but with her well known enthusiasm for everything she takes on, it probably won't be too long before she is seen among the cloth-capped crowds of *aficionados*, cheering her latest acquisition past the winning post.

It was in 1988 that the Princess was given a white-nosed greyhound whose racing name is a regal sounding Hardy King but who is known to all and sundry as Butch at the kennels in Compton Green, Gloucestershire where he is kept. The greyhound was a gift to the Princess from an anonymous donor and she accepted it in the name of the Save the Children Fund, which means that every penny Hardy King wins will go to the Fund. Before she would consider accepting the dog though, Princess Anne had to be convinced that greyhound racing was a good and professional sport. It had earned itself something of a bad name for some years because of claims of cruelty in the training methods. However, the Princess was persuaded that the conditions in greyhound racing had improved considerably and that the sport was being run efficiently and fairly, so she agreed to become the first royal owner since Prince Philip was presented with a dog called Camira Flash in 1967.

Hardy King had already won a couple of races before he was given to the Princess Royal, but on his first outing for her, he broke a toe; he still managed to come in third, reflecting his new owner's courage perhaps? If he continues with his winning ways, every time he flashes past the winning post, a child in need will benefit. Similarly, with the racehorse Bobby Kelly, which is owned by the Save and Prosper group, all prize money is donated to the Save the Children Fund.

PRIVATE LIFE

On the evening of Wednesday 21 December 1988 a very special dinner party was held at Gatcombe Park. It was the belated fortieth birthday celebration of Captain Mark Phillips, and his wife had seen to all the arrangements herself, making sure that he knew nothing about them. Jane Holderness-Roddam and a couple of the other ladies-in-waiting who are also friends of the couple helped to plan the event. Some seventy guests, including several from overseas, had been invited to join the Princess in wishing Mark a happy birthday, and Margaret Hammond, his secretary, was allocated the task of looking after the invitations and, even more importantly, ensuring he was kept in the dark. Mark said later, 'I began to suspect something was going on when telephones were suddenly put down if I entered a room, but I had no idea that such a grand affair was being planned. It was brilliant.'

It was also just as well that most of the guests were old friends because there was a bit of a crush as seven circular tables of ten were set up in the dining room. It also made the job of serving the meal slightly difficult for the extra help who had been recruited for the evening. The Georgian silver, a gift from the Queen, was polished and displayed, and when Mark arrived home from a business trip that afternoon, it was the first he knew for sure of the surprise party. The guest of honour made a short speech of thanks in which he said how delighted and surprised he was that so many had come, especially those from abroad. The evening was a tremendous success, with dancing on the flagstones of the hall until the early hours of Sunday morning. The only thing anyone in the village of Minchinhampton saw of the event was the large number of cars arriving on that Wednesday evening. The Princess had managed to keep it a secret and there was not a single leak to the press.

Next morning there was a shooting party at which the Princess was heard to remark, 'My feet haven't recovered from last night' – an indication of the amount of dancing she had done. Caroline Wallace's husband Malcolm said the invitations had been received six weeks earlier, so the planning was executed with typically royal efficiency – and there wasn't a single refusal. For the Princess it had been a triumph. An evening's entertainment, organized by her, on behalf of her husband, which had turned into a night to remember.

The Princess Royal's private life is just that – private. It is the way she wants it, and the way she gets it. Unlike her older brother, the Prince of Wales, and his wife, who appear to accept the publicity that surrounds them even in their private lives, outside her public commitments, the Princess Royal genuinely wants to be left to herself. She would be perfectly happy if there was never a mention in the press of any of her family or friends, or the way she entertains at home. She has been comparatively successful in maintaining her privacy and the only glimpse the public gets of her at home with her friends is when Gatcombe is open for the annual Gatcombe Horse Trials in August. Even then only the park is open; the house is securely guarded against any unwanted visitors by the Gloucester constabulary.

Common gossip, fed by newspaper reports, has it that the Princess Royal surrounds herself only with members of the 'horsey set', excluding anybody else. While there is a certain element of truth in the stories and people like Malcolm Wallace and his wife Caroline, Jane and Timothy Holderness-Roddam and David and Dinah Nicholson do form the nucleus of the circle of close friends who regularly visit Gatcombe or invite the Princess back to their houses, it is not exclusively so. She numbers men and women of many diverse talents among her circle of acquaintances; actors, racing drivers, businessmen, the Dean of Windsor and a sprinkling of old school friends are included in the exclusive group which gathers around the dining table at Gatcombe.

There are not all that many really close friends but quite a few whom Her Royal Highness calls 'good mates', while those whose names crop up in the press as 'close friends of Princess Anne' are usually no more than casual acquaintances with whom she may be only on 'nodding' terms. The genuinely close friends are rarely commented upon because they obey the one unwritten rule that binds them all – no talking. Whatever goes on behind closed doors at Gatcombe – or any of the other places where they meet – is strictly 'off the record', and the penalty for breaking this rule is banishment. There is no reprimand or official 'telling off', simply a drying up of invitations, not only from the Princess, but from all her friends also. No matter what their background, all the Princess Royal's friends have this one thing in common – they are totally discreet. It is an important point and one which allows the Princess to say whatever she likes, secure in the knowledge that it will go no further.

The older group, in terms of the number of years they have known Her Royal Highness, includes Lady Susan Hussey, a woman of the bedchamber to the Queen. In spite of the generation gap between them, she has remained the best of friends with the Princess since the days, more than twenty years ago, when she was 'loaned' by Her Majesty to the young princess before she had ladies-in-waiting of her own. Alison Oliver and her husband Alan, who now live in Oxfordshire, have retained Anne's friendship for the same number of years. They may not see one another as often as they used to but they still regard their friendship as one of the closest and longest standing relationships. The Marquis of Lothian's daughter Lady Cecil Cameron, who is a godmother to Zara, has known the Princess Royal since childhood, and today she and her husband are to be found on the guest list at many of the dinners given at Gatcombe.

Jackie Stewart's friendship with the Princess goes back to 1971, when they were both chosen as Sports Personalities of the year. Their friendship has blossomed to include both spouses and their respective families, and the Princess and her children enjoy the hospitality of the Stewarts at their charming home in Switzerland almost every summer. 'We don't make any special arrangements for them,' says Stewart. 'They always occupy the same guest accommodation and the only people who know they are coming are my secretary and the Palace.'

Jackie Stewart, the son of a Scottish garage owner who, on his own admission, did not have much of an education (he is slightly dyslexic) was the most successful racing driver Britain ever produced, winning twenty-nine Grand Prix races in his career. These days he is a multi-millionaire businessman with worldwide commitments. The secret of his success with the Princess Royal is that he has never tried to be anything other than himself. He knows he does not come from the landed gentry and it doesn't bother him in the least. His accent may not be the same as most of those who are usually in the company of the Princess, but that doesn't bother him either. He is what he is: a self-made man who can hold his head high in any company. The Princess admires excellence above almost anything else, and the fact that the Stewarts have been house guests at Gatcombe more often than any other couple speaks for itself. He is also a near Olympic standard rifle shot and enjoys a day's shooting at Gatcombe as much as any of the huntin' and shootin' set who were born to it. When Helen Stewart was chosen to be a godmother to Zara in 1981, she described the choice as 'a delightful surprise and an honour'.

Lieutenant Colonel Andrew Parker Bowles is Commanding Officer of the Household Cavalry. In his youth he was one of Princess Anne's escorts and he is also a fearless rider having completed the Grand National twice. He remains on good terms with Her Royal Highness, as does his wife Camilla, and at their home at Bolehyde Manor, some twenty miles from Gatcombe, they often act as hosts to the Phillipses.

Michael Tucker farms nearby and, with his wife, is another old friend who occasionally volunteers to put up a couple of Princess Anne's guests for the night when there's an overflow at Gatcombe. These friends make up a close-knit circle with its own status. The Princess does not care if they are famous or not, as long as they are loyal and unpretentious.

The Phillipses never did a great deal of entertaining at home; for the past ten years Mark has probably spent three months of the year abroad, either giving riding lessons, attending seminars where his presence commands high appearance fees, making television commercials (only in Australia and New Zealand, never in Britain) or attending to his many other business affairs throughout the world. He is said to earn over four hundred thousand pounds a year, but as twenty-five per cent of everything he makes goes to his agent Mark McCormack (or at least to McCormack's management company) he still needs to keep working constantly to support his lifestyle and that of his family, and to pay his share of the bills at Gatcombe Park.

The Princess Royal's programme is even more extensive, with two or three overseas tours every year and engagements almost every other day throughout the British Isles. So the time left for entertaining at home is strictly limited.

The Princess enjoys giving dinner parties which are fairly small and intimate affairs. As we have seen, the dining room is large enough to cope with up to seventy guests, but the usual number who sit down to eat is more likely to be between ten and fourteen. That's a comfortable number which enables conversation around the dining table to be enjoyed by everyone present.

An evening at Gatcombe is lively and relaxed, and while the talk may concentrate on horses to a certain extent, it can and often does veer widely from subject to subject. Films, television, sex are all discussed with great vigour, and no one has to wait for the Princess to speak to them first. The only subject that is taboo is the royal family itself. There is an unwritten rule that nobody ever mentions any member of the family unless the Princess does so, and that is unlikely. The Queen is always referred to as the Queen and never 'my mother' and similarly the Prince of Wales receives the full treatment rather than 'my brother'. When the Princess refers to her husband in conversation with outsiders, it has always been as 'the Captain', and rarely 'Mark' or even 'my husband'. Mark has been equally careful to refer to his wife as 'the Princess'. The couple have never shown a great deal of affection in front of others; with no 'darling' or 'dear' in their remarks to each other, un-like the Waleses and Yorks, whose conversations are peppered with such endearments. The guests of the Princess all call her Ma'am. Jackie Stewart made the mistake in the early days of their friendship of calling her by her Christian name. Nobody told him not to, but he soon got the message in the company of others who had been around a little longer. Today it is Ma'am at all times.

At Gatcombe informality is the order of the house. Guests who are invited for the weekend are advised, 'We aren't formal, just throw in a pair of jeans and a black tie.' Peter Gibbs says the Princess is a brilliant hostess: 'Nothing is too much trouble and she goes to endless lengths to see that everyone is comfortable, adding little personal touches which perhaps one would not ordinarily expect from a member of the royal family.'

The rules governing friendship with a member of the royal family are complex and difficult to understand, because they are implied rather than written on tablets of stone. With the Queen and the Duke of Edinburgh it is easy. There is never the slightest risk of overstepping the boundaries between friendliness and familiarity and one is never left in any doubt about how to address them. With the younger members it's a little more of a grey area. Prince Edward likes to be considered 'one of the boys', especially by those he works with in the theatre. The Duke and Duchess of York are equally informal, so much so that the Duchess has had to be reminded several times to remember who she is. She is such a gregarious and outgoing person that her natural friendliness and exuberance occasionally make her forget her position.

The Princess Royal is never anything other than royal. She was brought up in the most privileged of positions, surrounded by centuries of royal tradition, and it would be understandable if she had turned out to be the most conventional of them all. In terms of the royal family and the monarchy she is in fact a rigid traditionalist, seeing no reason for change for change's sake. It is in her outside life that her attitudes show how different she is from the rest of the family. She travels on scheduled train services between Gloucestershire and London, buying a ticket in exactly the same way as everyone else. Her policeman informs British Rail the night before so she is sure of a seat. She is met at Paddington station by a car from the Royal Mews, but it is not one of the Rolls–Royce limousines and is much more likely to be a Ford or Vauxhall estate car.

Similarly when she takes the children skiing she buys a package holiday and invariably travels on a scheduled flight without any of the privileges usually associated with royalty. In Switzerland or

France they stay in hotels, rather than private villas surrounded by security guards, as is the case when the Prince and Princess of Wales take their annual skiing holiday. Many motorists in Britain have been surprised to see a large horse-box overtake them on the motorway, driven by a slim young woman wearing an anorak and a peaked cap who turns out to be the Queen's only daughter. The number plate on the vehicle used to give a clue to the identity of the owner: 1 ANN. It has now been changed for security reasons and the vehicle is no different from any other on the road.

The Princess Royal's way of relaxing is to have something physical to do. Even on the long arduous overseas tours, she hates a day off, with nothing planned. Peter Gibbs says that on their recent visit to New Zealand there was one blank morning. The Princess asked him what they were going to do with it. His idea was to put his feet up and do nothing. She was appalled. 'I'm going sailing,' she said, and that's what she did all morning long. She has a low threshold of boredom and needs the constant stimulation of physical activity.

In the little free time she does get at home she involves the rest of the family in her sporting pursuits. Peter and Zara are growing up well used to life in the saddle, and their mother and father are delighted with their progress. They won't push them too quickly, but if either of them shows any promise they will get every support when they start to take part in competitions.

In her choice of friends the Princess is careful at first but loyal to a degree once the relationship has been established. She likes people to drop by unexpectedly, explaining, 'It's easier for them to know when I'm here than the other way around. They know they are welcome, and I like people to ring up or simply drop in if they are in the vicinity.'

Someone who 'drops in' more often than one might imagine is the Queen herself. She is her daughter's closest friend, her most loyal ally and trusted confidante. They talk frequently on the telephone and Her Majesty loves driving to Gatcombe to see the Princess and the two children. Peter of course, being the first grandchild, occupies a very special place in his grandmother's affections, but the relationship between mother and daughter is one which has not often been highlighted in the millions of words which have been written about the Queen and her family. It is an extraordinarily close relationship based on mutual love and trust. There is nothing the Queen could ask the Princess which she would not do willingly and the same would apply if it were the Princess who was seeking the favour.

Mother and daughter share many qualities; they are both compassionate and totally committed to duty. The Queen sees her position as a sacred trust. The Princess Royal accepts her role in the royal family as something she did not seek but which she would never dream of giving up. 'Opting out is not an option,' in her view. They are both countrywomen at heart, sharing a love of horses, dogs and nature. Ask each of them what their favourite holiday would be and the answers would be identical – two weeks at Balmoral. They also have an uncanny resemblance in other ways. Neither is a good sailor and both prefer the cold weather to the heat. Hours spent in the wind and rain do not bother them a bit and the thought of lying on a beach for an afternoon fills them with horror.

I once asked the Princess Royal if it was difficult for her to maintain a close relationship with her mother, bearing in mind the fact that her mother was also her sovereign? She didn't hesitate in her reply. 'I think you've got the question the wrong way round. It's much more difficult to remember that she is Queen than a mother. After all, I've known her longer as a mother than as a Queen, if you see what I mean. She has been Queen most of my life, but that's not how I think of her – it's the other way round really.'

The Princess has often been described as 'her father's daughter' because of their outspoken views and their shared distrust of the press. She has, however, inherited many of the Queen's best qualities including courage and determination. When the Princess survived the kidnap attempt in 1974 it was partly because she was able to keep her head and not panic; exactly the characteristics the Queen displayed in 1982, when an intruder got into her bedroom at Buckingham Palace and sat on her bed for some time before help arrived. In both cases there could have been tragic results if the ladies had not been calm and fast-thinking. Since the incident involving the Queen, her daughter has been even closer than before.

Obviously theirs were experiences shared by two women which could not be fully understood by any man.

When the Queen visits Gatcombe to see her daughter and grandchildren she always telephones in advance. Dropping in in royal terms does not mean that literally. There's no question of Her Majesty turning up on the doorstep unannounced for a friendly cup of tea. If she did she would be welcome of course at any time; it just doesn't work that way in the royal family, and the Queen's exquisite manners apply just as much to her own family as to strangers.

Almost since the year they were married, rumours have circulated on a fairly frequent, if irregular basis about the state of Anne and Mark's marriage. They were impossible to ignore because newspapers and magazines printed thousands of words on the subject week after week. The stories become monotonous because of their regularity, and invariably the quotes came from, 'a source close to the couple' – anonymous every time. First of all it was Mark who was apparently being seen in the company of an attractive woman – sometimes a different one three times in a week. If he attended a party without the Princess, it set off a storm of speculation, both at home and even more so abroad.

The most serious allegation concerned the former television newsreader Angela Rippon. She and Mark spent some time together during the period when Princess Anne was expecting Zara. The papers had a field day. The television star and the royal horseman. It was a natural for the headline writers. Photographs of them walking together at Badminton appeared in the national press and gossip columnists vied with one another to produce the most lurid tales.

The true story was a little more mundane. Miss Rippon employs the same management company as Mark – IMG – and one of their executives had the bright idea of bringing the two personalities together to produce a book. It was called *Mark Phillips – The Man and his Horses* and was written by Angela Rippon with cooperation from Mark. Much of the book concentrated on the technical side of Mark's riding career and looked in some detail at the various courses up and down the country. They were seen together walking the courses and the press put two and two together and made five.

It cannot have been very pleasant for the Princess, in the latter stages of her pregnancy, to read stories of her husband's alleged affair every day. When the book was published it received a great deal of publicity and was an immediate commercial success. Miss Rippon, with no reason to remain, disappeared from the scene and the reporters looked for new victims. The publicity did her career no harm whatsoever and probably accounted for much of the book's early success.

The Princess too has come in for her share of unwelcome attention from the gossip writers and rumour mongers. She and Mark have been friends for some years with the actor Anthony Andrews and his wife Georgina. Andrews is a handsome leading man who plays romantic roles in films and on television. He receives a lot of fan mail, most of it from women, and his name features frequently in the social columns of the tabloid newspapers. Being an actor means all publicity is good publicity and any association with the Princess Royal is always good for a mention. Andrews also enjoys shooting and riding and his wife is a particularly competent horsewoman, so they both have a lot in common with the Princess and Mark. And it is this last fact, the friendship with Mark, that is rarely commented upon. Neither is the fact that it was Georgina Andrews who knew the Princess and introduced her husband in the first place. The truth is that all four have enjoyed each other's company, and there is not, nor ever has been, any romantic entanglement between Anthony Andrews and the Princess Royal. Georgina Andrews has even arranged fund-raising cocktail parties at her family's department store in Piccadilly on behalf of the Royal Yachting Association, another of the Princess Royal's organizations, at which both King Olaf of Norway and King Constantine of The Hellenes have been present. They have all ignored the press stories but inevitably it has caused a certain amount of embarrassment, and it is to their credit that they have not allowed the rumours to spoil their friendship. The Princess admires loyalty above almost every other quality in her friends – and she returns it in full.

One of the most recent and by far the most unpleasant stories concerning the Princess Royal's private life came to light in April 1989. The *Sun* newspaper revealed that it had been given four letters written to the Princess. They were of a highly personal nature and the newspaper had informed the police immediately without publishing the details. An immediate high level investigation was ordered and every newspaper in Britain, and many abroad, carried the story. The fact that the contents of the letters had not been revealed added to the speculation about who had written them and what they contained. A few days later Buckingham Palace press office took the unusual step of issuing a statement which named the writer as Commander Timothy Laurence, Equerry-in-Waiting to the Queen. The letters were apparently of a friendly nature and written in familiar terms, but as no one in the Household had seen them, it was impossible to confirm or deny that they were any more than that. They had been stolen from the Princess's private office at Buckingham Palace and the investigation concentrated on those members of staff with easy access.

The story made headlines all over the world for nearly a week, coming as it did a few days after an Indian parliamentary research assistant claimed that she had had a relationship with Mark Phillips. The real truth of that story was quickly established when it was revealed that in fact this lady had paid to join one of his equestrian courses at Gleneagles in Scotland and she was one of thirty or so people in the group. So her claims about intimate private dinner parties for two were quickly dismissed. She also said she had stayed with the Princess and Mark at Gatcombe, when in fact she had enjoyed the hospitality of one of Mark's assistants in a cottage in the grounds – at a time when neither the Princess nor her husband were at home. But it all added to the Anne and Mark story.

The Princess carried on with her public duties in spite of the press reports about the breakup of her marriage, and her dignified manner in the days during and immediately following the Palace press statement, brought her tremendous support and sympathy from people from all walks of life.

In one newspaper poll conducted that week, she emerged as the most popular person in the royal family. Eventually those stories died down and the Princess continued to lead the sort of life she has led for the past sixteen years, as an independent woman who does her own thing, whether it is in her private life or one of her many public roles.

One of the most common questions posed by the press about Anne and Mark is, 'What did they have in common to make their marriage last sixteen years?' In the first place, of course, they shared a passion for horses which in the early years occupied so much of their time together. They also had a similar sense of humour, and the ability to laugh at the same things often saved awkward situations. But Mark has remained firmly immersed only in the equestrian world while the Princess has blossomed into a wide variety of different roles which have placed her on a different level altogether. And no matter what their differences are they have a lot of mutual respect: he regards her as a true princess in every sense, loyal, hard-working and regal, while she, in turn, admires the way he has refused to accept being a member of the royal family as an excuse to cash in on her position. He insists on earning his own living and realizes that his fame as a rider will not last forever, hence his long absences from home. As he says, 'I've got to do it while people still want me. The working life of a sportsman is short enough as it is.' The Princess spends more time with her children than their father does. Her nights away from Gatcombe are comparatively few. When she is involved in engagements in Britain she usually manages to get home, however late it is. Mark, however, needs to travel extensively with his varied business interests, frequently being absent from the estate for weeks at a time.

When Mark's mother died in 1988 he was devastated. The person he turned to for comfort was his wife, and she shared his grief, fully understanding what the loss meant to him. If there had been any coolness between them at the time, it could not have happened. Mark still misses his mother tremendously; she was his strongest supporter in every one of his enterprises. His wife helped to fill the gap and in her own undemonstrative manner quietly but firmly helped to heal the wounds he suffered at his mother's sudden death.

The Princess Royal has been fortunate in her friendships. None has so far let her down, probably because she is so selective in the first place. It takes a long time to be fully accepted by her; she is by nature suspicious and she has been brought up to be wary of making casual relationships. Even when she was at school she was slightly apart from her fellow pupils. They didn't know how to treat her at first and she had no experience of life outside the Palace.

When she learned to trust people and accept them for what they are, she became the most loyal of companions. Loyalty to her is all important and it has to work both ways. She gives it completely – if eventually – and expects it totally in return. This feeling of loyalty has been learned, as has everything else she knows, through her relationships with the other members of her own family. This is where she, and all the others, draw their strength. Throughout the year their paths do not cross all that much in the normal course of events, but they are all aware that in a crisis they can always call on one another. When Prince Edward made his controversial decision to leave the Royal Marines, contrary to what many newspapers reported at the time, the royal family was very supportive. If they were disappointed at his sudden withdrawal from service life, they gave no outward sign, and even privately there was little criticism in what was a most delicate period for the whole family, each of whom has strong associations with the armed forces. They accepted it as his decision – and his alone.

If the Princess needed advice and help she would ask someone in the family – never an outsider. Friends are all very well as friends, but when you are royal, the only people you can really trust are other royals – in other words, your own family.

CHAPTER
NINE

♦

ANNE: THE PRINCESS ROYAL

When the Queen created her only daughter The Princess Royal on 13 June 1987, she not only elevated Princess Anne to a unique and historically significant role within the royal family, she also bestowed on her the rarest of all royal titles.

Princess Anne is only the seventh person to bear the title Princess Royal in the three and a half centuries since King Charles I decided to make his daughter Mary the first Princess Royal in 1642. Since then the title has only been conferred on the eldest daughter of a sovereign, but the honour is by no means automatic. While every first born male child of the sovereign has succeeded to the title Prince of Wales (Prince Charles is the 21st while his wife is the 9th Princess of Wales), the title of Princess Royal has not been bestowed on eldest daughters in the same way.

The last Princess Royal was Princess Mary, Countess of Harewood, the only daughter of George V. She became Princess Royal in 1932 and held the title until her death in 1965. Of all the ladies who held the title, Princess Mary is acknowledged as the one who enhanced its dignity and style more than any of the others. She was a tireless worker for the causes she supported and a tremendous enthusiast in all the organizations, official bodies and military units with which she became associated throughout her life.

There are a number of remarkable parallels between the lives of Princess Mary and Princess Anne. The physical resemblance is there for all to see; just look at early photographs of Princess Mary and compare them with Princess Anne at the present time; the likeness is uncanny. But there are also other similarities. Princess Mary was the 'tomboy' of her family, much tougher and rougher in her play than any of her brothers when they were children. So too was Princess Anne. The stories about her taking the lead in all the games with Prince Charles when they were young, and how she used to be first up on their joint pony while he preferred the quieter pastimes, are all true. Princess Mary was a better rider than her brothers; Princess Anne's record speaks for itself. Princess Mary didn't mind in the least taking the messiest jobs in the operating theatre when she was a nursing probationer; similarly, Princess Anne has never flinched from the disease and dirt of the refugee camps of Ethiopia and the Sudan when she visits them as President of the Save the Children Fund. When Princess Mary's brother David abdicated as Edward VIII because of Mrs Simpson he was ostracized by his family – with the exception of Princess Mary, who kept in touch when he went to live in exile. Since Princess Margaret's divorce from Lord Snowdon, her niece Princess Anne has remained one of her staunchest supporters. As we have seen, the last Princess Royal was Colonel-in-Chief of the Royal Scots for more than fifty years, and when she died, the regiment declined to have anyone else as their titular head until the person they regarded as 'the rightful successor' should become available. Eighteen years later Princess Anne was appointed their Colonel-in-Chief. The Royal Scots knew it was only a matter of time before the Princess would receive the title they believed was rightfully hers.

The style of Princess Royal carries with it no other benefits. Unlike the Prince of Wales, Princess Anne does not inherit great estates or a large fortune with the title. Also there is no tradition within the royal family of any form of ceremonial investiture such as those accorded to Prince Charles at Caernarvon in 1969 or Prince Edward in 1911. Similarly, the Princess Royal is not required to make any solemn vows before the sovereign. In fact, apart from publication in the Honours List, there is no official presentation, simply a Royal Warrant. The only record of the creation of the last Princess Royal is the announcement by King George V in the New Year's Honours List of 1932.

Nevertheless it is still the highest honour that can be awarded to a female in the royal family, and the fact that Princess Anne accepted the title when her mother offered it has brought great happiness to all the other members of the family. The Duke of Edinburgh in particular had been anxious for his daughter's work to receive some sort of public recognition. She acts as a Counsellor of State whenever the Queen is out of the country for more than a few days and altogether Her Royal Highness is associated with nearly a hundred organizations both civil and military.

The Queen first raised the subject of making her daughter Princess Royal shortly before Princess Anne's thirty-sixth birthday in August 1986, but it was nearly a year later that the official announcement was made, on Her Majesty's Official Birthday in June 1987. So for all that time it was the best kept secret in Buckingham Palace, with only a handful of people – all very close to the Queen or the Princess – in the know.

There is often a lot of speculation in the press about the leaks which spring from the Royal Household. This particular incident showed that, when they want to, the royal family and their staff are able to remain as tight-lipped as the Kremlin.

Of course there had been a tremendous amount of good-natured lobbying by a number of Princess Anne's organizations and regiments, who had never hidden their wish for her to be made Princess Royal. When the announcement finally came they were all overjoyed, and secretly, although I have no evidence to support this theory, I believe Her Royal Highness was equally pleased. She had known for some years that there had been a move to have her created Princess Royal but her own well-documented attitude to titles had been made public many years earlier. Princess Anne once talked to me briefly on the subject, which was clearly an embarrassment to her at the time. I asked her if she had thought about being Princess Royal, and her reply was: 'All I know is that it is in the gift of the Queen. It is entirely a matter for her and apart from the fact that it is the sovereign's gift I know little about the precedents. The subject is nothing to do with me.'

In fact the whole subject of titles is one which the Princess herself cares very little about. She has never needed any extra honours to increase her status and she still does not think it necessary for her children to become 'Lord' or 'Lady' or even to have the prefix 'Hon.'

before their names. But Her Royal Highness's colleagues at the Save the Children Fund and the Riding for the Disabled Association are delighted at the honour the Queen has bestowed on their President. To them it's a long overdue and much deserved award. Similarly, the Princess's nine regiments – in Britain, Canada, Australia and New Zealand – all feel they too have a share in this unique sign of recognition.

But for thirty-six years she was known simply as Princess Anne, and the fact that she has now become The Princess Royal is unlikely to change this in the eyes of the general public. What the title has done is give Her Royal Highness a unique position within the royal family. There was just a slight possibility that she might become overshadowed by her glamorous sisters-in-law with their distinctive titles of Princess of Wales and Duchess of York. Although in reality Princess Anne is more than capable of holding her own with any of the other ladies in the royal family, the Queen, with a masterly stroke of royal diplomacy, ended any possible conflict by elevating her daughter to the one position which guarantees her continued prominence. It's a bit like a politician becoming Speaker of the House of Commons; it takes him out of the market place of common or garden politics and places him above the everyday competition for office which is the lifeblood of Britain's parliamentary system.

The title of Princess Royal also means that, apart from the Queen herself, Princess Anne is the only female member of the immediate royal family who does not have to rely on her husband's position for her title. When Prince Charles becomes King his wife will naturally become his Queen Consort; if the Duke of York ever changes his title, his wife will automatically do so as well. The Princess Royal is Princess Royal for life. It is possible for the Queen to take away the title if she wishes, but no British monarch has ever done so in the past and there is no reason to suppose that this should happen in this reign. Even when the Queen dies, the title of Princess Royal will continue to be held by Princess Anne. Her late great-aunt Princess Mary had been Princess Royal for only four years when her father King George V died in 1936; however, she held the title through three more reigns until her own death in 1965.

Princess Anne was almost thirty-seven when she became Princess Royal and some people thought that she had not been given the title earlier because she was considered to be too young. In point of fact the myth that all Princesses Royal have to be of mature age is just that – a myth. The first Princess Royal, Princess Mary, was just eleven years old when her father King Charles I created the title in her honour. And in 1840, Queen Victoria, who made her own rules anyway, dictated that her daughter Victoria should be known as The Princess Royal when she was less than eight weeks old.

Over many years in the past three and a half centuries there has been no Princess Royal. The first died in 1660, the year of the restoration of the monarchy in England, and the second, another Princess Anne, a daughter of King George II, did not become Princess Royal until his accession to the throne in 1727 when she was seventeen – a gap of nearly seventy years. The lady who held the title for longer than any of the others was Princess Victoria. Even though she later became Empress of Prussia, she continued to hold the title Princess Royal until her death in August 1901, more than sixty years in all.

Although there has never been a specific role for the Princess Royal – there still isn't a 'job description' as such – the early recipients of the title enjoyed a lifestyle far more luxurious than that of the present holder of the title. The first Princess Mary, at the age of eleven, was given a Household consisting of: A lady-in-waiting, a gentleman usher, a nurse, a governess, two pages, four footmen, five kitchen servants, a coachman, a groom, a seamstress and a laundress. She also had an income of £11,500 a year (about £10 million at today's rate). Princess Mary was married off at the tender age of nine to Prince William of Orange, who was five years older, and it was from the moment that she entered the Court of the House of Orange that she became known as 'Princesse Royale'. It was her father-in-law, Henry Frederick of Orange, who first addressed her as such. Prior to this moment, all princesses of the Royal House of Orange had been known simply as 'Highness' without the 'Royal' prefix. So what started as an affectionate, and perhaps snobbish courtesy, became a reality when Charles I formally conferred the title and all its style and dignity on his daughter in 1642.

Princess Mary died in London on Christmas Eve 1660 in the first year of the reign of her brother King Charles II. She was buried at Westminster Abbey, whose records for 29 December 1660 show that on this day took place 'the burial of The Princess Royal Mary, the King's eldest sister, mother to the Prince of Orange'. She was twenty-nine years old.

The second Princess Royal, Princess Anne, was allotted some £80,000 a year as living expenses from what was then, in the eighteenth century, the equivalent of the Civil List. As the salaries of her Household never totalled more than a thousand pounds a year, of which the largest single payment of two hundred pounds went to her music master, Handel, she was never short of money to indulge her interests. But her only extravagance was horses. She was a passionate and expert rider who liked to hunt as often as she could. It was claimed that she used hunting as an emotional 'safety valve' with a complete disregard for her own personal comfort. There were many times when she returned to the Palace with her face covered in scratches and bruises from the vigorous manner in which she pursued her sport. She did not care about her own appearance – or very much else for that matter. She certainly gave no indication of a social conscience in the way the present Princess Royal does today. In fact the only recorded incident of her charity occurred in 1737. She heard that Handel had been taken ill and it was Princess Anne who paid for him to travel to France to recuperate.

Theirs was a close relationship which became both personal and professional, and long after Handel had ceased to function as a private tutor, they continued to correspond. The Princess Royal and Handel died within three months of each other in 1759.

The third Princess Royal, Charlotte Augusta Matilda, was the fourth of thirteen children born to King George III and Queen Charlotte. She was born on 24 September 1766, the first royal princess to be born in Buckingham Palace, though in those days it was still known as Buckingham House. A month later she was christened as 'HRH The Princess Royal' but Princess Charlotte was twenty-two years old when the title was officially conferred on her by her father. The date was 22 June 1789 and the matter was decided because the King, realizing that she was no different in rank from any of her five sisters, resolved to single her out. Of course George

III suffered from mental illness for much of his life, but this was during one of the periods when he was temporarily recovered.

This Princess Royal acted as an unpaid private secretary to her mother Queen Charlotte for many years and it was not until she was thirty that she married. Her husband was Prince Frederick William of Württemberg, and they met for the first time just two weeks before the wedding in the Chapel Royal at Windsor. They then left for her new home and Princess Charlotte never saw her parents again. By the time she returned to England, for a visit in 1827, her brother William IV was on the throne; and when she died a year later, at the age of sixty-three, she was known as The Princess Royal Charlotte, Queen of Württemberg.

The fourth Princess Royal was born on 21 November 1840. Victoria Adelaide Mary Louise was the first child of Queen Victoria and Prince Albert, and it was her doting father who insisted on her being known as The Princess Royal. The Royal Warrant was issued on 19 January 1841 stating that henceforth she would be known 'by the style and title of Her Royal Highness The Princess Royal'.

She was married when she was seventeen, to Prince Frederick William of Prussia, heir to the Emperor. The marriage was seen as an alliance between two great dynasties, but fortunately for both participants, they found they liked each other on sight and grew to love each other greatly. Their home was in Berlin and Victoria gave birth to eight children, the youngest of whom, Princess Margaret of Hesse, survived two world wars before she died in 1954. It was only when it was realized that with Frederick's succession as Emperor, his wife would be Empress of Prussia, that steps were taken in England to create Queen Victoria Empress of India. It would have been unthinkable for the grandmother of Europe to have a title inferior to that held by her own daughter.

In fact Princess Victoria did not become Empress of Prussia until 1888 and then held the title for less than three months as her husband died shortly after succeeding to the throne. His widow became Dowager Empress. She outlived her husband by thirteen years, and died in 1901, the same year as her mother. She was sixty and had lived abroad for all her adult life; yet she still regarded herself as English and retained the title of Princess Royal until her death. As Princess Royal for sixty years she is still the one who has held the title for longer than any of the others. Her mother was of course Britain's longest reigning monarch, and her brother, later Edward VII, held the record for being Prince of Wales longer than any other man.

The fifth Princess Royal, and the first this century, was the eldest daughter of King Edward VII and Queen Alexandra. She was born in 1867 and her father succeeded to the throne in 1901. Four years later, on 5 November 1905, it was formally announced in the King's Birthday Honours List that 'His Majesty's eldest daughter Her Royal Highness, Princess Louise Victoria Alexandra Dagmar (Duchess of Fife) shall henceforth bear the style and title of Princess Royal.'

There is no evidence that the title made any significant change to the princess's status or lifestyle. She had never taken a major role in public life and she gave no sign that she intended to do so as Princess Royal. When in 1889 she had married the fabulously wealthy sixth Earl of Fife, who was known as Macduff, Queen Victoria had announced her intention of raising the earldom to a dukedom as she felt that it would not be appropriate for her granddaughter to be a mere countess. The princess could then be recognized as HRH Princess Louise, Duchess of Fife. But this did not actually take place until 1900, when the Earl became the First Duke of Fife. Even so Princess Mary of Teck (later Queen Mary) did not entirely approve of the union, writing: 'For a future Princess Royal to marry a subject seems rather strange.'

However, theirs was a happy marriage which produced two daughters: Princess Alexandra, who was to inherit the title of Duchess of Fife in her own right, and Princess Maud, who married the 11th Earl of Southesk.

The Princess Royal and her husband lived an intensely private life and such was the climate of the day that no one thought for a moment that they had not every right to do so. In the early part of this century the press and the general public were given only the barest details of the activities of the royal family and there was rarely any speculation about their private lives. The Princess Royal was not expected to have a high profile and if her public appearances were infrequent in her younger days, when she became married they were even more so. Apart from the King and Queen themselves, no one in the royal family undertook public duties and the people were content that this situation should remain.

Every winter the Princess Royal and her husband travelled to Egypt to escape the rigours of the British weather. In 1911 they set sail on the liner *Delhi* which ran into a severe storm off the coast of Morocco. The ship ran aground and the passengers were ordered to abandon ship. The Princess Royal refused to leave until all her fellow passengers had been evacuated and even then she and her husband had to stagger through the waves to the shore. This adventure was without doubt the most dramatic event in the Princess's life, and it would turn out to be the most tragic. The couple continued their journey to Egypt but the soaking in the freezing sea caused the Duke to catch pneumonia and within ten days he had died – in January 1912.

His widow became a virtual recluse for the remainder of her life. She survived her husband for nearly twenty years but rarely appeared in public, and most people had forgotten even that there was a Princess Royal when she died in 1931 at the age of sixty-three. By all accounts she was a pleasant woman and a devoted mother to her daughters. But she was of an age that had disappeared after the First World War and she never really cared for the twentieth century.

The sixth person to bear the title The Princess Royal was Princess Mary, Countess of Harewood, the only daughter of King George V and Queen Mary. She was born in 1897 and her full names were Victoria Alexandra Alice Mary. As we have seen she was the 'tomboy' of the family and the constant companion of her two older brothers David, (later King Edward VIII and Duke of Windsor) and Bertie (later King George VI). Mary was a better rider than either of them and she excelled at outdoor sports. She could run faster, jump higher and shoot straighter than her brothers and she enjoyed life to the full. Princess Mary lived through six reigns, Victoria, her great grandmother, Edward VII, George V, Edward VIII, George VI and Elizabeth II. She saw two of her brothers become King; David, the eldest, was Edward VIII, the King who was never crowned, and Bertie, born in 1895, became George VI.

She married Viscount Lascelles, Earl of Harewood, in Westminster Abbey in February 1922 and started a tradition which has been followed by most royal brides ever since: the public display of wedding presents at St James's Palace, with the proceeds going to charity.

Ten years after she was married, her father created her Princess Royal on New Year's Day 1932. The Princess Royal was a woman of extraordinary character. She was enthusiastic and energetic and incapable of snobbery – at a time when a rigid class system ruled in Britain. As with her great-niece, the present Princess Royal, she accomplished a number of royal 'firsts' in her life. She was the first royal princess to receive training as a nurse – in the operating theatre at Great Ormond Street Children's Hospital. She was the first woman in Britain to be appointed Chancellor of a university – hers was Leeds – and in 1948, she became the first woman to register her own racing colours, thereby anticipating both the Queen and Queen Elizabeth the Queen Mother. Her list of patronages and presidencies was among the most extensive in the royal family and she was one of its most active members throughout her life.

Princess Mary was Colonel-in-Chief of the Royal Scots for more than fifty years and bore the title of Princess Royal for the last thirty-three of them. If today the title carries with it an aura of dignity and distinction, it is due almost entirely to Princess Mary. She elevated it far beyond the realms of the courtesy title it had been for so many generations to the unique position it enjoys today within the royal family.

In her comparatively short life, Princess Anne has achieved much. She is respected for her work in international famine relief and childcare, and admired as a progressive, tough and dedicated member of the royal family. She has taken her chances in the world's sporting arenas, with no quarter asked or given, and come out on top. If she, in turn, can bring to the role of Princess Royal as much public affection as did her great-aunt Princess Mary, she will have achieved even more than all her predecessors put together.

♦

CHAPTER TEN

FINALE

As she approaches her fortieth birthday, the Princess Royal has moved up a gear in the pace of her life. She is taking on more and more responsibilities and spreading her interests far and wide. As a member of the International Olympic Committee, the British Olympic Association and the Fédération Équestre Internationale she has entered the administrative side of the competitive world of international sport at its highest level, with all the complex political problems that can involve. It is a world of big business, wheeler-dealing and image building where the glittering prizes for the winners sometimes mean they will use almost any method to get to the top.

An Olympic gold medal can lead to untold riches for an athlete, yet the difference between winning and being an also-ran can be less than one hundredth of a second; the ingredient that can make that difference could be a prohibited substance – drugs are a part of everyday life in most sports today, from football, swimming and wrestling to track and field events. The Princess knows that if she is to have any effect on the policies of the governing bodies she has joined, she must speak out on these issues, and it is not something from which she shrinks. 'My own position on drugs in sport is well known,' she says. 'Anybody who knowingly uses a drug to increase his or her performance, whether it involves taking it himself or giving it to a horse, is cheating. Wherever we find a sportsman taking drugs we must take the strongest action. If an

Olympic Gold Medallist like Ben Johnson can be suspended, it might deter others from doing the same thing.'

The Princess has brought to her organizations, sporting and others, the very characteristics that irritate some people, but which make her such an effective worker for the causes she espouses. She is tough, unwilling to take no for an answer – but never knowingly uses her position to get results. Other people sometimes use whatever influence they have for personal gain – in her case, she does it on behalf of others. Though it is clear from the amount of work she does for the Save the Children Fund, some sort of international recognition cannot be too far away. The year 1990 will see her celebrating 20 years as head of the fund – a Nobel Peace prize perhaps?

Facing up to her can be a disconcerting experience. She never backs down – and she does like to have the last word in any argument. Some people say it is a weakness on her part – that she refuses to see the other person's point of view. She sees it differently, believing passionately in what she does, and that it is her duty to speak out for what she believes in. She also claims to see too many points of view.

As far as her own public image is concerned she professes not to care, saying, 'It's too late now to do anything about it.' But she is honest enough to admit that 'It is pleasant when I see something nice written.' Her attitude to the media has changed considerably in the last ten years. Then she seemed to go out of her way to be uncooperative; today she gets on well with most reporters and cameramen even if she still refuses to do anything she suspects might be 'a stunt'.

When she appeared on television with Terry Wogan and Michael Parkinson she was relaxed, friendly – and looking at her best. Neither of these shows is an interview show as such – merely vehicles for their star presenters – but she managed to outshine her host on both occasions. The Princess told me she enjoyed appearing with them both, 'But I wish Parkinson would get away from his prepared script.' Wogan on the other hand used his Irish charm and natural wit to insert some shrewd questions into what appeared to be at first the usual innocuous and banal chat-show. Her Royal Highness said she had met Wogan a number of times before the television programme 'and I found him easy to get on with. That's why, when he invited me to appear on his show, I agreed.'

The most recent major television programme the Princess took part in was the 'Walden Interview' on Independent Television. Brian Walden is an experienced interviewer whose normal victims are equally experienced politicians and his programmes are usually perfect examples of serious 'talk-show' television. On this occasion, however, he appeared to fall under the spell of royalty and what could and should have been an enlightening programme turned out, disappointingly, to be no more than just another 'royal' interview. It was a wasted opportunity for which there could be no excuses. Walden's research team had spent weeks assembling material for their star, working with the Princess's private secretary and the Save the Children Fund, and she had expected the cut and thrust of a stimulating discussion between two well-informed individuals. When the recording of the interview was made it soon became obvious to the Princess that her interviewer wasn't going to be as tough as she expected. The result was that she appeared to be very much in control of the interview, which she was, but nothing very new emerged.

In her meetings with other public figures the Princess displays competence as well as confidence. She has always had the apparent confidence that comes with being born royal – as opposed to marrying into royalty – but the competence is something she has acquired over the years, as she has learned more and more about the business of her job. If you met her at a party you would hear no small talk; what you would get is a serious but entertaining discussion of subjects that interest and concern her. It would not be all Save the Children and the problems of the Third World, neither would it be all about horses – unless it was that sort of party. She will talk on almost any subject under the sun, but usually with the objective of getting her views across or learning something from whoever she is talking to. Her conversation does not normally include domestic problems like home decorating, children's feeding habits or aimless chit-chat about last night's television programmes. Which is perhaps why she is not an avid party-goer in the first place.

The Princess rarely shows any emotion in public, even annoyance. She does get irritated at times, usually because some small detail has not been planned on one of her engagements. Peter Gibbs says that when he goes on a 'recce' trip overseas, he always makes sure what footwear the Princess is going to need on every segment of the tour. This is because he was occasionally caught out in the early days by not paying enough attention to the sort of shoes that would be suitable. Whereas a man would probably not bother to change out of whatever he was wearing throughout the day wherever he was walking, for a woman it is important to know if 'high heels are all right in a muddy field or should one change into flat shoes or desert boots?' Her Private Secretary feels that this sort of minor irritation, which is peculiarly feminine, illustrates the sort of thing that annoys her. Her own attention to detail is legendary in Palace circles. She pays particular attention to the personalities of each of her staff – and each Christmas chooses their presents with special care. Sometimes it can be a gift with a humorous tag, such as a fun hat which carries the legend 'He thinks he's the boss.' The Princess likes to think of herself as being mean with money, and it is true that she does not throw her money around. But her staff say that meanness is an exaggeration – careful is the word they prefer.

If the Princess were interested in money for herself she could easily make a fortune by cashing in on her name. Her husband's agents have said that in terms of sheer exploitation she could make a million pounds a year with ease. It will never happen of course. The Princess Royal jealously guards against any possible commercial exploitation of her position; she even occasionally questions those organizations which use her to raise funds for charitable causes, and she is not entirely happy being associated with functions which are sold only on the basis of her name. There is always the danger of being considered to be in the 'Rent-a-Royal' business – and clearly she is not!

The Princess Royal receives £140,000 a year from the Civil List but she is insistent that it is not her pay and not a penny goes to her personally. The entire amount is used to pay the salaries of her staff and the expenses of running her office and organizing her public engagements. The £5,000 increase in her allowance this year (1989) was the lowest of any member of the royal family, apart from Prince Edward, who got no increase at all. And it meant a modest rise in pay for the people who work for her which was

actually less than the annual rate of inflation. There had been a
small amount of adverse publicity when she was said to have bought
a Bentley Turbo R motor car earlier this year. At nearly £100,000
it is one of the most expensive models in the world, and one
newspaper report asked the question: 'How can she justify spending
this sort of public money?' The truth is, she hasn't spent it at all.
The car was obtained on a three-year lease; it is going to be used
only as an official vehicle and it will also be a marvellous show-case
for the British motor industry. It is not a luxurious plaything for a
spendthrift princess with more money than sense. Her own private
car will remain a Reliant Scimitar, or Middlebridge as it is called
since the firm was taken over, of the same model she has been
driving for nearly twenty years.

The number of invitations the Princess receives has increased
five-fold in the last couple of years. Peter Gibbs feels this is partly
because of her television and radio appearances: 'People are at last
realizing that she is good-humoured and a warm personality and
not the ogre the press has made her out to be for so long.'

The fact that she carries out so many royal duties does not make
her universally popular with all her relations. There are occasional
grumbles from other Households that the Princess Royal is using
the Queen's Flight too frequently or that she is taking on jobs
which one of the others might have liked to accept. These are not
serious accusations but they do give an indication of the notice
taken throughout the royal family of the activities of its members.
The trouble is there is no 'clearing house' for royal engagements
at the Palace. If the Prince of Wales is invited to a function which
he is unable to attend it is never passed on to another member of
the family to see if they would like to do it. A separate invitation
must be sent to each individual; there is no cross-referencing. As a
former private secretary to the Queen has said: 'This is not a show
business agency with its stars available to the highest bidder.'

The Princess Royal says the reason for her increased activity is
simply the 'knock-on effect' from several of her organizations
having new projects in the pipeline, and, as she says: 'I've certainly
done a lot more talking in the last two or three years.' She has
always written her own speeches – in her own hand – but these
days rarely reads from a prepared text; she knows her subjects so

thoroughly she needs only a few notes jotted down for guidance. In her view one of the problems about public speaking is: 'If you know your subject too well, you're in danger of boring your audience to death.' She has also become expert in judging her audience, knowing almost to the second when to stop talking. This is something she has learned from others, particularly her father, who also learned very early on to recognize the danger signs of his listeners 'switching off'.

One occasion when her instinct did let her down was when she allowed herself to be persuaded to take part in the television programme *It's a Knockout*. The idea came from Prince Edward who recruited other members of the family, including Prince Andrew and the Duchess of York (the Prince of Wales refused point-blank). Princess Anne soon realized her mistake in agreeing to her brother's request but on the whole she came out of it better than the others in her family.

She's always had a reputation for 'having a go' – which has led to her driving a tank, scoring a series of bull's-eyes when firing an automatic weapon on an army firing range, and riding a motorbike at record-breaking speeds around the Earl of Lichfield's private circuit.

Today she is recognized as someone who has made a major contribution to the 'Royal Firm' – at the same time refusing to sink beneath the royal horizon. She is a tough, hardworking woman who, in spite of her own protestations to the contrary, has also become more compassionate.

Recently I spent several hours with Her Royal Highness at Buckingham Palace where we talked of a number of issues regarding her life and work. She was quite revealing about her own assessment of her character and the things which have helped to shape it. 'Maturity is a strange thing,' she said. 'You can meet children who are extraordinarily mature because of what they have seen and experienced – like those I meet from time to time in Riding for the Disabled and Save the Children; and I'm not talking only about those in the Third World but here in Britain as well – and then meet quite senior people who never mature. I think you need to have had an experience that has affected you deeply in order to mature. And perhaps a certain level of responsibility has something to do with helping your understanding of other people's problems. Having disappointments and learning to overcome them is another major factor in maturity. In my case, having spent a lot of time being involved with horses has meant getting used to disappointment. You spend years trying to achieve something and just when you think you are there, you are let down. It's not deliberate but it's a disappointment nonetheless – of a sort. In my early days as a competitor I lost Doublet – that was a traumatic experience, especially in the circumstances in which he went. But you have to learn to get on with life which is full of constant disappointments. The problem is that as a child one is rarely prepared for future let-downs. You expect everyone to remain the same – all the bosom friendships you made at school are expected to remain for the rest of your life; and it simply doesn't happen like that. People let you down and, let's face it, you let others down – it's human nature. The only advantage of getting older is that you learn a little bit more about understanding other people's problems as well as your own.'

The thought of letting anyone down is completely foreign to the Princess Royal's nature, even when something as cataclysmic as the assassination of a world leader interrupts her arrangements. In October 1984, the Princess visited Bangladesh and India on behalf of the Save the Children Fund. After completing the Bangladesh sector of the tour, she moved to India. On the fourth day, Her Royal Highness was visiting a settlement for Tibetan refugees in the foothills of the Himalayas in northern India at Mussooree. While she was there a message was relayed to her via the Indian police who were accompanying her that the Prime Minister, Mrs Indira Gandhi, had been shot and killed. The programme was completed and the Princess set out to return to Delhi, where, coincidentally, the Princess had been due to have had dinner with Mrs Gandhi that same evening. Before leaving the town of Dehra Dun, Princess Anne called at the home of Mrs Pandit Nehru to express her condolences. Mrs Nehru was badly shaken by the news and she asked the Princess if she and her two daughters could travel back to Delhi with her in the Andover of the Queen's Flight that was being used. The Princess immediately agreed and they set out in a convoy of cars for the airport – several of the vehicles being stoned on the way. The scene when they arrived in Delhi was chaotic, with buses burning, a pall of smoke hanging over the city and demonstrations in the streets. The Princess remained at the residence of the British High Commissioner, where she received a message from the Queen asking her to represent her at Mrs Gandhi's funeral. Amid the scenes of distress and barely concealed emotions, Her Royal Highness maintained a calm dignity as she walked with other world leaders including Margaret Thatcher and other British political figures. When the funeral was over, the Princess joined Mrs Thatcher for the flight back to Britain in the RAF VC10 that had been placed at her disposal. Before leaving, however, the Princess promised to return to India as soon as she could to finish the tour. She kept her word more quickly than anyone could have foreseen. Less than four months later, she was back in India and continuing the programme originally planned. The disappointment that had been felt when she had been forced to abandon her earlier visit disappeared as she moved among her hosts, spending even more time with them than would have been possible under the original programme. She was determined that they would not be let down – and they were delighted that she had kept her promise.

A great deal has been written about the Princess's relationship with her two sisters-in-law. Some 'informed' writers have said that Anne hates Diana and never speaks to her in private. The fact that she was not invited to become godmother to either of the Waleses' children is quoted as evidence of their antipathy. It has also been reported that Princess Anne has little in common with the Duchess of York, regarding her as frivolous and lacking a sense of responsibility.

The facts are slightly different. It is true that the Princess Royal and the Princess of Wales share few common interests; Prince Charles's wife is known not to favour country pursuits such as shooting, riding and hunting, but she does have a genuine affection for children, other people's as well as her own. She frequently includes Peter and Zara Phillips in her own family outings, without being asked, and in Princess Anne's eyes, anyone who likes her children is all right with her.

The relationship with the Duchess of York is even more subtle. She is the latest recruit to the 'inner-circle' of the royal family and as such is still learning the ropes. The Princess Royal could teach her a great deal about handling the press and how to behave in public. But of course she would never volunteer herself as a tutor. That would be too presumptuous and might be seen as condescending. What she has done is to let the Duchess know that if there is anything she can do to help, 'I am here if you want me.' That is as far as she would go. The Princess is not a demonstrative person but she is sympathetic to her sisters-in-law and realizes how difficult it must be to come from the outside into the cloistered world of royalty. She of course has never suffered from any of these crises of identity. But then she has never been anything other than royal. Her personality remains something of an enigma. She has inherited the characteristic of the 'royal freeze' when someone oversteps the mark, yet her face lights up when she smiles. Her laugh is natural, light and spontaneous, and her wit is rapier sharp to the point of hurtfulness at times. She has never been described as an intellectual but she is sharply intelligent with an ability to grasp the most complicated brief in the shortest time and is clearly the most articulate and self-possessed member of her family. What she does possess is the ability to get straight to the core of a problem and cut through any unnecessary waffle. It is a gift that she has had to use many times in recent years. The fact that she can put you at ease very quickly also means that she expects others to be equally relaxed in her company. If you are nervous it makes her uneasy. The Princess Royal is unlike any other lady in the royal family, or even any other person, in that she refuses to pretend. It has almost become her trademark. So that her failure, if it can be called that, is that she has never conformed to what the public has expected a 'proper' princess to be. When she took part in a BBC radio 'phone-in' programme she herself admitted that 'I have never been what some people seem to think a princess should be – wearing a crown and a long white dress.' But both the Princess and her husband are 'originals' – they may not be the most glamorous couple in the world, but the way in which they have both 'done their own thing' in the past sixteen years, has made them stand out in a royal family noted for its conventional attitudes. Who would have thought that the Queen's only daughter would speak out publicly on such a taboo subject as a sexually transmitted disease? And would be heard exchanging friendly profanities with her fellow jockeys as they lined up for the start of the 3.30 at Leicester? If they cared about convention she and Mark would have done something years ago to stop all the stories about their relationship. That they have never altered their programmes by a single day in order to quash the rumours, illustrates their independence of mind and individual outlooks. And whatever the future holds for her, the Princess will face it in her own uncompromising style; presenting a calm and dignified face to the world at large, while concealing any private emotions from all but her immediate family. If the Princess Royal wanted to be seen to comply with royal tradition, her children would probably be Prince Peter and Princess Zara by now. And if they ever are given titles it will be only because their mother will have finally given in to the wishes of her own mother, not because she feels they need any extra designation to enable them to keep up with their royal cousins.

She is emphatically a country person at heart preferring the company of animals to people, yet she has one of the highest profiles of any member of the royal family. Her devotion to duty means she is on show throughout the world for several months every year, but the style and confidence which she exemplifies has not come easily. She is not a natural performer who seeks the limelight, and the constant attention she attracts is something she has learned to accept with resigned tolerance. The job of being one of the most active and senior members of the world's most famous family has made enormous demands on her, and if determination is the word most people associate with her character, there is another which must feature very strongly – duty. If the Princess Royal has the ability to laugh at herself – and sometimes it is the only thing that keeps her going – she certainly takes her job very seriously indeed. She represents in many ways all that is best in the British monarchy – a modern, professional approach to a system which many people regard as anachronistic in the latter part of the twentieth century. She is who she is by an accident of birth; she has become what she is entirely through her own efforts – a princess for our time.

APPENDIX I

◆

THE PRINCESS ROYAL'S PROGRAMME

JANUARY – SEPTEMBER 1989

JANUARY

Wed 18 Jan	SCF – Million Pound Chain Reaction Promotion – meet manufacturers before a luncheon in Central London (1245–1430 hrs)
Wed 18 Jan	SCF – Industry and Commerce Group meeting at Buckingham Palace (1500–1630 hrs)
Wed 18 Jan	Receive John Sunderland (St John) at BP (1700–1730 hrs)
Wed 18 Jan	Woolmen – Alms Court Dinner at Tallow Chandlers' Hall (1920–2250 hrs)
Thu 19 Jan	HFT – attend Reception to open campaign for improvements of Frocester Manor & Old Quarries Minchinhampton Golf Club, (1830–1930 hrs)
Fri 20 Jan	Open Cattle Market, Louth, Lincolnshire (1130–1240 hrs) + Lincolnshire Agricultural Society AGM (1300–1600 hrs) Wessex (returning from Lincs to Sandringham)
Sat 21 Jan	Scottish Rugby Union – Scotland v Wales Match at Murrayfield, Edinburgh (1155–1610 hrs). BAe 146 (from RAF Marham & back to RAF Lyneham)
Sun 22 Jan	European Figure Skating Championship – Attend Closing Ceremony at The National Exhibition Centre, Birmingham (1350–1640 hrs)
Mon 23 Jan	Attend SCF Meeting in London to discuss SCF's work in the UK (1050–1400 hrs) IBM South Bank Office, London (no press release)
Mon 23 Jan	Receive Bob Scott (Manchester Olympic Bid) at BP (1500 hrs)
Mon 23 Jan	Attend the Duke Ellington Concert, Royal Festival Hall for Courtauld Institute of Art Fund (1925–2230 hrs)

Tue 24 Jan	Butler Trust – visit HM Prison and Remand Centre, Cardiff (1310–1605 hrs). Wessex
Wed 25 Jan	FEI – Statutes Revision Meeting, Berne, at the Hotel Bellevue Palace (depart LAP 24 Jan at 1855 hrs) (arrive LAP on 26 Jan at 1150 hrs)
Thu 26 Jan	Carmen – Court Luncheon at Ironmongers' Hall (1245 hrs approx)
Thu 26 Jan	Loriners – Installation Court at Vintners' Hall (1640–1840 hrs)
Thu 26 Jan	BKCEC – Apparel Export Awards at the Mansion House (1930–2230 hrs)

FEBRUARY

Wed 1 Feb	SCF – open and address Area Organizer's Annual Conference, Newington Causeway, SE1 (1030–1130 hrs)
Wed 1 Feb	Diplomatic & Commonwealth Writers Association of Britain – opening address & question time – Waldorf Hotel, Aldwych (1245–1440 hrs)
Wed 1 Feb	Visit Prison Service Headquarters, Cleveland House, Page Street, SW1 (1530–1730 hrs)
Wed 1 Feb	St John's Ambulance – reception for Grand Prior Cadets at BP (1745–1845 hrs)
Thu 2 Feb	Woolmen – Sitting for Mr Michael Noakes in the Yellow Drawing Room (0900 hrs)
Thu 2 Feb	SCF – Tower Hamlets Homeless Families, SCF HQ (1030–1200 hrs)
Fri 3 Feb	RN – visit HMS *Osprey*, Portland, Dorset (1000–1430 hrs). Wessex
Fri 3 Feb	National Autistic Society – Open new purpose built garden and woodworking centre, Somerset Court, Nr Highbridge, Somerset (1505–1610 hrs). Wessex
Fri 3 Feb	British Food & Farming 1989 banquet in Cheese Pavilion, The Royal Bath and West Showground, Somerset (arrive Showground 1625 & retire) Dinner (1930–2210 hrs)
Sat 4 Feb	England v Scotland Rugby Match at Twickenham (1225–1645 hrs)
Mon 6 Feb	BKCEC – SEHM Menswear Exhibition and luncheon, Paris (1155–1600 hrs). Andover. Stay at GP.
Tue 7 Feb	WRNS – visit Historical Collection at RN Museum, Portsmouth, Hampshire (1100–1415 hrs). Wessex
Tue 7 Feb	Attend Farewell Party for Captain of the Queen's Flight (early evening) at BP
Tue 7 Feb	Address St Thomas's Hospital Medical & Physical Society, followed by dinner at St Thomas's (1830–2230 hrs)
Wed 8 Feb	SCF – Adams Childrenswear Staff Conference – Nuneaton, Warwickshire (1215–1420 hrs). Wessex
Wed 8 Feb	Open Centenary Business Centre, Nuneaton (1425–1455 hrs)
Tue 14 Feb	BKCEC Visit Gini Pearl – Staines, Middlesex (1000–1040 hrs)
Tue 14 Feb	Road Haulage Association Ltd – open new Head Office in Weybridge, Surrey (1145–1230 hrs)

Tue 14 Feb	W. & H. Gidden Ltd – visit workshops & premises, Tabernacle Street, EC2 (1400 hrs)
Tue 14 Feb	Presentation of cheque for SCF from Junior Orange Association of the United Kingdom at BP (1700 hrs)
Tue 14 Feb	HFT – Reception to recruit new support from industry commerce for HFT Development Trust (1830 hrs) at BP
Wed 15 Feb	Woolmen – Sitting for Mr Michael Noakes in the Yellow Drawing Room (0900 hrs)
Wed 15 Feb	BKCEC – visit Michael Ross (Knitwear) Ltd, Hayes, Middlesex (1100–1200 hrs)
Wed 15 Feb	LU – Kings College London, WC2 – inaugurate new Computer Centre (1400–1600 hrs)
Wed 15 Feb	RYA – Council Meeting, Knightsbridge (1630–1830 hrs)
Wed 15 Feb	Dinner with New Zealand High Commissioner at 43 Chelsea Square (prior to visit to NZ)
Fri 17 Feb	SCF Gypsy Work in Wales – visit 2 traveller sites in Cardiff (1200–1500 hrs). Wessex
Mon 20 Feb	Interview for magazine *Yachts & Yachting*
Mon 20 Feb	BKCEC – visit IMBEX Exhibition at Olympia (1330–1445 hrs)
Mon 20 Feb	Manchester 1996 – evening reception at the Mansion House (Address) (1700–1900 hrs)
Wed 22 Feb	Tasmania & New Zealand (Depart LAP 1200 hrs 22 Feb) (Arrive Hobart 0945 hrs 24 Feb)

MARCH

Tue 7 Mar	(Arrive LAP 1215 hrs)
Wed 8 Mar	LU – Presentation Ceremony of new graduates, Royal Albert Hall (1400–1630 hrs)
Thu 9 Mar	RYA – official launch of the sponsorship of the National Windsurfing Schemes, Alexandra Palace (1500–1600 hrs or earlier if necessary)
Mon 13 Mar	Butler Trust – Award Ceremony, Lambeth Palace
Mon 13 to Tue 14 Mar	Royal Scots – visit to 1 RS at WERL (arrive evening 13th and depart 1500 hrs on 14th to see Warrior APC conversions) Andover on 13th, HS 125 on 14th
Wed 15 Mar	Badminton Association of England Ltd – attend 1989 All England Badminton Championships, Wembley Arena (1245–1520 hrs)
Wed 15 Mar	RYA – Council Meeting, Knightsbridge (1630–1830 hrs)
Thu 16 Mar	Present Ritz Club Trophy at Cheltenham Racecourse (P.M.)
Fri 17 Mar	South Warwickshire Health Authority – open New District General Hospital, Warwick, (1030–1130 hrs). Wessex
Fri 17 Mar	Open new factory of Kaybe Conveyors Limited, Tamworth (1210 –1405 hrs) and visit Probus Limited (domestic Kitchen Equipment) Staffordshire (1415–1530 hrs). Wessex
Sat 18 Mar	French Fédération de Rugby – Scotland v France International, Paris – arrive late A.M. Andover

Sun 19 Mar   MTS – visit new centre in Fos-Port de Bouc (50 Km from
                Marseilles). Andover. Depart Marseilles 1500 hrs for Budapest

19–24 Mar   Budapest – FEI General Assembly & Bureau Meeting. Andover

Thu 30 Mar   SCF – Visit the Consumers' Association Laboratories & SCF Shop,
                Harpenden & Tring, Hertfordshire (1340–1630 hrs)

Fri 31 Mar   Attend VSO Reunion at Commonwealth Institute (evening) – fly
                from Doncaster Racecourse by Wessex early P.M. to BP or KP.
                Wessex to GP

APRIL

Mon 3 to   Visit 8th Canadian Hussars at Lahr, West Germany (1200 hrs
Tue 4 Apr   arrival – 1500 depart) BAe 146

Thu 6 Apr   SCF – chair the 9th Industry and Commerce Group Meeting, BP
                (0900–1030 hrs)

Thu 6 Apr   SCF – Council Meeting and 'Thank You' Reception, SCF
                Headquarters, London SE5 (1115–1430 hrs)

Thu 6 Apr   RYA – AGM Inn on the Park (1600 hrs tea) AGM (1630–1715 hrs)

Thu 6 Apr   British Atlantic Committee – Attend seminar on North Atlantic
                Treaty and the formation of Nato, Queen Elizabeth II Centre
                (1730–1930 hrs)

Fri 7 Apr   Academic Awards Ceremony, Institute of Civil Engineers, Great
                George Street, SW1. 1200 hrs + lunch

Mon 10 Apr   Open new Colourfast Plastics factory, Eccles, Manchester (1000
                hrs approx). Wessex

Mon 10 Apr   COT – address meeting on caring for terminally ill. Liverpool
                (1200–1430 hrs). Wessex

Mon 10 Apr   Wimpey Property Holdings Ltd – open Clayton Square Shopping
                Centre, Liverpool City Centre. (1500–1530 hrs). Wessex

Mon 10 Apr   Liverpool Housing Trust – open newly refurbished terraced houses
                for the elderly at Florence Court, Liverpool. Wessex

Tue 11 Apr   LU – Institute of Neurology, WC1 – Open Day to mark appeal
                for funds for research in neurology and the neurosciences (1430
                –1600 hrs)

Tue 11 Apr   NAC Rural Trust – attend launch of Village Homes for Village
                People Guides at 35 Belgrave Square (1630–1730 hrs approx)

Tue 11 Apr   BAFTA – evening event to launch Corporate Membership (possibly
                at St James's Palace)

Wed 12 Apr   High Wycombe and Amersham Health District – Scannappeal –
                open the Scan facilities at High Wycombe, Bucks. (1000–1100
                hrs from BP). Drive

Wed 12 Apr   Windsor Parish Church All Saints. Open new Parish Hall Windsor,
                Berks (1130–1300 hrs)

Wed 12 Apr   Open The Queen Anne First School, Windsor, Berks

Wed 12 Apr   Farriers – Craft Committee meeting, London (1400 hrs)

Wed 12 Apr   Gala Evening hosted by US based National Amusements in
                conjunction with Peterborough's *Evening Telegraph* to benefit SCF

	– Showcase Cinema, Mallory Road, Peterborough. Wessex. HRH to stay overnight.
Thu 13 Apr	RAF Wattisham – 50th Anniversary. Present new Squadron Standard to No. 74 Squadron, Ipswich, Suffolk (1100 hrs approx.) Wessex to BP or LHR
Fri 14 to Sun 16 Apr	American Horse Shows Association – 1989 Volvo World Cup Finals for Jumping, Tampa, Florida (depart 14 Apr from Gatwick at 1120 hrs) (arrive LAP 0845 hrs on 17 Apr – to be confirmed)
Mon 17 Apr	SCF Africa Review Group Meeting at BP 1000 hrs
Mon 17 Apr	MTS – Lunch for Lord Leathers, Royal Thames Yacht Club (1245 hrs)
Wed 19 Apr	Open Equestrian Centre at Brackenhurst Agricultural College, Nr Southwell, Notts. Wessex
Wed 19 Apr	Open Brushwood Residential Unit (for physically and mentally handicapped) at Chiswell, Notts. Wessex
Wed 19 Apr	TG – deliver the final Dame Margery Corbett Ashby Memorial Lecture at the Royal Overseas League, Park Place, SW1 (1500 hrs)
Thu 20 Apr	SCF – open new Peat Marwick McLintock offices – Birmingham (1700–1800 hrs) followed by Dinner Dance at the Metropole Hotel (1900–2230 hrs). Drive
Fri 21 Apr	Open the Spring Meeting of the Intensive Care Society at Château Impney Hotel, Droitwich Spa, Worcestershire (0915 hrs). Wessex
Fri 21 Apr	BKCEC – visit Gossard, Blackwood, Gwent & Berli, Ebbw Vale, Gwent. Wessex
Mon 24 Apr	NFU/Nat West – present VENTURECASH Awards, London (1030–1400 hrs)
Mon 24 Apr	Signals: Receive Maj. Gen. Alexander (on relinquishing his appointment as Signal Officer in Chief) and receive Maj. Gen. Cook on taking up this appointment (BP 1500 hrs)
Tue 25 Apr	Voluntary Organizations Liaison Council for Under Fives – attend 10th anniversary conference The Ismaili Centre, 1–7 Cromwell Gdns (1500 hrs)
Tue 25 Apr	British Telecom – present Marconi International Fellowship Award and Young Scientist Award. (1830 hrs followed by dinner), Stationers' Hall
Wed 26 to Thu 27 Apr	IOC – Barcelona: Executive Board Meeting with International Summer Sports Federations BAe 146
Fri 28 Apr	Visit Royal Society of Medicine – address as President of SCF (1400–1630 hrs)
Fri 28 Apr	MTS – fundraising dinner in the Painted Hall at Royal Naval College, Greenwich (stay BP)
Sat 29 Apr	Royal Signals – visit 34 Signal Regiment (Volunteers) at Middlesborough A.M. (visit + lunch departing 1500 hrs). Wessex
Sat 29 Apr	Visit site of National Garden Festival, Gateshead (1530 hrs). Wessex

MAY

Mon 1 May	Bank Holiday
Tue 2 May	SCF – Launch of SCF Week, SCF HQ (1100–1200 hrs)
Tue 2 May	BKCEC Vivienne Bannister, Hastings, E. Sussex, (P.M.) Wessex
Tue 2 May	HFT – open new workshop in grounds of Lympne Place, Hythe, Kent – (1500–1600 hrs). Wessex
Tue 2 May ·	SCF – Chair public seminar 'Juvenile Justice: Better Ways' at IBM South Bank, SE1 (1800–2030 hrs)
Wed 3 May	Visit The Unity Centre, Unity Centre Ltd, Unity House, 161 Arundel Gate, Sheffield (0945–1030 hrs). Wessex
Wed 3 May	BKCEC visit Joseph Dawson, Bradford (1100–1200 hrs). Wessex
Wed 3 May	COT – address meeting on some aspect of recent legislation relating to disability such as Disabled Persons Act and Education Act, plus exhibition York (1245 hrs, lunch + P.M.) Wessex
Wed 3 May	Weatherby (David Nicholson) – evening
(Thu 4 to Sun 7 May)	FEI – Badminton Three Day Event
Thu 4 May	CIT – Conference & Exhibition at Olympia 'Combating congestion – relieving transport's bottlenecks' P.M.
Thu 4 May	CIT – Dinner at the Royal Garden Hotel, W8
Fri 5 May	Solway Foods Limited – open hi-tech food factory, Corby, Northamptonshire. Wessex
Fri 5 May	SCF – Exhibition of Homemade Blankets, Guildhall Northampton (1100–1200 hrs). Wessex
Fri 5 May	SCF – open first SCF shop in Warwickshire 45 mins P.M. Wessex
Mon 8 May	CIRED – open International Conference on Electricity Distribution, Brighton, Sussex (0930 hrs approx) Wessex
Mon 8 May	LU – visit the Royal Holloway and Bedford New College, Egham, Surrey (1430–1700 hrs). Wessex
Mon 8 May	Address Annual Dinner of the Consular Corps of London on SCF, Intercontinental Hotel, W1
Tue 9 May to Fri 12 May	NIGERIAN STATE VISIT (9th: Arrival/Lunch/Banquet)
Tue 9 May	Meet the 1989 ASE/RI Australian Science Scholars at Royal Institution of Great Britain, 21 Albemarle Street, W1 (1530 hrs)
Wed 10 May	BKCEC – visit Drendie Girl, London N7 A.M.
Wed 10 May	Windsor Horse Trials Press Conference, Berkeley Square (1200–1300 hrs)
Wed 10 May	LU – Presentation of new graduates at the Royal Albert Hall (1400–1630 hrs)
Wed 10 May	St John – attend Greyhound Race, Wembley Stadium – evening
Thu 11 May	Bourneville College of Further Education – Open Day on 76 years of Further Education as part of City's Centenary Celebrations, Birmingham (1030-1200 hrs). Andover
Thu 11 May	RDA – Picnic and Ride at Solihull Riding Club, Dorridge, West

	Midlands – to celebrate 21st anniversary of the Lapworth Group (1230–1345 hrs). Andover
Thu 11 May	COT – attend opening ceremony of Occupational Therapy Course at Coventry Polytechnic, West Midlands and visit OT Department at Coventry and Warwickshire Hospital (1415–1615 hrs). Andover
(Thur 11 to Sun 14 May)	Royal Windsor Horse Show
Fri 12 May	LU – United Medical & Dental Schools of Guy's & St Thomas's Hospitals, SE1 – Visit Dental School, Guy's, London Bridge SE1, attend Service of Thanksgiving, Southwark Cathedral, followed by lunch at Glazier's Hall (1000–1430 hrs)
Sat 13 May	Girl Guides – address the AGM on SCF Westminster (1500–1700 hrs)
Mon 15 May	Christies Panel Products Ltd, Bristol, Avon (1100–1210 hrs)
Mon 15 May	National Head Injuries Association – open new building at Headway House, Frenchay Hospital, Bristol, Avon (discussion over buffet lunch) (1300–1430 hrs approx)
Mon 15 May	Royal Scots – Royal Caledonian Ball, London
Wed 17 May	Open St Michael's, Sandhurst, Pastoral Centre, Sandhurst, Surrey (1130–1230 hrs)
Wed 17 May	WRNS – attend AGM of WRNS Benevolent Trust at Victory Services Club, London (1430 hrs)
Wed 17 May	RYA – Council Meeting Knightsbridge (1630 hrs)
Wed 17 May	Incorporated School of Tropical Medicine – attend Dinner in London
Thu 18 May	Open new Hall at Felsted School, Felsted, Dunmow + Open new Abbeyfields Association Complex, Felsted (A.M.)
Thu 18 May	COT – attend Opening Ceremony of Occupational Therapy School, Witham, Essex (lunch + P.M.). Wessex
Thu 18 May	East of England Agricultural Society – Council Meeting, Peterborough (1700 hrs). Wessex
Fri 19 May	Open 'West Wilts 89' Exhibition, Trowbridge, Wiltshire. Wessex
Fri 19 May	Open new Hydrotherapy Pool at Larkrise School, Trowbridge, Wiltshire. Wessex
Fri 19 May	Open new clubhouse of the Trowbridge & District White Ensign Association. Wessex
Fri 19 May	Open new unit at Burton Hill House School, Malmesbury (time permitting – to be confirmed)
Fri 19 to Sun 21 May	Conference at St George's House, Windsor (beginning 1700 hrs on 19th)
Mon 22 May	Chelsea Flower Show P.M.
Tue 23 May	Visit Ford New Holland Basildon Tractor Plant on their Silver Jubilee, Basildon, Essex (1100 hrs). Drive
Tue 23 May	BKCEC – David Evans & Co., Crayford, Kent
Tue 23 May	HFT – Gilbert & Sullivan evening, Savoy (part of centenary celebrations) – dinner.

Wed 24 May	RYA – unveil plaque on TS *Astrid* at Southampton (A.M.)
Wed 24 May	Visit the Dame Hannah Rogers School, Nr Plymouth, Devon (P.M.). Wessex
Wed 24 May	Open new premises of Royal Western Yacht Club of England, Queen Anne's Battery, Plymouth
Wed 24 May	RN – visit HMS *Vivid*, Royal Naval Reserve Unit at Mount Wise, Plymouth, Devon (1930–2200 hrs). Wessex
Thu 25 May	Loriners – Annual Livery Dinner – Mansion House
Fri 26 May to Sun 28 May	Windsor Horse Trials
Sat 27 May	SCF – Biggest Birthday Party in the World to celebrate SCF's 70th Anniversary at Alton Towers (1430–1630 hrs). Wessex
Mon 29 May to Tue 6 June	SCF visit to Ethiopia. BAe 146 (Cancelled due to political situation)

JUNE

Wed 7 Jun	Derby
Wed 7 Jun	FANYs – visit 3 element display at HQ 1900–2000 hrs
Thu 8 Jun	Butler Trust – visit Winchester Prison, Hampshire (A.M.) Wessex
Thu 8 Jun	Visit National Centre & Exhibition of Tools for Self Reliance, Netley Marsh Workshops, Southampton (1400–1500 hrs). Wessex
Fri 9 Jun	Oxford University – Open Institute for Molecular Medicine, Oxfordshire (1030 + lunch). Wessex
Fri 9 Jun	SCF – watch short displays of music, dance & drama given by children at the Children's Festival to Celebrate 70 years of SCF – Devizes, Wiltshire (1400–1600 hrs). Wessex(?)
Sat 10 Jun	Attend Ball for The Peper Harow Foundation at Goodwood House (1930 hrs). Wessex
Mon 12 Jun	The Duke of Edinburgh's Dinner Party at BP
Tue 13 Jun	GA Property Services/General Accident – Summer day at Knebworth Herts (1200–1800 hrs). Wessex
Wed 14 Jun	RDA – Shropshire County Competition and Fun Day at West Midlands Show Ground, Shrewsbury (1000-1200 hrs). Drive to Shrewsbury then BAe 146
Wed 14 Jun	Open new Forth Hostel at Oatridge Agricultural College, Uphall, West Lothian. BAe 146 – to be confirmed
Wed 14 Jun	Hamilton – evening meeting
Thu 15 Jun	SCF – visit SCF Children's display + buffet lunch at Chester, Cheshire (1130–1430 hrs) + present awards to winners of Golf Competition at Royal Liverpool Golf Club at Hoylake, Merseyside 1500–1600. BAe 146 (into Hawarden/depart from Formby)
Fri 16 Jun	Timeform – fundraising dinner on eve of Timeform Charity Day at Gimcrack Rooms, York Racecourse, North Yorkshire (1945 hrs: return by train to Southampton/or BAe 146 from Leeds Bradford)
Sat 17 Jun	Round the Island Race, Isle of Wight

Sun 18 Jun	RYA – present prizes at East Midlands Youth & Junior Championships, Rutland Water, Leicestershire (1730 hrs). Wessex
Mon 19 Jun	Visit Royal Highland 150th Show Edinburgh (1000–1800 hrs). BAe 146
20–24 Jun	Royal Ascot
Wed 21 Jun	RYA – Council Meeting, Knightsbridge (1630 hrs)
Wed 21 Jun	MTS – Fund Raising 'The Last Night of the Proms' concert at Guildhall, Portsmouth. Wessex
Thu 22 Jun	Gold Cup Day
Fri 23 Jun	SCF – visit City of London Mediaeval Fair, Broadgate Centre, EC2 (1000–1100 hrs – Windsor for lunch)
Sat 24 Jun	SCF visit Plymouth Shop (1145–1210 hrs) & present Princess Anne Awards and attend Children's Festival (1230–1630 hrs). Wessex
Sat 24 Jun	Dorset County Branch of the British Legion – attend Gala Music Hall in aid of Legion's charities at the Pavilion in Weymouth, Dorset. (evening). Wessex
Sun 25 Jun	Dog Trials Gatcombe – Graham Cummins
Mon 26 Jun	Visit Staffordshire: Marchington Church on the village's 900th anniversary; New Scout HQ, Rolleston on Dove; JCB Excavators Ltd; Sheltered Housing Scheme; Uttoxeter Leisure Centre Sports Hall (1000–1630 hrs). Wessex
Mon 26 Jun	Open Cheadle Hospital, North Staffordshire. Wessex.
Tue 27 Jun	MTS – attend Annual Service at St Michael Paternoster Royal, followed by lunch at Grocers Hall, AGM and Council Meeting (1130–1500 hrs)
Tue 27 Jun	LU – Charing Cross & Westminster Medical School, W6: opening ceremony for new lecture theatre & seminar rooms (1530–1730 hrs)
Tue 27 Jun	Transaid – attend Reception, Portland Place (1745–1915 hrs)
Wed 28 Jun	TG – AGM, Royal Albert Hall (Lunch & P.M. meeting)
Wed 28 Jun	Woolmen – Annual Ladies Banquet at Drapers' Hall
Thu 29 Jun·	Visit Whitby celebrating 450th anniversary of Closing of Whitby Abbey. Ecumenical Service in MTS building + exhibitions, N. Yorkshire (1000 hrs + Lunch). Wessex
Thu 29 Jun	Malton Agricultural Society Show, N. Yorkshire (1400–1630 hrs). Wessex
Thu 29 Jun	HFT – Ball at Grosvenor House in aid of HFT
Fri 30 Jun	McArthur Group Ltd (ironmonger and tool manufacturers) – 150th anniversary, exhibition and luncheon, Bristol (1100–1330 hrs). BAe 146
Fri 30 Jun	Salisbury City Almshouse & Welfare Charities – open new almshouse(s) of 17/18 units at Trinity Hospital and New Brympton House, Salisbury (1430–1600 hrs). BAe 146 into Boscombe Down/return to Northolt
Fri 30 Jun	Carmen – Ball at Grosvenor House (proceeds to SCF)

JULY

Sat 1 July to Fri 7 July	Holyrood
Sat 1 July	Visit Troon Fete (for 'WaterAid'), SCF shop & RDA Rally on Ayr Race Course. BAe 146 or train
Mon 3 July	RDA – Visit Buchan Group Menzie, Aberdeenshire (1130–1430 hrs). Wessex
Tue 4 July	RDA – Visit Group at The Stables, Veensgarth Tingwall, Gott, Shetland Islands (1330–1530 hrs). Wessex
Wed 5 July	Open the Antartex Visitors' Centre at The Edinburgh Woollen Mill, Alexandria (early A.M.). Wessex
Wed 5 July	Visit Strathcarron Hospice, Denny, Stirlingshire
Wed 5 July	Scottish Business Achievement Award Trust Ltd – Annual Lunch, Edinburgh (1245 hrs)
Wed 5 July	Visit Trefoil Holiday & Adventure Centre for the Handicapped, Gogarbank, Edinburgh (1500 hrs)
Wed 5 July	Royal Scots – meet representatives of Golden Jubilee reunion of 8th Battalion at a reception at the Prestonpans Branch of the Royal British Legion, Nr Edinburgh (1800–1900 hrs)
Thu 6 July	BKCEC – visit Bairdwear (Kilbride) Ltd, East Kilbride, Glasgow
Thu 6 July	BKCEC – visit Rally-Klad Limited, Glasgow
Thu 6 July	Garden Party – Holyrood P.M.
Thu 6 July	Address Royal Scottish Geographical Society on travels as President of SCF, Usher Hall, Edinburgh – evening
Fri 7 July	BKCEC – visit Clan Douglas Knitwear Ltd, Hawick, Roxburghshire (return by Shuttle/Wessex/Royal Train)
Sat 8 July	RYA – Parade of The Cutty Sark Tall Ships, London (0800 hrs)
Sat 8 July	Spinal Injuries Association – auction luncheon sponsored by Coral racing – Present Coral Eclipse Trophy at Sandown Park
Sat 8 July	SCF – attend third Sham-E-Bahar Charity Ball, Osterley, Middlesex (2015–2300 hrs)
Sun 9 July	Guards Polo Club – charity match in aid of HFT
Mon 10 July	SCF – 10th Industry & Commerce Group Meeting (1630–1800 hrs) & Corporate Membership Reception, (1800–1900 hrs) at BP or a Corporate Member's HQ
Mon 10 July	The Duke of Edinburgh's Dinner Party at BP
Tue 11 July	BSO – Annual Award Ceremony, Institute of Electrical Engineers + buffet reception at BSO (1100–1330 hrs approx)
Tue 11 July	Loriners – Livery Static display of artefacts relating to its Loriners trade in celebration of 800 years of the Mayoralty in Guildhall (1400–1500 hrs)
Tue 11 July	Garden Party – BP
Tue 11 July or	COT – attend concert & reception to further the New College Information and Study Centre London
Tue 11 July	COT – attend Special Fashion Show and reception in London
Wed 12 July	United Engineering Steels – open Aldwarke Bloom Caster

	Development, Rotherham, South Yorkshire (A.M. + lunch). BAe 146 to RAF Finningley
Wed 12 July	Visit James Neill Holdings Factory, Handsworth, Sheffield
Wed 12 July	Brook Advisory Centre – 25th anniversary celebration St Martin's Terrace, New Zealand House (1730–1900 hrs)
Thu 13 July	Evening at Savvas Nightclub, Nr Usk, Wales (1900–midnight). Wessex (originally 12 June)
Sat 15 July	SCF – visit the Princess Royal School, Batley on their 50th anniversary (1100–1145 hrs). Attend reception in Wakefield Town Hall followed by 'Wakefield Whoppa Weekend' – sports gala and Branches Fair + Wakefield Citizens Advice Bureau West Yorkshire (also possible visit to new SCF shop in Wakefield) (1030–1550 hrs). BAe 146 to Leeds
Sun 16 July	British Racing School's Fundraising Gymkhana Newmarket (1430–1700 hrs). Wessex
Mon 17 July	Take Salute at the Royal Tournament – evening (to be confirmed)
Tue 18 July to 26 July	UNITED ARAB EMIRATES STATE VISIT (Arrival/Lunch and State Banquet)
Tue 18 July	SCF/St John – formally accept a James Osbourne sculpture in aid of both charities at Osbourne Studios, Covent Garden, WC2 (1530–1615 hrs)
Wed 19 and Thur 20 July	East of England Show, Peterborough. Wessex
Thur 20 July	HFT – Dinner to celebrate completion of the Bedfordshire Herald Appeal at RAF Henlow, Hertfordshire. Wessex.
Fri 21 July	Order of St John Banquet at Brighton Pavilion, Sussex. Wessex
Mon 24 July	FANY Visit HMGCC Pounden, Bicester
Mon 24 July	Freight Transport Association – banquet in the Mansion House to mark centenary
Tue 25 July	SCF – Tesco Pro-Am Charity Golf Classic, RAC Golf & Country Club, Epsom, Surrey (1830–1930 hrs)
Wed 26 July	RYA – Royal Ocean Racing Admiral's Cup 1989 Race programme – attend reception on RYA Lawn at Royal Yacht Squadron, Cowes (1800–2000 hrs). Wessex
Thu 27 July	Racing at Cowes
Fri 28 July	RN – Royal Naval Engineering College, Plymouth, Devon. Review Ceremonial Divisions, present The Queen's Sword (1000–1630 hrs). Wessex
AUGUST	
Tue 1 Aug	Redcar Races – open new Stable Block and new Entertainment Building. BAe 146 to Teeside
Sun 6 Aug	FEI – European Senior Dressage Championship, Mondorf-les-Bains, Luxembourg. BAe 146 (subject to availability)

11–13 Aug   Gatcombe Horse Trials
Mon 14 Aug   Open World Veterinary Poultry Congress, Brighton, Sussex (1000
               hrs/lunch). Wessex (subject to availability)
Tue 29 Aug   Attend Westminster and London Horse Show – to be confirmed
Tues 29 Aug   IOC – San Juan, Puerto Rico – 95th IOC Session. BAe 146
to Fri 1 Sept
Returning   Belize, Honduras, Ecuador & Bolivia. BAe 146
Fri 15 Sept

APPENDIX II

♦

OFFICIAL APPOINTMENTS

1950	1,000,000 (millionth) Member of the Automobile Association
1969	Patron, Benenden Ball
1970	Hon. Member, Young Adventure Club
1.1.70	President, Save the Children Fund
17.11.70	Commandant in Chief, St John Ambulance and Nursing Cadets
Jan 71	Member, Reliant Owners Club
June 71	Hon. Member, Island Sailing Club
Nov. 71	Patron, Riding for the Disabled Association (RDA)
Nov. 71	Hon. Member, Royal Thames Yacht Club
21.3.72	Hon. Life Member, Flying Doctor Society of Africa
1.4.72	President, British Academy of Film and Television Arts (BAFTA)
12.9.72	Patron, Jersey (CI) Wildlife Preservation Fund
June 74	Hon. Member, British Equine Veterinary Association
1976 only	President, The Hunters' Improvement & Light Horse Breeding Society
27.2.76	Freedom of the City of London
May 76	Vice Patron, British Showjumping Association
15.6.76	Visitor of Felixstowe College
21.10.76	Patron, Gloucester and North Avon Federation of Young Farmers' Clubs
Jan 77	President, Windsor Horse Trials
April 77	Patron, Royal Port Moresby Society for Prevention of Cruelty to Animals
April 77	Patron, Horse of the Year Ball
Nov. 78	Hon. Member, Minchinhampton Golf Club
27.10.79	Patron, Royal Lymington Yacht Club
Nov. 80	Patron, All England Women's Lacrosse Association
1981 only	President, Three Counties Show
June 81	Hon. President, Stroud District Show (show discontinued 1983)
17.2.81	Chancellor of London University
March 82	Patron, Home Farm Trust (until September 89)

May 82–85	Patron, Bourne End Junior Sports and Recreation Club (3 years only)
Sept. 82	Patron, National Union of Townswomen's Guilds (6 years)
1983 only	Commonwealth Universities Congress
March 83	. Visitor of the Strathcarron Hospice, Denny
14.4.83	President, British Olympic Association
7.10.83	Patron, British School of Osteopathy
1984 only	Patron, Surrey Agricultural County Show
Feb. 84	Patron, Spinal Injuries Association
Feb. 84	Hon. President, Chartered Institute of Transport
April 84	Patron, Riding for the Disabled Association, Australia
May 84	President, Missions to Seamen
1.6.84	Hon. President, British Knitting and Clothing Export Council
1984/5 only	Patron, Oxford House, Bethnal Green
May 85	Patron, Suffolk Horse Society (Hon. Life Member July 82)
May 85	Hon. Associate, Royal College of Veterinary Surgeons
July 85	Patron, Butler Trust
1985/6 only	President, Royal Bath and West Show
Sept. 85	President, Patrons of Birmingham Olympic Council
Sept. 85	Patron, the Lady Jockeys' Association of Great Britain
Oct. 85	Patron, Canadian Therapeutic Riding Association
16.1.86	Patron, College of Occupational Therapists (5 years)
28.2.86	Patron, Association of Combined Youth Clubs (3 years)
20.3.86	President, Riding for the Disabled Association
21.5.86	Hon. Life Member, Royal Yachting Association
1.6.86	Patron, Scottish Rugby Union
5.6.86	Patron, British Executive Service Overseas
1.10.86	President, Royal Agricultural Society of England (until 30.9.87)
25.11.86	Hon. Life Member, Royal Corps of Transport
Dec. 86	President, Fédération Equestre Internationale
8.12.86	Hon. Member, The Jockey Club
1986 only	Patron, Amateur Rowing Association
1986 only	Patron, Suffolk Sheep Society
1986	Member, Beaufort Hunt
1986	Hon. President, The Royal Caledonian Hunt
1986	Hon. Member, Sussex Agricultural Society
1986	Hon. Member, Royal Yacht Squadron
1986	Vice President, Royal Bath and West and Southern Counties Show
22.1.87	Patron, Australian Veterinary Association
12.2.87	Fellow, Royal Society
6.3.87	Patron, Intensive Care Society (3 years)
31.3.87	Hon. Fellow, Institution of Electrical Engineers
12.5.87	Hon. Member, Road Haulage Association
26.5.87	Patron, British Olympic Medical Trust

17.6.87	Fellow, Royal Veterinary College
29.6.87	President, East of England Agricultural Society (1989 only)
13.7.87	Patron, Caldecott In Hand Show (1988 only)
23.7.87	President, Royal Association of British Dairy Farmers (1990 only)
3.9.87	Hon. Member, Amateur Riders Club of America
19.8.87	Hon. Member, Associazione Nazionale Italiana di Riabilitazione Equestre (ANIRE)
Nov. 87	Patron, British Women's Gasherbrum II Expedition 1989
31.12.87	Patron, Scottish Business Achievement Award Trust Limited (until 31.12.92)
12.2.88	Member, International Olympic Committee
18.3.88	Patron, William Lee Quatercentenary
6.5.88	President, National Agricultural Centre Rural Trust
12.5.88	Patron, Royal Scots Club and Flying Scot Club
16.6.88	Patron, World Student Debating Championships 1990
July 88	Patron, The Cranfield Trust
1.8.88	President, Medical Equestrian Association (3 years)
15.8.88	Fellow, King's College, London (from 1989)
19.8.88	Patron, Ulster Sports and Recreation Trust
19.8.88	President, Royal Norfolk Agricultural Association (1990 only)
25.8.88	Patron, British Racing Schools Race Day
9.11.88	Patron, Home Farm Trust Development Trust
14.11.88	Patron, World Junior Cycling Championships (taking place 14–22 July 1990)
14.11.88	Patron, National Association of Prison Visitors
14.11.88	Patron, Gateshead National Garden Festival
24.11.88	Patron, 6th International Conference on Equine Infectious Diseases, Robinson College, Cambridge 7–11 July 91
29.11.88	President, REDR – Engineers for Disaster Relief (5 years)
30.11.88	President, Council for National Academic Awards (6 years)
16.1.89	Patron, Save the Children Fund Corporate Fund Raising Committee, Hong Kong
10.2.89	Patron, University of the West Indies Relief and Development Fund
10.2.89	Patron, ECCS Congress 1989 (International Conference on Steel Construction)
17.2.89	Patron, Gloucestershire Rugby Union
14.3.89	Patron, British Nutrition Foundation (5 years)
22.3.89	Patron, United Kingdom/New Zealand 1990 Organization
30.3.89	Patron, Animal Diseases Research Association (ADRA) Equine Research and Grass Sickness Fund
10.4.89	Patron, International Literacy Year 1990 (to be run in England and Wales under the auspices of the Adult Literacy and Basic Skills Unit – ALBSU)

SERVICES

9.6.69	Col-in-Chief, 14th/20th King's Hussars
28.2.70	Col-in-Chief, Worcestershire & Sherwood Foresters Regiment (29th/45th Foot)
24.6.72	Col-in-Chief, 8th Canadian Hussars (Princess Louise's)
25.6.74	Chief Commandant, Women's Royal Naval Service (WRNS)
18.8.74	Patron, Association of Wrens
18.8.74	Patron, Army and Royal Artillery Hunter Trials
14.10.74	President Women's Royal Naval Service Benevolent Trust
Oct 74	Life Member, Royal Naval Equestrian Association
1975–1990	President, Royal School for Daughters of Officers of the Royal Navy and Royal Marines (Haslemere)
22.6.77	Col-in-Chief, Royal Corps of Signals
	Col-in-Chief, Canadian Forces Communications & Electronics Branch
	Col-in-Chief, Royal Australian Corps of Signals
	Col-in-Chief, Royal New Zealand Corps of Signals
	Col-in-Chief, Royal New Zealand Nursing Corps
	Col-in-Chief, Grey and Simcoe Foresters Militia – Canada
June 77	Patron, Royal Corps of Signals' Institution
June 77	Patron, Royal Corps of Signals' Association
June 77	Hon. Air Commodore, RAF Lyneham
June 78	Life Member, Royal British Legion Women's Section
Aug 78	Hon. Life Member, RNVR Officers' Association
Nov 78	Patron, Canadian Forces Communications and Electronics Branch Institution
18.8.81	Commandant in Chief, Women's Transport Service (FANY)
1.7.82	Col-in-Chief, Royal Regina Regiment
Jan 83	Patron, The Royal Tournament
30.6.83	Col-in-Chief, Royal Scots (The Royal Regiment)
18.1.85	Joint President, Lowland Brigade Club
15.10.88	Col-in-Chief, Royal Newfoundland Regiment

LIVERY COMPANIES

30.11.71	Yeoman of the Saddlers' Company
6.12.71	Hon. Freeman of the Worshipful Company of Farriers
	Master, Sept. 84–Sept. 85
	Immediate Past Master, Sept. 85–Sept. 86
	Past Master, Sept. 86 onwards
15.3.72	Hon. Freeman of the Worshipful Company of Loriners
	Hon. Liveryman, Feb. 79
	Hon. Assistant, 6 Oct. 86
	Under Warden, Oct. 89
10.5.72	Freewoman of the Fishmongers' Company

8.6.76	Hon. Liveryman of the Worshipful Company of Farmers
April 82	Hon. Liveryman of the Worshipful Company of Carmen
	Hon. Assistant, Dec. 83
	Senior Warden, Oct. 85
	Master of the Company, 6 Oct. 86
	Immediate Past Master, 6 Oct. 87
20.10.88	Lady Liveryman of the Worshipful Company of Woolmen

PHOTO CREDITS

COLOUR PICTURES

Section I

Doublet's headstone *Anwar Hussein*

The Princess Royal going into the water at Badminton *Photographers International*

Helping pull a ferry across the river Gambia *Tim Graham*

At a feast in Dubai *Anwar Hussein*

Shopping in the local souk *Anwar Hussein*

Dubai Horse Show *Tim Graham*

Tribute from slum dwellers in Bangladesh *Photographers International*

Visiting a refugee camp in the Sudan *J.S. Library*

The Princess Royal leaving a hut in the Sudan *Anwar Hussein*

Portrait of The Princess Royal in the Sudan *Anwar Hussein*

Visiting a clinic in North Yemen *J.S. Library*

Giving the President of the Sudan a signed photograph *Anwar Hussein*

Riding a camel in Qatar *Photographers International*

At Ascot *Anwar Hussein*

Inspecting camouflaged soldiers at Warminster *Glenn Harvey*

Awarding Bob Geldof an honorary doctorate *Rex Features*

Section II

Gatcombe Park *Anwar Hussein*

The entrance hall at Gatcombe Park *Anwar Hussein*

Driving a 50-ton Chieftain tank *Tim Graham*

The Princess Royal at a charity fashion show *Anwar Hussein*

Posing for a portrait by John Ward *Rex Features*

The Princess Royal riding Cnoc Na Cuille *Tim Graham*

At the BAFTA awards: meeting Robert Powell and Denholm Elliot *Rex Features*

Joking with fellow jockeys *Anwar Hussein*

The Princess Royal awarding her husband with a medal at Seoul *Colorsport*

Portrait taken at a celebrity shoot-out *Camera Press*

With Billy Connolly at a celebrity shoot-out *Camera Press*

Skiing with Zara *UK Press Ltd*

The Princess Royal sailing *Yachting Photographics*

Informal portrait *Terry O'Neill/World Press Network*

BLACK AND WHITE PICTURES

Section I

Four generations of royal ladies *Popperfoto*

Coronation Day *Popperfoto*

Princess Anne with Prince Charles at Braemar Games *Popperfoto*

Princess Anne with Suzie Babington-Smith and Caroline Hamilton *Hulton Deutsch Collection*

Princess Anne meeting the headmistress of Benenden *Popperfoto*

Portrait of the Princess on her sixteenth birthday *Rex Features*

With Prince Charles at Covent Garden *Popperfoto*

The Princess's first car *Popperfoto*

Section II

The Princess and Mark Phillips at Chatsworth *Popperfoto*

The Royal Wedding *Popperfoto*

Visiting her detective *Popperfoto*

Mark Phillips with Anthony Andrews and his wife, Georgina *Rex Features/Richard Young*

The Princess with Mark Phillips at Montreal *Rex Features*

Going over a water jump *Rex Features*

Visiting a Norfolk branch of the RDA *Eastern Daily Press/by courtesy of the Riding for the Disabled Association*

The Princess Royal at the China Coast Bar *The Missions to Seamen*

INDEX